Praise for *Agile IT Organization Design*

"Continuous delivery is often described from the perspective of the technicians. This is understandable because that is where it started, but it does the process a disservice. Continuous delivery is a holistic approach. It requires change across the organization and it encourages such change, to the betterment of the groups that practice it. This book addresses that problem and looks at CD from an organizational perspective. It starts from Dan Pink's ideas of intrinsic and extrinsic motivators and describes how to structure an organization for success—how to encourage a focus on autonomy, mastery, and purpose that will motivate your teams and produce high-quality results. This book takes a look at all aspects of organizational design that impact the ability to deliver regular, small, high quality changes. If you follow the advice in this book, your organization will be the better for it."

—*Dave Farley, author of* Continuous Delivery

"A number of years ago, Silicon Valley marketing guru Geoffrey Moore quipped, 'A bank is just a computer with a marketing department.' Today, technologies—cloud, social, big data, the Internet of Things, and mobile—continue to drive this unprecedented digital transformation in organizations. As such, the need for agility has moved from software development to corporate boardrooms. Sriram's book makes the case that to thrive in these fast and uncertain times, enterprise leaders need to rethink how IT, not just software development, is organized, structured, and measured. His book provides guidelines, not prescriptions, which enable innovation, adaptability, and responsiveness at scale."

—*Jim Highsmith, Executive Consultant, ThoughtWorks, Author of* Adaptive Leadership

"Very hands-on and operational book for management of Agile-based development. Provides valuable insight for IT practitioners. A must read for IT professionals."

—*A.V. Sridhar, Founder, President & CEO Digite, Inc.*

"Agile IT Organization Design is an engaging, enlightening, and immensely practical book. While many authors have addressed Agile software development, very few have tackled the wider topic of the more systemic changes necessary to move from Agile software to an agile organization, and onwards to 'digital transformation.' Even fewer have done so at more than a very theoretical level. Drawing heavily upon his substantial practical experience, Sriram Narayan's book explores the pitfalls of many of our current 'organizational wisdoms' and gently, but convincingly, suggests appropriate and relevant alternatives to try in their place—all the time backed up by real-world examples. I highly recommend the book to anyone interested in, or struggling with, the challenges and opportunities of achieving organizational agility."

—*Chris Murphy, President and Chief Strategy Officer, ThoughtWorks*

"Agile and continuous delivery transformations require changes in technology, process, and people. This book is the first to tackle the people aspect in depth, and it does this very well. A must read for those taking the journey!"

—*Anders Wallgren, CTO, Electric Cloud*

"Agile IT Organization Design tackles all the problems that we just want to ignore. Relying heavily on hands-on experience rather than theoretical exercises, Sriram provides concrete actions to address the issues with Agile software development and continuous delivery at a structural and organizational level. He clearly addresses issues of finance, accountability, and metrics, not just team structure and team processes, and gives many examples and scenarios to help understand how these issues manifest and how the proposed steps work to resolve the issues. Organizational transformations to Agile often fail, not because the individual processes and practices break down, but because the organization itself—its power structure, its organizational norms, and its culture—fight against the gains that Agile has the potential to bring. Sriram focuses our attention on the systemic problems, but then provides action steps to allow us to address these problems in our context. This book presents no silver bullet, as those don't exist. However, Sriram provides for organizations a way to start facing reality and moving towards an organization that supports not only Agile software development but organizational and business agility."

—*Rebecca Parsons, Director at Agile Alliance & CTO at ThoughtWorks*

"Sriram's book addresses the rarely-approached topic of Agile organization design in a very pragmatic and thorough manner. It does a great job of explaining the value brought by Agile and DevOps approaches in enterprise-scale organizations, and gives strong details on the 'how' to get there. It also paints a very practical picture of how the different processes of the company (budgeting, staffing, metrics, etc.) will be affected by the Agile organizational choices. I see it as the perfect companion book for a large-scale Agile transformation effort."

—*Regis Allegre, VP Software Engineering, Cloudwatt*

"Businesses today are discovering that if they are to build 'digital first' experiences for their customers, they need to rethink how their product, marketing, and technology teams work together. Sriram's book pulls aside the curtain to reveal that the best-kept secrets of the world's top performing digital organizations are actually very accessible to all. It serves as a pattern language for management of the modern digital enterprise."

—*Adam Monago, VP Digital Strategy, ThoughtWorks, @adammonago*

"Agility is so much more than stand-ups and test driven development. Even the best practices won't yield results unless backed by the right leadership. Sriram's book is an important contribution to the all-too-bare bookshelf on leadership of IT organizations. He mixes theory and practical insights in the right measures and the result is as readable as it is full of usable insights."

—*Nagarjun Kandukuru, VP Global South Strategy, ThoughtWorks*

"Sriram covers everything the Scrum coach didn't tell you. Most books on Agile stop at a team and project level, and that's exactly where the organizations tend to get lost in the real world of pre-existing organization structures and procedures—which in turn become blockers to achieving ultimate business agility. If you ever wonder why your attempt at Agile is floundering, this is one book where you'll find some answers for sure."

—*Puneet Kataria, Vice President Global Sales, Kayako*

"The field of Agile is an evolving, moving target and there is little in terms of guidance for managers and staff that are trying to implement it within an enterprise context. This book provides a complete guide to all of the organizational aspects of implementing Agile within the enterprise context, as well as providing extremely useful examples and cogent advice. I would recommend this book to anyone with a general interest in Agile through to senior managers looking to reenergize their enterprise organizations using the principles and practices of Agile."

—*Ken Robson, Global Head of Trading Technology, Danske Bank*

"Sriram has pulled off an audacious attempt at a unified theory of IT. This work led me through the incredible range of issues that I recognize, slotting each one into context and building a vision of how things can and should be. If you want to be elevated above the trenches of Agile and DevOps—to get a better view of where they fit in the digital world that includes sales, finance, governance, resourcing, delivery, and most importantly, people—then read this book. A compelling read that I'm already referring back to."

—*Duncan Freke, Development Director, thetrainline.com*

"Sriram makes a convincing case that digital transformation efforts need IT agility. He also does a great job of explaining how IT agility is more than just engineering and process. This book is a valuable read for those on the digital transformation journey."

—*Shashank Saxena, Director, Digital and eCommerce Technology,*
The Kroger Co.

"Adopting Agile software development practices is not just an IT change, it is an organization-wide change. Sriram goes through every aspect of what this means to an organization and gives options for how to bring changes in, including hard-to-change areas like project funding. This book is thought provoking, an easy read, and includes great examples."

—*Jeff Nicholas, Director, PB & WM IT Digital Banking APAC, Credit Suisse*

"This book is for anyone who is looking for clear and focused guidance in the pursuit of modern product delivery. Any transformational leader will find this book a great tool that provides answers to many of the problems of Agile transformation at scale. A great jump start for those looking to improve their effectiveness and responsiveness to business, Sriram's book recognises that people leadership is the DNA of any Agile transformation."

—*Marcus Campbell, Delivery Director, Semantico*

"Entrepreneurial organizations thrive on continuously adding value, rapidly innovating, and staying close to their customers. Similarly, Agile software development emphasizes continuous, incremental improvements, quick response to change, and close collaboration. Sriram makes a compelling case for Agile design of IT organizations in large enterprises. He goes well beyond describing how an IT organization can adopt Agile development methodologies to explain how any successful digital transformation within a large enterprise must encompass strategy alignment, project portfolios, IT staffing, budgeting, and more. This book is a great read for those who want a digital transformation to have impact both within and beyond their enterprise IT organization."

—*Ron Pankiewicz, Technology Director, VillageReach*

"Organizational structure is a key enabler for a company to achieve its raison d'être. This book lays out the rationale for organizing IT organizations around Agile software development concepts. It provides practical guidance on wide-ranging success factors including tangible org elements such as structure, team design, and accountability, and intangible cultural elements such as alignments and norms. These concepts will certainly help IT companies turn the tide on huge cost and time overruns that are typical on large IT projects."

—*Paul Kagoo, Engagement Manager at McKinsey & Co.*

"Outcomes matter in an increasingly 'winner takes all' digital arena. A true digital transformation undertaking, driven by the need to build competitive advantage, is marked by an increase in responsiveness, insights, and engagement, not just cost effectiveness. IT organization is a key partner in this transformation but is seldom structured to succeed in most enterprises. This book makes a case for how IT organization needs to be weaved within outcome-based teams, not activity-based teams, to drive agility and competitive advantage. In general, organizational design is very expensive to engineer in real world situations but this book takes on this tough problem by providing some frameworks and considerations for the reader to evaluate the validity of outcome-based structure in their organization."

—Vijay Iyer, Sr. Product Manager, NetApp

"I found Agile IT Organization Design to be well organized with an in-depth knowledge of challenges that IT organizations face, while providing possible ways to address those challenges. Moreover, it was eminently readable and I found myself readily recognizing the problems described within. It may seem odd to describe a business-oriented book as such, but I found this to be an enjoyable read!"

—Randy R. Gore, Program Manager, IBM

"As enterprises try to ramp up their digital transformation initiatives, there will be an ever-increasing need for better collaboration between IT and business. New org structures will fuel this collaboration. Sriram's book is a timely elaboration of the importance of org structures for the success of digital initiatives large and small."

—Dinesh Tantri, Digital Strategist, @dineshtantri

Agile IT Organization Design

Agile IT Organization Design

For Digital Transformation and Continuous Delivery

Sriram Narayan

✛Addison-Wesley

New York • Boston • Indianapolis • San Francisco
Toronto • Montreal • London • Munich • Paris • Madrid
Capetown • Sydney • Tokyo • Singapore • Mexico City

For information about buying this title in bulk quantities, or for special sales opportunities (which may include electronic versions; custom cover designs; and content particular to your business, training goals, marketing focus, or branding interests), please contact our corporate sales department at corpsales@pearsoned.com or (800) 382-3419.

For government sales inquiries, please contact governmentsales@pearsoned.com.

For questions about sales outside the U.S., please contact international@pearsoned.com.

Visit us on the Web: informit.com/aw

Library of Congress Cataloging-in-Publication Data
Narayan, Sriram.
  Agile IT organization design : for digital transformation and continuous delivery / Sriram Narayan.—First Edition.
    pages   cm
Includes bibliographical references and index.
  ISBN 978-0-13-390335-5 (pbk. : alk. paper)
  1. Organizational change. 2. Strategic planning. 3. Information technology—Management. I. Title.
HD58.8.N37 2015

004.068—dc23

2015010984

ISBN-13: 978-0-13-390335-5
ISBN-10: 0-13-390335-4

Text printed in the United States on recycled paper at RR Donnelley in Crawfordsville, Indiana.
First printing, June 2015

For dear departed Amma and Appa
&
For Swati—my wonderful wife and elixir of my life

Contents

Preface

Enterprise IT has mostly underperformed. It's been a struggle to deliver IT-as-enabler, to say nothing of IT-as-differentiator. Partly as a result, it is common to hear of strained relationships between business and IT. This doesn't augur well for digital transformation initiatives. I submit that a prime reason for the sorry state of affairs is poor organization design. A June 2014 McKinsey Global Survey[1] also bears this out. It found at larger companies that structural issues are viewed as the top hurdle to meeting digital goals.

Organization design is traditionally considered from an industry-agnostic point of view. Although perceived to be the domain of HR, this is rarely the case when planning re-orgs. In contrast, this book explores organization design by IT leadership for IT organizations. It aims to provide a sound basis for IT organization design. This is essential because, in practice, IT organization design is rarely thought out from a baseline of principles. The prevailing design is mostly a product of happenstance, mergers or acquisitions, people-retention compulsions, and the ideas of whoever is in charge at various levels in the organization. It resembles how software accumulates technical debt over time unless we periodically step back and reassess the design.

Organization design in the 21st century is not merely structural but also cultural, political, operational, and physical. I draw upon several sources—my industry experience; the existing literature on organization design, Lean, and Agile; and several well-regarded works on individual and team psychology to present a synthesis for an Agile IT organization design. Many of the structural and operational configurations I suggest are already in place at several new-generation ISVs. I explain how the rest of enterprise IT could benefit from them. On the other hand, the chapters addressing politics and culture are equally relevant to ISVs and the rest of enterprise IT.

A number of reviewers suggested (in good faith) that I use Lean instead of Agile in the title in order to improve marketability. Apparently, Lean is "in" whereas Agile is jaded. However, I chose Agile because its strong people-orientation credentials are core to the solutions I offer.

---

1. http://www.mckinsey.com/insights/business_technology/the_digital_tipping_point_mckinsey_global_survey_results

Running counter to the trend of inflating an article-length topic into a book, I have packed a wide range of topics into a single book because I believe they are interlinked and a synthesis is required. It is also a sign of the wide scope of an IT leadership role. Yet the coverage isn't exhaustive. Topics such as innovation, knowledge management, people diversity, and performance reviews are not covered or are only mentioned in passing.

Many of the topics covered here come under the scope of IT governance. But conventional IT governance gets into discussing standards and frameworks too soon. The discussion in this text is mostly standards and frameworks agnostic. Besides, the cultural aspects I address are not generally considered part of the scope of IT governance.

This isn't a cookbook. I describe problems, explore causes, and offer solutions. However, I stop short of detailing steps to implement solutions. In a few sections, steps for migrating from existing situations are provided. In addition, the last chapter has a section that suggests a sequence of adoption of various recommendations. But overall, planning migration tends to be contextual. I expect that the intended audience will be able to draw upon the advice provided here and plan their own migration. Besides, I might be available for consulting.

Many of my recommendations here have succeeded in some shape in the real world. Wherever evidence of success or failure is publicly available, I have included it. In other cases, the recommendations are supported by reason and examples from first-hand experience. Once we accept that conventional approaches haven't delivered needed results, it gets easier to consider the alternatives suggested seriously.

I provide many short, example scenario narratives to illustrate problems with the status quo. They are inspired by real situations, but names of companies, people, and other details have been altered. Any resemblance to real entities is coincidental and unintentional. They aren't full stories in that they don't include a resolution. However, the chapter content that follows the narrative provides ways to deal with the problem. The more you are able to relate the scenarios to your own experience, the more you will find the rest of the chapter to be illuminating. Many other inline examples are drawn from e-commerce ("e-tail") so that they remain accessible to a diverse readership.

The first four chapters are a prerequisite to reading the rest of the book. Chapters 8, 9, and 10 on projects, finance, and staffing, respectively, go together. The rest of the chapters may be read independently. There are many cross-references between chapters despite my efforts to keep all the related arguments together. This is a sign that the topics are interdependent.

Given the broad scope, I had to bring up several subsidiary topics without going off on an explanatory tangent. To compensate, I have provided footnotes that link to freely available explanatory material from credible sources on the Internet (rather than offline or behind a paywall). Readers of the physical version may access these links from the book's companion website at agileorgdesign.com.

Who This Book Is For

- Execs and others who decide on matters of IT organization design or governance
- Senior management at ISVs and Internet businesses
- VP or director or head of IT, product management, engineering, or software development
- Business heads who interface with IT and IT-business partners
- Finance controllers, IT finance analysts, and investment managers
- Investors in digital businesses
- Techies who have the ear of executive leadership
- ICT strategists
- Members of IT governance groups
- Process quality/SEPG group members, process consultants, and coaches

This book is meant for medium to large IT organizations (50 to thousands of IT staff) that are facing challenges with IT and business agility. By IT organizations, I mean those that serve their own business directly (software is the business; e.g., ISV) or indirectly (Internet businesses, enterprise IT). That said, IT suppliers (IT services companies) might be able to use the contents herein to engage more effectively with their clients.

Why have I included investors in the target readership? Problems in organization design do not show up promptly in financial statements. Yet, in the long run, they have the potential to make or break business outcomes. Since investments tend to have a longer tenure than executives do, investors in digital businesses would do well to understand this topic and hold executives accountable.

If you have already achieved IT and business agility, the stuff here may seem obvious or old news. However, you are likely to encounter some new angles, arguments, or techniques. That said, this is not an introductory book by any means. It is assumed that the reader has some experience of software delivery and has at least a passing familiarity with Agile methods like Scrum or XP and the basic ideas of DevOps and continuous delivery.

Acknowledgments

Although I don't have first-hand experience of caring for a newborn baby, writing this book did seem like how it might be. I could not imagine how my first draft of about twenty thousand words would grow into a healthy one-year-old of more than seventy thousand. And just like any IT project worth its overrun, I (and my editors at Addison-Wesley) have had to deal with scope creep and effort and schedule overruns. But staying true to the advice in this book, we tried to be value driven rather than plan driven. I believe that you will find value in it as well. A lot of it is due to the support, guidance, and encouragement of several people kind enough to help me. I am grateful to all of them.

Pramod Sadalage, a friend, colleague, and author of a number of books on applying Agile engineering techniques to data, was first to help. He recommended my work to Bernard Goodwin at Addison-Wesley, who then became my editor until his retirement at the end of 2014. Christopher Guzikowski then took over and brought this book to a successful launch. Michelle Housley provided great support throughout via developmental editing, coordinating with reviewers, and helping me get through paperwork. Stephanie Geels provided excellent copyediting, and Kesel Wilson and several others at Addison-Wesley ably helped with the production process. There are also others who I didn't personally interact with, like the cover designer, compositor, and the proofreader. They have all been instrumental in bringing this work to fruition.

Pramod also reviewed my manuscript more than once. Early in this process, I was fortunate to receive a gracious offer of guidance from Jim Highsmith—a famous Agilist and also a colleague at ThoughtWorks. Thank you, Jim, for mentoring me over Skype calls and several e-mails. Dinesh Tantri who used to be digital strategist at ThoughtWorks helped crystallize my understanding of the digital transformation phenomenon. Ulrich John Solomon and Suresh Kumar Bellala from ThoughtWorks finance team helped me better understand the nuances of IT finance and validated some of my recommendations. Duncan Freke, development director at Trainline, enthusiastically supported my writing through several reviews and conversations around his own pioneering IT re-org efforts.

Special thanks to full-length reviewers who, despite their busy schedules, took time to read and offer detailed feedback: Aman King, Dave Farley, Dougal

Watt, Gil Broza, Keith Dodds, Randy R. Gore, Nagarjun Kandukuru, Sebastian Silva, Shyam Kurein, and Tom Poppendieck. Thanks also to other reviewers who managed to give the manuscript what time they could: Dave Whalley, Marco Abis, Puneet Kataria, Rajesh Babu, Rebecca Parsons, Sitaraman Dharmarajan, Sagar Paul, and Sunil Mundra. And of course, thanks to all those who read my manuscript and provided endorsements. Several colleagues helped obtain endorsements: Alagu Perumall, Anand Vishwanath, Vishwanath Nagrajarao, and Sagar Paul.

ThoughtWorks and my office general managers provided invaluable support by granting me time to work on it. Jeremy Gordon offered friendly guidance on some legal aspects. Big thanks to Shabrin Sultana who is the creator of some of the better looking illustrations in this book. Thanks also to Siddharth Asokan from the ThoughtWorks marketing leadership team for making Shabrin available. The research team at ThoughtWorks also helped me with my research for the book.

I'd also like to thank Alanna Krause of Enspiral for permission to quote and use screenshots from her projects, Jo Freeman for permission to quote from her essay, and Henrik Kniberg for permission to quote from his writings and adapt one of his illustrations.

In a book on the evolution of buildings called *How Buildings Learn,* author Stewart Brand offers thanks to a "vast network of uncredited influence" that helped shape his work. I am similarly indebted to networks within ThoughtWorks and in the Lean and Agile community at large.

About the Author

Sriram Narayan, an IT management consultant with ThoughtWorks, has provided IT agility guidance to clients in telecom, financial services, energy, retail, and Internet businesses. He has also served as a leadership coach and a director of innovation. He was a founding member of the ThoughtWorks technology advisory board—the group that now authors *Technology Radar*. During a two-year stint at the products division of ThoughtWorks, he helped with product innovation and advocacy on Go—a tool that helps with continuous delivery. He has also worn the hats of a developer, open-source contributor, manager, product owner, tester, SOA architect, trainer, and Agile coach. An occasional blogger and speaker at conferences, his writings, talks, and contact information are available from sriramnarayan.com. The opinions in this book are his own.

Glossary

Note: *The definitions here convey the sense in which a term is used in this book. They may not always be industry-standard terms or definitions.*

Activity Action that contributes to an outcome.

Activity-oriented team A team that is responsible for a single activity. Usually a team of specialists (e.g., marketing, sales, support, development).

Agile In the context of this book, the word *Agile* (capital A) is used to refer to a mindset or methodology that is aligned with the values and principles outlined in the Agile Manifesto. It is not used in the sense of the common English adjective.

Asynchronous communication Channels of communication that don't require parties to the communication to be available simultaneously. For example, e-mail and online forums are asynchronous while phone, VOIP, tele/web conference, chat, and face-to-face meetings are synchronous.

Build vs. buy or make vs. buy A decision to build an IT solution (using in-house or outsourced talent) versus buy an off-the-shelf solution (increasingly in the form of SaaS).

Capability In the context of this book, *capability* refers to the people and systems that make up a business-aligned IT capability.

CapEx Expenditure of capital toward creating or enhancing assets (IT assets). It is recorded in the balance sheet. It shows up in the income statement only as an annual depreciation.

Continuous delivery (CD) An approach to delivering software that reduces the cost, time, and risk of delivering incremental changes *to users* through seamless automation from development to deployment that makes production releases uneventful and frequent.

Continuous integration A practice followed by Agile software development teams of frequently checking-in code under development into a version control system, which then auto-triggers a comprehensive suite of fast-running tests after each check-in. It ensures that the codebase retains its functional integrity in the face of rapid development.

Cross-functional team An interdisciplinary, outcome-oriented team. It may consist of hard-core specialists, generalizing specialists, or generalists.

Cycle time The elapsed time for an item (feature) to progress through the complete value stream. Elapsed time = value-added time + wait time.

DevOps DevOps (development + operations) aims to improve collaboration between the development organization and IT-operations by locating these skills within a single team and by emphasizing culture, automation, measurement, and sharing.

Digital business A business that offers its customers a transaction space that seamlessly bridges digital and physical worlds.

Digital transformation Digital transformation is a change program that aims to transform a primarily brick-and-mortar business into a digital business.

Function lead A catch-all term in this book for people who provide leadership for specialist functions (e.g., VP or director or head of marketing, sales, development, architecture, quality, or program management).

Handoff The act of handing over a work item from one specialist or team to another. A value stream with a series of N specialist activities will have N − 1 handoffs.

Internal scope Scope internal to a feature. Flexible internal scope is key to leveraging a problem-solving approach as opposed to a deliver-to-planned-scope approach.

Internet business A business that doesn't sell software but whose revenues are all (or mainly) via Internet transactions (contrast with ISV).

ISV Independent software vendor (increasingly of the SaaS variety). New-generation examples include companies such as Atlassian, Box.com, and GitHub.

IT-B The part of the IT organization that creates value. The people in charge of conceiving solutions and building (and running) software. Wages of IT-B personnel are mostly treated as CapEx.

IT-I The part of the IT organization that protects value. The people in charge of IT infrastructure and assets. Wages of IT-I personnel are mostly treated as OpEx.

OpEx The ongoing, running cost of IT systems and infrastructure, including the wage cost of people dedicated to this. It shows up as expenditure in the income statement.

Outcome An independently valuable and achievable business outcome.

Outcome owner A catch-all term in this book for someone (below the rank of an exec) who is accountable for and dedicated to a business outcome. For example, product manager/owner/champion, chief product officer, or program/project manager.

Outcome-oriented team A team that has autonomy and accountability for an outcome (e.g., a cross-functional product team).

SaaS Software-as-a-service is a model of distributing software in which the vendor hosts the solution for the customer rather than it being installed on customer's infrastructure.

Silo Organizational silos are units or departments that tend to protect themselves and not work well with other units.

Systems of differentiation or engagement The IT applications that help differentiate a business offering in the market or help drive engagement with customers.

Unscripted collaboration Collaboration between teams is unscripted when it occurs outside of regular, scheduled meetings and without prior planning, permission, or approval.

UX (XD) User experience (experience design).

Value stream A value stream (in this book's context) is a series of activities required to deliver a business outcome.

Chapter 1

Context

In order to scale Agile we need a scalable, yet Agile-friendly, organizational architecture. That's the subject of this book. Granted, several practices of Agile software development have gone mainstream. Even enterprise IT has adopted them. The industry has come a long way from 2001 when the Agile Manifesto was authored. But the pioneers have made further progress during this time. They have gone from continuous integration to continuous delivery, from quarterly releases to daily releases, from manually configured infrastructure to automated infrastructure, from incremental development to iterative development, from points-based estimation to no estimation,[1] and so on.

Progress hasn't been limited to engineering practices and delivery processes. It has begun to touch IT governance and beyond. It has begun to influence aspects such as project finance, portfolio management, team design, metrics, and culture. For example, one of the themes of the movement called *DevOps* is the merger of development and their downstream IT operations teams into a single build-it-and-run-it team. DevOps requires reorganization, not just changes to engineering techniques and delivery processes.

Team-level agility is relatively well understood. But middle managers grapple with how to translate team-level agility into IT agility. They need direction, leadership, and support from IT governance groups and the execs. The execs have usually bought into the idea of Agile but are somewhat short on concrete actions they can take to help middle managers. They will find many recommendations here. With the authority vested in them, they can initiate organization-wide changes.

The need of the hour is business agility, not just delivery process and engineering agility or even IT agility. Both business and IT agility need internal

---

1. http://www.cio.com/article/2381167/agile-development/-no-estimates-in-action-5-ways-to-rethink-software-projects.html

1

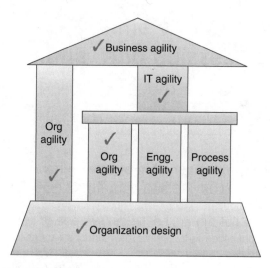

Figure 1-1 *Scope of this book*

organizational agility. In the context of this book, organizational agility is internal facing—it serves all members of an organization. IT agility serves the business. Business agility serves the market. Organizational agility is essential for IT and business agility (Figure 1-1). This book shows how organization design can help deliver organizational agility and in turn help IT and business agility.

The term *organization design* is used here in a somewhat expansive sense. I cover not only structure and culture but also aspects of governance and finance. I also touch upon business engagement with IT because IT cannot be effective by itself without appropriate engagement from business. IT agility is irrelevant if it doesn't translate into successful business outcomes.

This first chapter sets the tone for the rest of the book. It explains why this topic is important, the scope of coverage, and the angles of coverage.

1.1 Focus

Before we proceed, note that the term *IT organization* has a specific meaning here. Usually, IT organization refers to a mix of:

- IT-I—Infrastructure and pure operations:
  - People in charge of procuring, provisioning, and maintaining IT infrastructure for the whole organization (e.g., cloud, laptops, servers, storage, network, security, end-user software).
  - People in charge of running commercial off-the-shelf (COTS) systems.

- IT-B—Build and operate:

  - People in charge of developing and running internal systems. **Enterprise IT** tends to have many people in this category.

  - People in **Internet businesses** (e.g., e-retail, travel, financial services, aggregators) in charge of building and running customer facing technology platforms.

  - People in charge of building commercial software products as in the case of independent software vendors (**ISVs**).

This book is aimed at **IT-B**. Sometimes, the term *development organization* is used to refer to the range of IT specialists (developers, testers, analysts, data scientists, etc.) required to develop a product/solution. IT-B is bigger than this. It includes the program management office (PMO), product management organization, and IT operations people in situations where they are part of the product teams (e.g., DevOps). For readers more familiar with the terms *strategic IT* and *utility IT*, IT-B is mostly the former.

The recommendations herein are most applicable where IT-B represents in-house IT capability, although they may be tailored to adapt to outsourced scenarios. Speaking of outsourcing, note that an IT services firm (IT appdev supplier) typically only has IT-I and perhaps a little IT-B for its internal needs. Its consultants usually form part of the IT-B teams of its clients.

1.2 Business, IT, and Shadow IT

Who is the business when we speak of business and IT? It depends. An ISV may have few businesspeople other than marketing staff, salespeople, and the product manager. On the other hand, an Internet business has many more businesspeople, such as retail sourcing people, commercial managers at aggregators, etc.

Enterprise IT, by definition, is a big organization distinct from a big business organization. Does it have to be so? Doesn't it reinforce the business–IT divide when we speak of business and IT as two different entities? Can't we just embed IT folks into the business organization and avoid the need for a separate IT organization? It is a question worth asking, although one can imagine the dismay of IT managers as they consider it.

It's possible to achieve this embedding of IT in case of ISVs, harder with Internet businesses, and extremely difficult with enterprise IT. The reasons are varied:

- IT is labor intensive and highly specialized. Centralizing IT under a separate organization helps recruitment and staffing. Otherwise, every business unit has to worry about recruiting and managing its IT team. Given the demand–supply gap and the high mobility of the IT workforce, this is not something for which business typically wants to take responsibility.

- Being labor intensive, it needs a relatively large number of people. Seating them along with businesspeople in the central business district can get very expensive in terms of floor space rentals. This calls for at least a geographic separation if not a separation in the org chart. Then again, this may be false economy given the benefits of co-located, cross-functional teams.

- IT-B work is necessarily forward looking—medium to long term. Business is mostly immediate term, especially when bound by quarterly targets. Embedding IT with business risks focusing all IT on the immediate term. For example, there is a risk that instead of building a platform of extensible capabilities, we end up with a ton of smart, unmaintainable spreadsheets attempting ad hoc integration with legacy systems.

- In many businesses outside the world of start-ups, IT culture is distinctly different from business culture.

Thus, although a merger of business and IT is desirable, for the vast majority of big organizations it isn't going to happen anytime soon. That said, there are changes on the horizon. A clandestine merger of business and IT is underway in the form of what is termed *rogue IT* or *shadow IT*.[2] For better[3] or worse,[4] business has begun to take IT matters into its own hands. The availability of inexpensive infrastructure-as-a-service (IaaS) and software-as-a-service (SaaS) solutions means that business units don't have to wait for IT to attend to their infrastructure (IT-I) and development (IT-B) needs, respectively.

Besides, the fragmentation and proliferation of personal computing devices such as tablets, smartphones, and smartwatches has forced IT-I to draw up Bring Your Own Device (BYOD)[5] policies. What's more, the IT department is no longer the owner of all IT expenditure. Already, SaaS marketers are seeking

2. http://en.wikipedia.org/wiki/Shadow_IT
3. http://www.huffingtonpost.com/vala-afshar/cios-stop-chasing-shadow_b_4239465.html
4. http://www.cioinsight.com/security/slideshows/shadow-its-growing-footprint.html
5. http://www.cio.com/article/2396336/byod/all-about-byod.html

the attention of business unit heads rather than CIOs. Back in 2011, one of Gartner's predictions for 2015 was that 35% of enterprise IT expenditures for most organizations will be managed outside the IT department's budget.[6]

Although shadow IT is largely frowned upon as irresponsible by CIOs today, it is possible that business units will evolve to responsibly own their own IT systems. But speculation aside, as things stand, it is still pertinent to talk of improving business-IT effectiveness.

1.3 Business-IT Effectiveness

Medium to large IT organizations frequently struggle to bring new capabilities to the market. Product development efforts continue to languish—it's not just budget and schedule overruns; there are significant issues of product (or solution) adoption and performance. This happens irrespective of whether the product is for internal use or market facing. This is a problem of business-IT effectiveness, not just IT effectiveness. But let's consider IT effectiveness first.

Most IT organizations attempt to improve delivery effectiveness with improvements to build, test, deployment, release, and operations engineering. For instance, Humble and Farley's book *Continuous Delivery*[7] offers great advice on the engineering aspects of effective IT delivery. Continuous delivery is an approach to delivering software that reduces the cost, time, and risk of delivering incremental changes *to users*. It advocates practices such as continuous integration and deployment pipeline, test automation, test-driven development, building once and deploying to multiple environments from the same binary/package, version-controlled configuration, infrastructure on demand, zero downtime deployments, and automated rollbacks.

Teams that adopt the above practices report greater test coverage, more reliable deployments, better reproducibility of bugs, etc. But they may still need to work toward fewer bugs overall or a smooth, even flow of work from requirements to deployment. In places where engineering is organized by functional verticals such as development, testing, and deployment, the head of each vertical is able to report some progress on specific metrics but, frequently, the business does not perceive any overall improvement in IT responsiveness.

Long development cycle times continue to haunt big organizations with hundreds of IT staff members (in-house/contractors/outsourced). Many banks, telecom companies, and big retailers face this issue of frustratingly slow and unreliable IT delivery. Many older-generation ISVs with multiple product lines

6. http://www.gartner.com/newsroom/id/1862714
7. (Humble and Farley 2010)

struggle to compete and retain product leadership. To people slogging in these big organizations, all this talk by start-ups and leading-edge companies of multiple production deployments per day seems like a mirage.

Next, we turn to the larger issue of business-IT effectiveness. Let's start with a scenario.

Scenario 1-1 Delivery Continues, Growth Is Discontinued

Gestalt Inc. is a vendor of knowledge management tools. It is facing tough times with falling sales and rising competition, not to mention open-source alternatives, across its line of products. Five to six years ago, business was good even with just one release per year. Today, they find it difficult to attract new customers even with a release every month. Clearly, they are delivering continuously. But that is not enough for the success of the product. Old customers still swear by their products, but the newer ones keep demanding more features and better usability. Many prospects complain of poor documentation. Insiders complain of politics between marketing, sales, product development, and support. Others point out that the traditional high-touch sales model is obsolete. Prospects today look for content-rich documentation, tutorials, videos, and demos so that they can sell themselves on the product.

A well-oiled IT delivery setup is not enough for a successful business outcome. Continuous delivery and DevOps are irrelevant if they don't improve business outcomes. Business outcomes don't improve just by getting development and IT operations to work better together. As indicated in Figure 1-2, marketing, sales, support, training, product management, development, IT operations—all functions have to work better together. Getting each function right is necessary but not sufficient. Improving interactions between functions boosts organizational agility. This yields bigger benefits as we reach a point of diminishing returns from individual function optimization. We'll see how interactions can be improved through better organization design.

> The automobile is not the sum of its parts. It is the product of their interactions.
> —Russell Ackoff

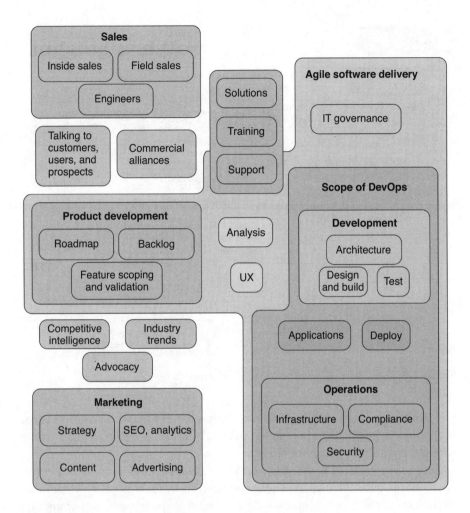

Figure 1-2 *Organizational agility touches everything*

1.4 Digital Transformation

Organizational agility is also an important ingredient for *digital transformation*[8]—changes to business that blur the line between offline (real/physical world) and online interactions with customers, thus offering them a seamless, enriched experience. Although it is often cast as just digital marketing, it usually involves tactical or strategic changes to the business that are

---

8. http://www.capgemini.com/resource-file-access/resource/pdf/Digital_Transformation__A_Road-Map_for_Billion-Dollar_Organizations.pdf

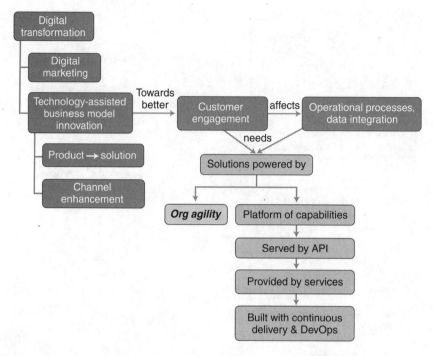

Figure 1-3 *Digital transformation—face of the space*

mediated by technology (Figure 1-3). Deep changes may be required across functions on the road to becoming a digital business. These changes cannot take place without organizational agility.

Technology-assisted business model innovation usually begins with a review of the status quo. We map as-is (existing) and to-be (enhanced) customer journeys. A customer journey map describes the touch points that a customer has with the business throughout the lifecycle of her relationship.

In a typical digital transformation exercise, the to-be journeys may have more digital touch points and enhanced functionality at existing touch points—for example, a regular radio-taxi service may decide to add a new digital touch point in the form of a mobile app for booking a taxi. It may also decide to enhance existing touch points. For instance, perhaps their web site was informational only. You could go there to get the phone number of their call center but not make a booking over the web. They may decide to enhance this by also permitting online bookings, providing history of bookings, and offering a means to submit feedback for completed trips. This type of tactical change to the business may be termed *channel enhancement*.

On the other hand, a business may realize that it can better engage with its customers by offering a more complete solution beyond the sale of its core product; for example, Nike+[9] allows users to track their runs, record statistics, and then try to improve. This amounts to a strategic change from consumer goods (products) to consumer solutions.

These tactical and strategic maneuvers may require changes to existing operational processes and IT systems. For example, click and collect is a new retail customer journey that allows the customer to buy online and pickup from the store. It requires changes to how in-store inventory is managed. It also requires a unified pricing strategy.[10]

Another trend is the increasing acknowledgement of the need for a mobile-first approach to building customer-facing (or even field personnel-facing) applications. However, a mobile-first strategy risks becoming a mobile-only strategy unless we invest in an API[11] capable of serving other channels. The API may be delivered by services that in turn would be built and run based on the practices and principles of continuous delivery and DevOps.

Digital marketing is a common and important component of a digital transformation initiative. It aims to improve reach through different digital marketing channels such as email, search and social advertising, display advertising, events, webinars, and communities. Web and mobile analytics are leveraged to effectively target sections of customers via these channels.

What if I don't see my business going digital, one may ask? Well, the way software is eating the world,[12] there may not be a choice. The pervasiveness of the Internet has made it economically viable to build huge companies in single domains, where their basic, world-changing innovation is entirely in the code.[13] These domain-specific digital businesses have already disrupted their nondigital incumbents in domains as diverse as travel and hospitality, media, personal finance, retail, and home décor. The boundary between online (Internet) and offline (physical world) transactions is increasingly blurred. As noted earlier, digital transformation is an effort to offer a seamless, integrated customer experience between the two worlds. More than ever, it calls for closer collaboration between business and IT.

When business and IT collaborate well, it results in a rewarding journey from product or solution concept to cash (or internal adoption). The journey may face inherent challenges from the market and from the changing technology landscape, but it will be relatively free of frustrations and delays because of internal factors. We have fairly well understood methods to deal with the

---

9. https://secure-nikeplus.nike.com/plus/products/
10. http://hbr.org/2014/09/digital-physical-mashups
11. https://hbr.org/2015/01/the-strategic-value-of-apis
12. http://online.wsj.com/article/SB10001424053111903480904576512250915629460.html
13. http://www.wired.com/2012/04/ff_andreessen/5/

inherent challenges in this journey. Lean product discovery techniques (for start-ups and enterprises) help with the first mile. Continuous delivery and DevOps help with the last mile. Agile software development has become mainstream for the miles in between. So much for the inherent challenges. But there are accidental, organizational challenges as well. These challenges of organizational agility, described in chapters to follow, permeate every mile of the journey and threaten the success of digital transformation efforts.

1.5 Bimodal IT and Dual Operating Systems

In a 2014 report[14] titled "Bimodal IT: How to Be Digitally Agile Without Making a Mess," Gartner advocates a two-speed IT organization that I summarize as:

- A business-as-usual IT organization that continues to be concerned with predictability, change control, and cost-efficiency.
- A high-speed IT organization to stay relevant in the face of changes in the market and in the technology landscape.

A two-speed IT organization may well be a non-ideal but necessary alternative to having a single high-speed IT organization. In a similar and broader vein, in his book called *Accelerate,*[15] Kotter expands on an earlier HBR article[16] to make the case for two-speed *business* organization. He describes an organization's hierarchies and processes as its operating system and advocates a dual operating system. The first operating system protects and sustains the core business. The second operating system, modeled on Agile principles, is tasked with the design and implementation of strategy. For those who relate to the bimodal or the dual operating system approach, this book is about realizing the high-speed or second operating system IT organization.

1.6 Angles of Coverage

As depicted in Table 1-1, the rest of this book address the topic of organization design from structural, physical, cultural, operational, and political angles. Some topics are relevant from more than one angle; for example, the chapter on accountability is relevant from a structural and a political angle. These angles are explored through a common lens of three themes set out in Chapter 3.

---

14. https://www.gartner.com/doc/2798217
15. (Kotter 2014)
16. https://hbr.org/2012/11/accelerate

Table 1-1 *Chapters and Angles*

Chapters		Angles of Coverage				
		Structural	Cultural	Operational	Political	Physical
Ch4	Superstructure	X				
Ch5	Team Design	X				
Ch6	Accountability	X			X	
Ch7	Alignment	X		X		
Ch8	Projects			X		
Ch9	Finance			X		
Ch10	Staffing			X		
Ch11	Tooling		X	X		
Ch12	Metrics		X	X		
Ch13	Norms		X			
Ch14	Communications		X		X	
Ch15	The Office					X

1.7 Summary

- This book describes how organization design can help deliver organizational, IT, and business agility. Organizational agility is internal facing—it serves all constituencies in an organization. IT agility serves the business. Business agility serves the market.

- The focus of this book is IT-B—where systems are developed and where most of the CapEx wage is incurred.

- The distinction between business and IT is greater in traditional enterprise IT than in ISVs and Internet businesses. Notwithstanding shadow IT, which continues to blur this distinction, it is pertinent to talk of business-IT effectiveness rather than just IT effectiveness.

- Business agility is affected not just by issues in IT or engineering. Overarching issues of organizational agility are a big factor across the business value stream.

- Digital transformation is a lot more dependent on Agile transformation than is apparent from high altitudes.

- For those who relate to Gartner's bimodal approach or Kotter's dual-operating-system approach, this book is about realizing the high-speed or second operating system IT organization.

- The chapters to come address issues of organization design from structural, cultural, political, physical, and operational angles.

Chapter 2

The Agile Credo

This book embraces Agile values and principles and some Lean techniques as well. But what does this have to do with organization design? Isn't Agile just a software development methodology?

Well, if we examine the value statements in the Agile manifesto (reproduced in Section 2.1), we find that only one of them (i.e., *working software over comprehensive documentation*) directly refers to software, and even that can be recast more generally as *a working product over comprehensive documentation*. These principles are applicable to all of IT (not just the development organization) and even beyond to business in general. Steve Denning[1] calls it "the best-kept management secret on the planet."[2]

For IT to have an impact on business agility, the Agile credo has to spread beyond engineering technique and delivery process. An organization design that is out of step with Agile principles will get in the way of IT agility. Therefore, it is useful to understand these principles using the context of software development. Although I assume that you have some familiarity with Agile principles and practices, this chapter covers some underlying ideas that are treated as a given in the chapters ahead.

Agile veterans may skip this chapter except maybe for Section 2.3.

---

1. http://www.stevedenning.com/About/default.aspx
2. http://www.forbes.com/sites/stevedenning/2012/04/09/the-best-kept-management-secret-on-the-planet-agile/

2.1 Understanding the Agile Manifesto

Let's begin with what is called the Agile Manifesto. It is reproduced below.

Manifesto for Agile Software Development[3]

We are uncovering better ways of developing software by doing it and helping others do it. Through this work we have come to value:

Individuals and interactions   over processes and tools
Working software   over comprehensive documentation
Customer collaboration   over contract negotiation
Responding to change   over following a plan

That is, while there is value in the items on the right, we value the items on the left more.

Kent Beck	James Grenning	Robert C. Martin
Mike Beedle	Jim Highsmith	Steve Mellor
Arie van Bennekum	Andrew Hunt	Ken Schwaber
Alistair Cockburn	Ron Jeffries	Jeff Sutherland
Ward Cunningham	Jon Kern	Dave Thomas
Martin Fowler	Brian Marick	

© 2001, the above authors this declaration may be freely copied in any form, but only in its entirety through this notice.

As it says regarding the four value statements, the things on the right aren't unimportant, it's just that they are to be traded off for the things on the left as and when situations demand. Let's take a couple of examples.

2.1.1 Example #1

When a tester finds a bug, she is generally expected to first log it in a bug-tracking system. A developer can then look into it. This is the default process. However, Agile software development teams often follow a practice called *dev-box testing,* in which a developer calls a business analyst or tester over for a quick verification of newly developed functionality before it can be called dev-complete or ready for testing. The verification is conducted on the developer's workstation in the presence of the developer. Bugs found during dev-box testing are not logged. The developer just makes a mental note (or a scribbled-down note) of it and fixes it immediately. This may seem like a violation of due

---

3. http://agilemanifesto.org/

process and a gap in documentation. But it turns out to be effective in practice and so in this case individuals and interactions take precedence over process. The fact that fixing the bug is considered more important than logging it is an example of preferring working software to comprehensive documentation.

2.1.2 Example #2

Usually, Agile software development teams showcase incremental progress in functionality to product owners, business stakeholders, or end-user representatives at regular intervals. The showcase is as much about soliciting feedback as it is about demonstrating progress. As it happens, people tend to get better ideas when they see things in action than when it is just a concept on paper or a prototype. Showcases generate change requests. Some requests can be quite disruptive. Agile software development contracts (formal or informal) with the customer (external or internal) have room for scope negotiation so that the change requests can be accommodated without extra paperwork (contract negotiation). This is an example of customer collaboration over contract negotiation. The changes also disrupt the plan, but that's okay because as we shall see in Chapter 8, the plan isn't sacrosanct. Responding to pertinent change is considered more valuable than sticking to a plan.

2.2 Continuous Delivery and DevOps

Even though the industry has latched on to Agile, it is mainly being adopted by the development organization. The journey from development to production—called the last mile of software delivery—still remains a long, drawn out process in many enterprises. Continuous delivery (CD) is an approach that improves the speed and reliability of the last-mile journey. CD is integral to Agile software *delivery* just as continuous integration is integral to Agile software development.

"Delivery" implies that software is delivered to end users or consuming systems. It is not enough for software to be just developed and waiting for testing or integration or approval/certification or production deployment. Neither is it enough for software to be deployed and waiting to be consumed or used. Even if everything is ready and just waiting for an announcement from marketing or internal comms, it still isn't delivered.

"Continuous" implies that software is always in a deliverable state. No separate *hardening* phase[4] is required. A release is only a decision away. Releases

---

4. https://www.scrum.org/Forums/aft/307

are boringly uneventful. Loosely coupled architectures, loosely constrained and backwards compatible API ensure that frequent releases aren't held back by dependencies. This takes away the need for an elaborate release calendar that gingerly navigates dependencies. The CD approach incorporates stage-gates, build promotions,[5] audits, and operational controls into an automated software delivery pipeline with manual latches where necessary.

DevOps helps CD by encouraging deep cross-pollination (in a figurative sense) between developers and sysadmins and other IT operations engineers. Often, development and IT operations share an uneasy relationship in enterprise IT. Developers commonly write code with scant consideration for operational aspects such as availability or monitorability. Sometimes they are pressured into deprioritizing work on operational considerations in favor of functionality. On the other hand, IT operations may set constraints on matters such as deployment windows, approved software and versions, and computing resources. DevOps makes both parties part of the same team. This helps them understand each other's concerns better.

DevOps recognizes the importance of culture. The acronym CAMS (culture, automation, measurement, and sharing) is used to encapsulate its key themes. Culture is acknowledged as all important in making development and IT operations work together effectively. But what is culture in this context? It is not so much about an informal dress code, flexible hours, or a free in-house cafeteria as it is about how decisions are taken, norms of behavior, protocols of communication, and the ways of navigating hierarchy and bureaucracy to get things done.

2.3 Agile Culture

> The brand is just a lagging indicator of a company's culture.
> —Tony Hsieh, founder of Zappos.com[6]

You might find yourself reading some of the recommendations I make and thinking that other approaches are equally valid. For example, I recommend against encouraging internal competition although there are many successful

---

5. http://www.thoughtworks.com/insights/blog/build-promotion-go
6. (Hsieh 2010)

counterexamples. It boils down to what we mean by Agile culture. Sahota[7] argues that Agile is mainly a fit for organizations with a collaboration culture or a cultivation culture. This terminology is from Schneider's culture model[8] for organizations. Here's a brief explanation based on Figure 2-1. An organization is a living social construct with an existing culture that exhibits dominant traits in one of the four quadrants shown in Figure 2-1. The horizontal axis represents how the organization makes decisions, and the vertical axis represents what the organization pays attention to. Control and competence cultures have impersonal processes of deciding—detached, formal, and policy driven. By contrast, collaboration and cultivation cultures (fit-for-Agile cultures) decide informally and participatively, always giving importance to people and context. Schneider argues for recognizing and making the best of one's culture rather than attempting interventions to change the culture, especially diagonal transitions in Fig-ure 2-1—wise counsel though somewhat conservative.

Besides, culture cannot be changed directly. It changes as a result of changes to organizational beliefs and rituals. Many of the recommendations in this book are about propagating the Agile culture that has taken root in development teams to the surrounding IT-B organization by changing the way the organization works.

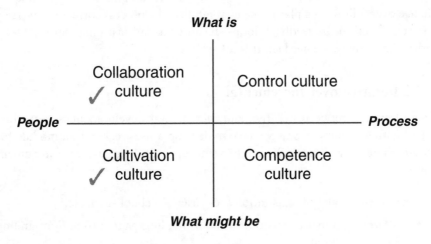

Figure 2-1 *Agile Culture = collaboration or cultivation*

---

7. http://www.infoq.com/minibooks/agile-adoption-transformation
8. http://www.parshift.com/Speakers/Speak016.htm and (Schneider 1994)

2.4 Common Themes

Let's now turn to a few lower-level principles commonly understood by the Lean and Agile community. A quick overview of these principles provides the background for points made in later chapters.

2.4.1 Fail-fast

Lengthy development processes combine high upside potential (successful delivery and benefits realization) with high downside risk (lots of money wasted). The idea with failing fast is to reduce downside risk while maintaining upside potential. We do things in such a way that we quickly know if we have it wrong. When the cost of failure is small, it lets us do more things on an experimental basis and negotiate unknowns better.

For example, the practice of continuous integration helps a development team fail-fast in integrating code under development. A corollary of failing fast is to aim for fast feedback. The practice of regularly showcasing (demoing) features under development to product owners and business stakeholders helps them verify whether it is what they asked for and decide whether it is what they really want. The Agile Manifesto emphasizes adaptability (responding to change over following a plan). The adaptability of a process correlates inversely with the length of its feedback loops. In order to fail-fast (and learn quickly) rather than slowly, we need short feedback loops.

2.4.2 Iterative over Incremental

The difference between iterative and incremental development is best illustrated with an example. Say we have to develop a user registration module for an e-commerce web app. We could write up a 20-page use case document covering:

- Different modes of registration (new-user, Facebook-user, etc.)
- Different points of registration (main landing page, promotion landing page, at checkout)
- Confirmation of registration
- Login audit trail
- Rules for valid usernames and passwords, password strength indicators, and so on

This use case would then be taken up by a developer and completed in four to six weeks. The developer would then move on to the next use case while the registration use case is taken up for testing. This is very coarse-grained incremental development. There is little or no feedback or learning from other roles (analyst, tester, product owner) during the four to six weeks of development.

To shorten the feedback loop, we split the registration use case into perhaps a dozen user stories. These stories are usually developed sequentially and sometimes as two, or at the most three, parallel streams of development. Being small, each story can go through an analyze-develop-test cycle in, say, two or three weeks. After that, they are showcased (demoed) to the product owner for feedback. Thus, when we develop iteratively, this week's development is informed by the feedback from last week. In case of continuous delivery, where features could be incrementally made available to users over multiple releases, this feedback could even be from production.

Feedback is what makes it iterative; otherwise, it is just mini-waterfall. Merely splitting use cases into stories does not make for iterative development if we wait until all stories are developed before we seek feedback. The point of splitting is to get feedback faster so that it can be incorporated into ongoing development. However, seeking stakeholder/user feedback for small batches of functionality (stories) is often not feasible with formal stage-gate processes.[9] They were conceived with linear flows of large batches in mind.

It takes more work to include end users rather than just product owners inside short iterative feedback loops. To take it all the way, we need to sequence the stories in such a way that the functionality is just about usable from an early stage. We rejig the feature's *internal scope* so that the feature can be delivered over several usable increments.

So, for example, instead of developing all modes of registration before taking up username and password validation, we'd start with the most common mode of registration and the most basic of validations for the first release. Features like just-in-time registration, login audit trail, and password strength indicator can wait until later. This provides users with a just-about-workable solution early on with soon-to-follow improvements that can also take advantage of their feedback. This approach is depicted in Figure 2-2. While this approach is safe to use with internal customers, in the case of market-facing applications, we may need to rope in a few willing beta customers because the market typically won't care for a just-about-workable solution.

---

9. http://www.pmhut.com/conducting-successful-gate-meetings

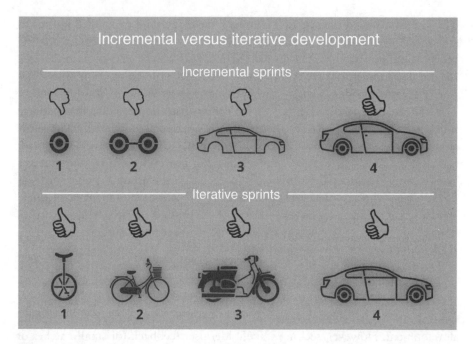

Figure 2-2 *Incremental versus iterative development (adapted from drawing by Henrik Kniberg)*

2.4.3 Value Stream Optimization

A value stream is a series of activities required to deliver an outcome. The software development value stream may be described as: validate business case, analyze, design, build, test, deploy, learn from usage analytics and other feedback—rinse and repeat. Note that it is an iterative rather than a linear series of activities. It is preferable to optimize the whole value stream rather than parts of it. Thus, end-to-end cycle time is more important than IT delivery cycle time or development velocity. When we optimize a value stream for end-to-end cycle time, we are optimizing for responsiveness over cost-efficiency. By contrast, when we optimize a part of the value stream without considering how it affects the whole value stream, it is called suboptimization or local optimization. The following chapters approach organization design with the aim of optimizing the whole value stream.

2.4.4 Information Radiators

Information radiators are giant public displays of information—electronic or paper. For example, they could be story card walls (Kanban boards), burnup charts, sales funnels, marketing events calendar or statistics, retrospective action items, standup meeting punctuality indicators, architecture diagrams, domain models, build pipelines, and so on. The idea behind a public (internal to the organization) information radiator is twofold. One, it promotes transparency of good and bad news. Two, it makes the information more accessible compared with information available by logging in and querying an application or looking up a report or dashboard. Good information radiators spark conversation.

It is common to find Agile teams using up any wall space they can find with information radiators. Sometimes, they amusingly run afoul of corporate guidelines that require all public displays to be approved by the internal communications (corporate communications) team. Although the ones created by the latter are also technically information radiators, in reality, they are better classified as notices, internal marketing, or promotions. Besides, they usually are slow-changing information compared to those relevant for IT-B work.

Information radiators have largely been used to *track* execution. But they can also be used to radiate information about business-IT alignment, chain of accountability for outcomes, portfolio mix and status, and organizational norms. These *organizational* information radiators are described in the chapters to follow.

2.5 Isn't Agile Dead?

It is claimed that Agile in the enterprise has hit the trough of disillusionment[10] in the hype curve.[11] Many problems stem from a premature attempt at *scaling* Agile within the organization. The nature of the transformation is such that it is unrealistic to plan upfront for an 18-month organization-wide change program to go from status quo to continuous delivery. People try nevertheless, and when the outcomes don't materialize, they say Agile doesn't work.[12] When the word spreads enough, the label of Agile gets a bad reputation and the community tries to move away from discredited labels to newer labels.

With apologies to Mark Twain, reports of the death of Agile are greatly exaggerated. If anything, Agile has yet to experience a legitimate birth in places that proclaim its demise. The word *development* in Agile software development does not just refer to developers. This may be obvious, yet many places focus only on reskilling developers and testers. They try a spurious implementation of

10. http://blogs.gartner.com/nathan-wilson/the-trough-of-disillusionment
11. http://www.gartner.com/technology/research/methodologies/hype-cycle.jsp
12. http://www.forbes.com/sites/stevedenning/2012/04/17/the-case-against-agile-ten-perennial-management-objections/

Agile and give it a bad name when it fails to improve business-IT effectiveness. Some may argue that there isn't just one right road to agility and so it is wrong to speak of spurious implementations. But the fact that Agile isn't prescriptive doesn't mean there is no such thing as a spurious implementation. Some adaptations go against basic principles so much that they can hardly be called Agile.

2.5.1 Spurious Implementations

For example, a common anti-pattern is to have separate activity-oriented teams of architects, analysts, developers, and testers and call it an Agile setup by having the team of developers adopt a few practices. We may argue that there is no injunction against activity-oriented teams in Scrum. But this falls into the trap of doing Agile rather than being Agile. To one who has internalized the idea of individuals and interactions over processes and tools, it is clear that an IT organization based on separate activity-oriented teams discourages free interaction and encourages process.

Another common anti-pattern is to tolerate the product owner not being a full-time participant in the development effort. Part-time product owners don't cut it because a user story is meant to be a placeholder for further conversation. One of the attributes of a good story is that it be negotiable (the N in INVEST[13]). It is imperative that someone with the power to negotiate be present for the conversation, not just a diffident analyst acting as a lame proxy for an absent product owner.

Many Agile implementations are compromised by well-meaning but misinformed people who first confuse the proper noun Agile (methodology) with the common English adjective and then make an incorrect mental substitution of the adjective *flexible* for agile. They go about brokering questionable compromises by saying, "Let's be agile about it." Most of the time, this is meant to dissuade a supposedly dogmatic adherence to Agile principles or practices. But mere adherence doesn't make it dogmatic. A levelheaded discussion may reveal that it is informed adherence.

2.6 Summary

- Agile principles are relevant for overall IT agility, not just engineering or process agility. They can be used to guide the design of an Agile IT organization.

---

13. http://xp123.com/articles/invest-in-good-stories-and-smart-tasks

- Continuous delivery is integral to Agile software delivery just as continuous integration is integral to Agile software development. DevOps helps continuous delivery by encouraging deep cross-pollination between developers and sysadmins as well as between developers and other IT operations engineers.

- When viewed through the frame of Schneider's culture model, an Agile culture/mindset is a good fit for collaboration and cultivation cultures, not so much for competence and control cultures. This is just model terminology; it doesn't imply that Agile cultures are incompetent.

- The adaptability of a process correlates inversely with the length of its feedback loops. In order to fail-fast (and learn quickly) rather than slowly, we need short feedback loops.

- Simply doing sprints or iterations doesn't make it iterative development if feedback is not sought in between or is ignored in deference to a release plan.

- Whole value stream optimization is far more important than optimizing activities that constitute the stream.

- The word *development* in Agile software development does not just refer to developers.

- Agile isn't prescriptive. That doesn't mean there is no such thing as a spurious implementation. Some adaptations go against basic principles so much that they can hardly be called Agile.

- Encourage the use of information radiators beyond development teams. As described in later chapters, they can be used to radiate information about business-IT alignment, chain of accountability for outcomes, portfolio mix and status, business metrics, and organizational norms.

Chapter 3

Key Themes

This chapter explains three key themes that form the basis for arguments in the rest of this book. All the organization design recommendations made in subsequent chapters can be traced to one or more of these themes. Here's a short summary:

- **Govern for value over predictability:** Software development is a design process rather than a production process. This has several implications for how we go about managing it. In particular, it is futile to chase predictability and important to chase value. More detail is provided in Section 3.1.

- **Organize for responsiveness over cost-efficiency:** Short IT delivery cycle time is the big promise of continuous delivery. Digital transformation requires this and more to achieve a short time to market. What does this mean for IT organization design? It is important to organize for responsiveness rather than cost-efficiency. Cost-efficiency is important, but it is to be traded off for responsiveness when needed. More detail is provided in Section 3.3.

- **Design for intrinsic motivation:** Digital transformation and continuous delivery require high levels of *unscripted collaboration* (Section 3.4.4) between teams. This requires a workforce that is motivated intrinsically rather than extrinsically. We'll see why this means designing an organization that fosters autonomy, mastery, and purpose.

3.1 Software Development Reconsidered

In order to understand the first theme—govern for value over predictability—we need to step back and reconsider software development. The IT industry is relatively new compared to the manufacturing or construction industry. Under the impression that software development is a production or construction process, IT managers have drawn parallels to manufacturing or construction (and continue to do so[1]) while seeking guidance for the management of software delivery. With this mental model, it is natural to expect predictability. However, expectations of predictability as expressed through project plans and release plans have never materialized.

A project plan is a prediction. It predicts that a team of N people will complete X amount of work by Y date. And how well have these predictions fared? The CHAOS Manifesto 2013[2] reports average cost and time overruns for sub-million dollar projects since 2004. Average overruns have never dipped below 45% for cost and 70% for time. Larger projects fare worse! Traditionally, we have tried to avoid overruns by doing even more analysis and upfront design and by tracking progress ever more closely. Given that the last ten years of this approach haven't yielded great results, it is worth questioning the assumption that software development is fundamentally predictable.

The assumption appears reasonable when we think of software development as a production process. As we will see, it is not so. But for this assumption, we might be less persistent in chasing predictability in the face of repeated failure. We might be more willing to move away from plan-driven projects. To question the assumption, let's see what this supposed production process produces. What is the product?

3.1.1 Source Code, Binary Is Not the Product

> In software all the effort is design.
> —Martin Fowler[3]

We don't get the product after the coding phase; we just get some source code. The source code is only the design. Yes, artifacts such as design diagrams, system architecture diagrams, and network diagrams are also design, but source code is the most detailed design. I'll explain this in a moment but this

1. http://www.business-standard.com/article/management/it-is-difficult-to-talk-of-value-when-you-cannot-measure-the-value-you-are-delivering-rohan-murty-114121400510_1.html
2. http://www.versionone.com/assets/img/files/CHAOSManifesto2013.pdf
3. http://martinfowler.com/articles/newMethodology.html

observation was made back in 1992 in *C++ Journal*.[4] It has generally been accepted as correct by the programming intelligentsia. But its profound implications have been largely underappreciated by the project management and IT governance communities. For example, one implication is that software bugs are not defects of production—they are defects in the design. Another implication is that the notion of a development team as a software factory[5] is a false metaphor. A factory manufactures or assembles product; development teams only produce the design (source code and/or binary). Understanding this helps us reset expectations of predictability from what we'd expect of a production/construction process to what we'd expect of a design process.

3.1.2 The Product Is What the User or Client Uses

> Product development produces the recipes for products, not the products themselves.
> —Don Reinertsen[6]

If software development were really a production process, it would culminate in a usable, finished product and not in a repository of source code or binaries. The product is what the user/client uses. Therefore, it is what we get when the deployed/installed software services a request. In case of web applications, for example, every page rendered on the user's browser is a product.

Production in software is realized at the very last moment. It is completely automated and usually error free (unless the server runs of resources, there is a network partition, etc.). If users find the product defective, they can ask for a replacement (in case of web apps) by simply refreshing the page—a new copy of the product is instantly made available. Because it does its job so silently, quickly, cheaply, and automatically, it escapes our attention as the real production phase—the phase where millions of identical/customized units of the end product are manufactured in response to millions of identical/unique requests.

Recall that the final environment where software runs is called *production*, whereas the environment in which coding takes place is called *development*. Coding is not production! All software is design. The hardware hosting the software is a factory capable of manufacturing the product on demand. The smartphone we hold in our hands is an example of a real software factory. The device is a factory; the various apps installed on it are but detailed designs for producing widgets and forms, graphics and layouts, interfaces and interactions.

---

4. Reeves, J. W. 1992. What is software design? Retrieved from *C++ Journal*: http://www.bleading-edge.com/Publications/C++Journal/Cpjour2.htm
5. http://en.wikipedia.org/wiki/Software_factory
6. (Reinertsen 2009)

The raw materials for production are the resources used by the smartphone—CPU cycles, memory, storage, display real estate, and bandwidth. Production is realized when we bring up an app and interact with it.

3.1.3 Software Development Is a Design Process

If software development were a production process, we wouldn't be allowed capitalize development cost. CapEx is only meant for nonconsumable items such as design. This is why the running cost of a data center is treated as OpEx. Development is a design process. Design processes are generally evaluated by the value they deliver rather than a conformance to plan. Therefore, it makes sense to move away from plan-driven projects and toward value-driven projects. This has implications for IT budgeting and staffing and is explored at length in Chapters 8, 9, and 10.

So what if it is a design process, you may ask. Why shouldn't it be predictable? Why can't we be plan driven and value driven? To answer this, consider why software features routinely take much longer to develop than estimated. A characteristic of software development is that we learn at least some of what it takes as we go about development. For any given team, there are always things in the third quadrant of Figure 3-1. During the course of development, the team encounters unanticipated challenges and moves from quadrant III to II and finally to I. Some of these challenges may simply have to do with the fact that the team lacks experience or skill in certain very specific technical areas. Training can only go so far; for example, classroom training with identifying performance bottlenecks using a profiler is very different from identifying a problem in a real production environment. So in general, it is not possible to do upfront work to eradicate unknown unknowns. You can't prepare for what you can't anticipate.

The realization that the source code is part of the design, not the product, fundamentally rewires our understanding of software. It is often shocking at first, much in the spirit of a remark attributed to the great Danish physicist, Niels Bohr: "Anyone who is not shocked by quantum theory has not understood it."

3.2 Govern for Value over Predictability

In view of the preceding arguments, it is better to try to maximize adaptability and chase value instead of chasing predictability. This is what the Agile Manifesto means when it says responding to change over following a plan. To maximize adaptability, it is essential to have good, fast feedback loops. This is why there is so much emphasis on iterative development (Section 2.4.2).

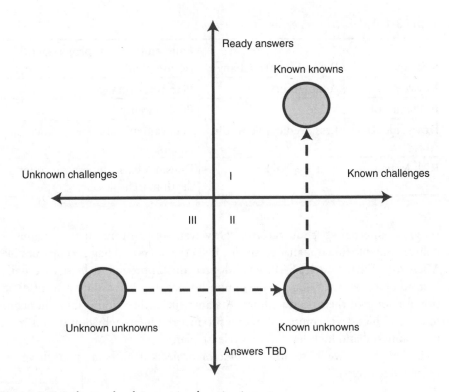

Figure 3-1 *Software development is a learning journey.*

How does a value-driven approach differ from a plan-driven approach? Table 3-1 provides a summary. A value-driven team can be set up to deliver relevant and useful functionality in steady increments, but it may not be possible to predict exactly what will be delivered by what date. It's a bit like the uncertainty principle—you can determine either exact scope or exact time, not both. In value-driven mode, we do not define the full solution upfront, only the problem. Even the understanding of the problem grows with time. Wearing a plan-driven hat, we ask: By when can you do this? or What will it cost to do this? Wearing a value-driven hat, we ask: How thoroughly can we solve this problem by that date? The power of this question cannot be understood unless we grasp the concept of internal scope. As described in the registration module example in Section 2.4.2, internal scope is scope internal to a feature. It is usually more negotiable than the feature itself.

Many leading software companies (e.g., GitHub, Box.com, Atlassian) operate in value-driven mode. They don't publish a release plan or even a product roadmap. Even internally, the roadmap does not have precise dates, only a target quarter. Where dates are honored—for example, for marketing

Table 3-1 *Value-driven versus Plan-driven*

Strategy	Responding to Change	Following a Plan (project plan, release plan)
Key Metric	Adaptability	Plan conformance
In Pursuit of	Value	Predictability
Downside Risk	Less predictable results	Less valuable and less predictable results
Risk Mitigation	Fast feedback	Does not exist (unless we count a death march[7] as one)

reasons—internal scope is variable. However, we can rely on their teams to deliver valuable functionality regularly. Even the old guard (e.g., companies like Microsoft, IBM, Oracle, SAP) has adopted this approach at least externally. Instead of a product roadmap, they publish what they call a statement of direction for some of their product lines. A statement of direction is more noncommittal and high-level compared with a product roadmap, which in turn is more noncommittal and high-level than a release plan.

In Chapter 8, we'll see how to refactor projects from being plan driven to being value driven.

3.3 Organize for Responsiveness over Cost-efficiency

> While companies may strive to achieve both, one of these factors must be the driver, the objective, and the other a constraint. Constraints help guide companies, but they are different from objectives and the two shouldn't be confused. Responsiveness is a business strategy. Agility and adaptability achieve that strategy.[8]
>
> —Jim Highsmith

An efficiency-oriented consumer bank will erect a multilevel interactive voice response (IVR) fence around the human agents in its call center. One that is responsiveness oriented will minimize IVR and always provide you an easy option to talk to a human. IT-B organizations face a similar tradeoff, but one that is way more justifiable in favor of responsiveness. They can choose to organize for responsiveness or cost-efficiency. In the IT-B world, cost-efficiency usually translates into a focus on staff utilization and/or productivity (delivery

---

7. http://en.wikipedia.org/wiki/Death_march_%28project_management%29
8. Highsmith, J. *Adaptive leadership: Accelerating enterprise agility,* 1st Ed., ©2014, p. 5. Reprinted and electronically reproduced by permission of Pearson Education Inc.

throughput). Given the increasing pressure on IT-B to reduce delivery cycle times, it is important to recognize and utilize opportunities to improve responsiveness even if it comes at the cost of some efficiency. Here is an illustrative scenario.

Scenario 3-1 Balancing Roadmap Fulfillment with Responsiveness to Users

GreatApps is a vendor of productivity apps on the Apple AppStore. One of their popular apps is an eBook reader called BookBliss. Alagu is the product manager, and Riya is the delivery manager on the Book-Bliss team. Buoyed by the success of version 1.0 (V1), they are working toward adding support for PDF files in the next major release. But this is a big feature and it will take a few months before even a minimum viable product (MVP) can be released. Riya is keenly aware of this and is trying to keep the team focused on PDF support. However, users of V1 are more interested in embellishments to existing support for epub and mobi formats. They keep pounding the forums with requests for improvements to annotations, bookshelf organization, syncing between devices, etc.

Alagu realizes that the current user base doesn't care as much about PDF support as they do about improvements to current features. He cannot appear to be unresponsive to their needs even as he goes after a new category of users in the next release. So he suggests that Riya carve out some team capacity for addressing the demands of V1 users. Riya feels that this will be a distraction from PDF support. She wants to maximize delivery throughput, and this is best achieved by having the whole team work on a single big feature. Spinning off some capacity for improvements would mean a net drop in velocity because the loss from the PDF stream wouldn't be made up by the initial slow velocity of the improvements stream.

Alagu agrees with Riya from an efficiency (productivity) maximization perspective but points out that the market situation called for prioritizing responsiveness over delivery efficiency. He agrees that they have to guard against any further fragmentation of capacity and avoid the risk of having too many streams of work in progress with far out completion dates.

Team design greatly influences responsiveness. Separate maintenance teams and matrix organizations for IT-B work against responsiveness. Chapter 5 deals with this in detail. As another example, manual processes of verification and control come in the way of responsiveness. In an essay called "How cadence determines process,"[9] Mary Poppendieck argues that weekly or shorter release frequencies demand a different process than monthly or longer ones. A continuous flow approach is used instead of checkpointing with the help of estimates, iterations (sprints), and commitments. Continuous delivery emphasizes automation and higher standards of engineering. It isn't easy, but market forces may leave little choice.

It Works!

Here is a successful business example of trading off cost-efficiency for responsiveness. In his account[10] of how he built Zappos—the online shoe retailer that Amazon acquired in a deal valued at $1.2 billon—Tony Hsieh reveals that he ran his warehouse round the clock even though it wasn't the most cost-efficient approach.

A cost-efficient approach would minimize the cost of servicing (picking) an order in the warehouse; that is, it would minimize the ratio: (hourly cost of running a warehouse) / (number of orders picked per hour). This would drive cost-optimizers to let orders pile up so that the picking density is higher and pickers have less of a distance to walk between orders. But piling up orders would mean that they aren't shipped (dispatched) as soon as possible, thus reducing responsiveness perceived by customers. The round-the-clock approach (among other things), while not the most cost-efficient, creates in Hsieh's words, "a WOW experience, which our customers remember for a very long time and tell their friends and family about."

Thus, a mindset of responsiveness considers time efficiency from the customer's or requestor's point of view rather than cost-efficiency from the service provider's point of view. A responsiveness mindset isn't born of altruism—it just makes good business sense overall even though it may not make for the best possible operational scorecard for any particular component of the business value stream (the warehouse in this case).

---

9. http://www.leanessays.com/2011/07/how-cadence-determines-process.html
10. (Hsieh 2010)

3.4 Design for Intrinsic Motivation and Unscripted Collaboration

Individual drive (motivation and energy) is essential for collaboration. Individual drive depends on personal and external factors. Personal factors include the emotional, mental, and physical health of the individual. External factors include things like working conditions and pay.

Most organizations attempt to provide a safe and comfortable physical space for their employees. Many offer attractive compensation packages and incentives like bonuses or variable pay. Some run rewards and recognition programs throughout the year. All of them have periodic performance review cycles to provide feedback and to hand out raises and promotions. Besides, there is the occasional team lunch, outing, or off-site event. Collectively, these measures act as *extrinsic* motivators—they are external to the content of the work, and they are out-of-band with respect to business as usual.

But what about having intrinsic motivation for the job at hand? What about doing the job well for its own sake or because it's satisfying? What about taking initiative even when there is no discernible personal payoff? This isn't new age idealism about artisans or craftspeople. Don't we hear at performance reviews that so-and-so is a self-motivated person? In his book *Drive,* Dan Pink[11] convincingly argues that intrinsic (self) motivation works better than extrinsic motivation. Extrinsic motivators may wear out or lose their novelty, but the intrinsically motivated individual is unstoppable.

Is self-motivation completely up to the self? Does organization design matter in this regard? If the best people motivators are intrinsic, what sort of organization design sustains intrinsic motivators? Pink argues that self-motivation arises under conditions of autonomy, mastery, and purpose. Taking this to be true, let's evaluate organization designs based on how well they promote autonomy, mastery, and purpose.

3.4.1 Autonomy

In the context of an organization, to have autonomy is to *be* empowered, not just *feel* empowered. Exactly how, we shall see later. But it does not mean being a lone wolf or being siloed or cut off from the rest of the organization. For example, entrepreneurs are autonomous but they are dependent on their investors, customers, suppliers, and employees. Autonomy to decide and execute can be very motivating.

---

11. http://www.ted.com/talks/dan_pink_on_motivation

3.4.2 Mastery

Mastery is the pursuit of excellence. We develop a liking for what we can do well. When in the zone,[12] work is its own reward. We feel motivated to do it even better. We feel great when our efforts bear fruit. This pursuit of excellence need not be confined to a designated part of the organization called a center of excellence. We'll explore some aspects of organization design that come in the way of mastery and see how to deal with them.

3.4.3 Purpose

It is natural for humans to seek out purpose. We want our lives to mean something. Those who labor under a strong belief in the larger purpose of their work can withstand all manner of hardship. We can often figure out whether someone is working purposefully or listlessly. A complete lack of purpose drives people into depression. The more we buy into the purpose of our team/product, the greater our resolve to work toward it. It helps if we can relate how our day-to-day tasks contribute to the larger cause. As we'll see later, this is easier to achieve in outcome-oriented teams (e.g., a self-sufficient product team) than in activity-oriented teams (e.g., testing team) because the work content in activity-oriented teams tends to be further removed from the business outcome (the purpose).

3.4.4 Unscripted Collaboration

Collaboration between teams is unscripted when it occurs outside of regular, scheduled meetings and without prior permission from or approval of team managers. Although scripted collaboration has it place, unscripted collaboration is essential for cultivating initiative, enabling innovation, and improving responsiveness. Trouble is, the traditional view of a manager is one who *owns* the time of those who report to her. However, this *manager-as-supervisor* persona is ill suited for an Agile workplace. Unscripted collaboration requires managers who are comfortable when their team members collaborate with other teams without their knowledge or permission. The manager's job is to anticipate problems, help achieve tradeoffs, help resolve disputes, and facilitate execution. Territorial control freaks need to be coached out of their comfort zones, and the incorrigible ones are better let go.

---

12. http://www.ted.com/talks/mihaly_csikszentmihalyi_on_flow

By its very nature, unscripted collaboration often goes unrecognized and unrewarded. What might motivate people to engage in unscripted collaboration despite such a bleak prospect? Intrinsic motivation! Unscripted collaboration needs an intrinsically motivating climate. What are the characteristics of this salubrious climate? Autonomy, mastery, and purpose.

3.4.5 An Organic Approach

A poor organizational climate stifles individual initiative and erodes the fertile soil of intrinsic motivation. Once the soil loses its inherent fertility, we have to resort to a never-ending regimen of external fertilizers. Accordingly, we will look at organization configurations that afford greater autonomy, respect mastery, and set people up with a shared purpose. As explained in Section 1.6, these configurations have structural, physical, cultural, political, and operational aspects. The chapters that follow examine these aspects in detail.

3.5 Summary

- Software development is a design process, not a production process. This makes it very hard to predict scope, development time, and effort. The track record of projects in the industry bears this out.
- We proceed on the following three themes:
  - Govern for value rather than predictability.
  - Organize for responsiveness over cost-efficiency.
  - Design for intrinsic motivation to encourage unscripted collaboration.
- Autonomy, mastery, and purpose are intrinsic motivators. They work better than traditional extrinsic motivators do. The following chapters suggest an organization design that fosters these intrinsic motivators.
- Organizational agility needs a culture of unscripted collaboration. It needs managers as facilitators and anticipators rather than managers as supervisors.
- Stop chasing the elusive goal of predictability. Chase value instead. This has implications for how we govern IT.
- When time to market is the first priority, structure teams for responsiveness first and cost-efficiency later.

Chapter 4

Superstructure

This chapter takes a macro-level view of the structure of organizations. It examines the pros and cons of centralized and decentralized structures through the lens of responsiveness and autonomy. It also introduces the notion of a silo and explains how it obstructs effective engagement between and inside business and IT. The next chapter builds on the foundations laid here.

4.1 Business Activities and Outcomes

This book lays a lot of emphasis on having teams *responsible for business outcomes* (outcome-oriented teams) as opposed to being *responsible for activities* (activity-oriented teams). To understand why, let's first review what qualifies as business outcome. Selling a product and generating revenue is an example of a business *outcome*. The outcome is the result of a long chain of *activities* like market research, lead generation, product design, development, testing, and customer support. To achieve the outcome, it is often necessary to adopt a divide-and-conquer approach and break the outcome into suboutcomes, as shown in Figure 4-1. However, the suboutcomes aren't so valuable by themselves, only in the larger context. For example, doubling leads is not useful if conversion halves. As outcome subdivision unfolds, we end up with merely contributory activities (e.g., development of marketing case studies).

The difference between outcomes and activities is similar to that between user stories and tasks in Agile software development. Table 4-1 illustrates that outcomes may be split into suboutcomes just as a feature may be split into several stories. But unless we are careful about how we split, we may end up with

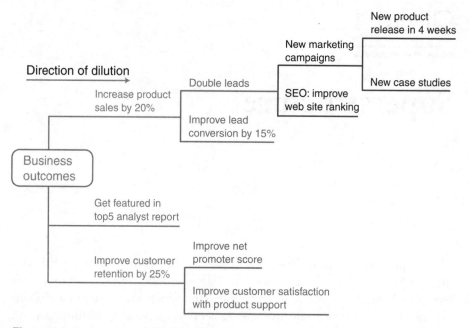

Figure 4-1 *Progressive subdivision dilutes outcomes into activities.*

Table 4-1 *Understanding Activities and Outcomes*

High-level outcome		Feature/Epic
Lower-level outcome	*maps to*	Story
Activity		Task

an activity instead of a suboutcome just as we may end up with a task instead of a story.

How do we determine whether the division of an outcome results in a sub-outcome or an activity? It is important to know this because, as we'll see soon, it is okay to form a team around a suboutcome but not around an activity. We could seek guidance from the criteria used for user stories and tasks. Good user stories are expected to be independent, negotiable, valuable, estimable, small, and testable (mnemonic INVEST). Good tasks are expected to be specific, measurable, achievable, relevant, and time-boxed (mnemonic SMART). The key difference is that tasks need not be independent or valuable by themselves.

These criteria can be adapted to organizational outcomes and activities as well. Good business outcomes are testable, valuable, independently achievable, and negotiable (TVIN). As we split higher-level outcomes into suboutcomes, we ask whether they continue to be independent and valuable business outcomes. If the answer is no, it is an activity rather than an outcome. Here is a hypothetical list of pending outcomes for an independent software vendor (ISV). As we go down the list, they begin to look less like business outcomes and more like activities.

- Increase product sales by 20%
- Improve Net Promoter score for a product by 10 points
- Improve customer satisfaction with product support
- Improve web site ranking in search results
- Ship the next release by a certain date
- Double the average number of leads in the pipeline

4.1.1 Outcome Orientation Allows for Autonomy

Why is the distinction between outcomes and activities important for organization design? Recall that we set out with the premise of designing an organization that allows for autonomy (Section 3.4). When we grant autonomy to a team, we run the risk of local optimization—the team cares much more about its own success than the success of the business as a whole. As it turns out, it is less risky to grant autonomy to outcome-oriented teams. Since outcomes (or suboutcomes) are independently valuable and achievable, local optimization is less of an issue. Therefore, a greater degree of autonomy can be afforded to a team that is responsible for an outcome. As long as they are accountable for the outcome, they can have some leeway in how they go about achieving it. This is not true for activities. Since they aren't independently valuable, optimizing at the level of an activity doesn't help at all. On the contrary, activity-level optimization is a common cause of silos and the lengthening of end-to-end cycle times.

   Owning an outcome also gives a team a sense of purpose—they can see how their efforts result in business value. It turns out to be intrinsically motivating. Figure 4-2 illustrates the two configurations. In both cases, a set of activities (a1..a5) cater to a set of outcomes (O1..O3). When we organize by outcome, each team owns one outcome and all the activities needed for it. By contrast, when we organize by activity, no single team owns an outcome. Each team owns just one of many activities that contribute to an outcome. Activity-oriented teams are often single-specialty teams—each member is a specialist in one activity, for example, a testing team or a vendor-management team. Outcome-oriented teams are multispecialty teams because the outcome needs the coordinated effort of multiple disciplines.

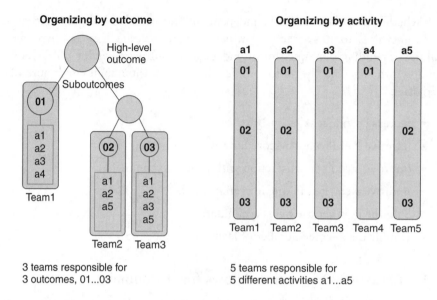

Figure 4-2 *Two ways of organizing teams*

For example, within IT, a project is usually a suboutcome that requires activities like development, testing, and support/maintenance. The latter are activities because they aren't independently valuable. It is suboptimal to form teams around these activities. It is better to group all the needed competencies into a project team or, even better, a stable long-lived capability team. Chapters 5, 8, and 10 cover this in detail.

4.1.2 The Outcome Owner

Outcome-oriented teams need clear leadership to make the best use of their autonomy. Otherwise, internal divisions may surface over important decisions. Responsiveness is affected when decisions are stalled. Designating one person as the outcome owner helps break stalemates. It also helps fix accountability. We'll dive into this in Chapter 6, where we also discuss balancing mechanisms that discourage outcome owners from abusing their decision rights. Note that this is not a new job title or a new rung in the hierarchy. Depending on the situation, the outcome owner might be a product manager, marketing or sales manager, product owner, project manager, head of change program, etc. By contrast, heads of activities such as a test manager, marketing-content manager, or VP/director of engineering would not make good candidates for the label of outcome owner.

4.1.3 Outcome Design

Not only are good business outcomes independently valuable, they are also independently achievable (just as good user stories can be independently taken up for development). This makes it possible to assign a single outcome owner and provide her with a team (organization) to realize the outcome. Otherwise, we run into avoidable structural dependencies that reduce responsiveness and challenge autonomy.

For example, take the case of a brick-and-mortar retailer who has begun testing the e-tailing waters. They bring on a chief digital officer (CDO) who puts together a digital transformation team. They sign up to deliver 5% of total revenue via digital channels in 18 months. So far so good. However, they go on to create suborganizations for web and mobile and hire separate product owners for capabilities such as catalog, search, personalization, and loyalty. This results in a matrix organization where neither the verticals (channels) nor the horizontals (products/ capabilities) represent independent outcomes. Catalog, search, and personalization cannot be delivered effectively as independent streams as they are too closely related. Digital loyalty cannot be developed independent of store loyalty. Given the organization, the original outcome of 5% revenue loses its way when subdivided into non-independent outcomes like catalog, search, personalization, and loyalty. Interdependent streams need a common outcome owner. Digital loyalty probably works better as a subunit of store loyalty. Introducing organizational boundaries between web and mobile hurts integration and UX. The next two chapters will provide us with a sound basis for better organization.

4.2 Centralization and Decentralization

> Many people approach this question as a problem to be solved once and for all; in truth, the question is a classic paradox that has a resolution, not a solution. Resolutions are temporary, not permanent, and change from time to time as the situation changes.[1]
>
> —Jim Highsmith

The fundamental challenges of organization are the same whether it is a corporate, a nonprofit, or a state. Centralized configurations have a tendency to disempower local units. On the other hand, subunits in decentralized configurations tend to jealously guard their local level autonomy. When they pose problems

---

1. Highsmith, J. *Adaptive leadership: Accelerating enterprise agility,* 1st Ed., ©2014, p. 12. Reprinted and electronically reproduced by permission of Pearson Education, Inc.

for coordinated action across units, they are labeled as silos. It is apparent that the choice of organization ought to be situational. One size doesn't fit all. What is less obvious is that *one size doesn't even fit any one (unit) at all times.*

For example, it makes sense for a new product development effort to be independent and autonomous (decentralized) until it achieves some maturity in the market (success of the first order). Later, some functions like marketing and sales may be partially centralized to exploit synergies with other products and achieve some consistency of messaging (success of the second order). Designing for second-order success from the beginning runs the risk of compromising first-order success.

If we accept autonomy as desirable for intrinsic motivation, then we need to design for adequate autonomy at a local level. This means centralized configurations won't work. The question then is how much to decentralize and along what dimensions. Typical dimensions are product or line of business, region, and function. Business outcomes are usually defined by product (or line of business) and then subdivided among regions. Decentralizing along product or region usually retains alignment with business outcomes. Functional decentralization (e.g., marketing, sales, product development, and support), on the other hand, does not align with business outcomes because each function represents only one of several activities required to achieve the outcome. Thus, autonomous products or regions work better than autonomous functions. Autonomous functions are the most common cause of silos.

4.3 Silos

A silo is a common symptom of decentralization gone wrong. In everyday English, a silo is a cylindrical tower used for storing grain. It is also used to refer to an underground military structure where ballistic missiles can be stored and fired. In either case, silos serve to protect what's within from intruders, be it pests, the weather, or the enemy. Corporate vocabulary has co-opted the word to mean an organizational unit that exhibits similar characteristics:

> Organizational silos are units (e.g., teams, departments) that tend to protect themselves and not work well with other units.

As much as this book is about an organization design oriented toward autonomy, it recognizes that silos are a case of misplaced or runaway autonomy. Silos show up at different levels and different internal boundaries of the organization. Here are some examples of high-level silos:

- Functional silos: Sales and marketing don't talk to each other. The notorious business-IT divide is a sign of a business silo and an IT silo.

- Regional silos: Europe sales and North America sales argue over who should support a transcontinental deal.

- Product silos: Cross-selling attempts by sales are continuously frustrated by inadequate integration between products. Consistent messaging and branding attempts by marketing are thwarted by product teams with a mind of their own.

Some silos are worse than others. For example, functional silos are worse than the regional and product-level silos. The latter, being organized along outcomes, are at least able to contribute to the business independently. Using this frame, let's reconsider business and IT.

4.3.1 Business-IT Divide

An IT organization is itself a functional vertical and a potential silo. It isn't market facing. It is often viewed as a cost center and as a support function by the business. Although there is some truth to this view, it is detrimental for IT-B work. IT-B work is generally only commissioned when there is a business case for making over buying. Making is as much about making the right thing (the what) as it is about making the thing right (the how). In case of a design process like software development (Section 3.1.3), determining the right thing is not a one-off upfront activity. It is iterative and it requires intense, unscripted collaboration between business and IT. A mentality of profit center dictating terms to cost center does not work; it results in comments such as "business doesn't know what it wants" or "if only IT could deliver on its promises."

The dreaded business-IT divide also shows up in digital transformation efforts. When the chief marketing officer (CMO) and chief information officer (CIO) do not partner well, it results in a bolt-on[2] digital solution—a veneer of social media presence and mobile apps without data integration. The rise of the CDO[3] role is an attempt to bridge this divide by bringing digital marketing and IT under one executive. But even a CDO is likely to have a background in business and marketing rather than leading strategic IT. A *McKinsey Quarterly* article[4] suggests that it is time to introduce the position of chief of software development in addition to CDO and CIO.

---

2. http://www.thedrum.com/news/2014/05/06/
   ceos-favour-bolt-digital-strategies-over-digital-transformation-says-forrester-study
3. http://www.forbes.com/sites/lisaarthur/2013/09/03/why-you-should-consider-hiring-a-chief-
   digital-officer-and-why-now/
4. http://www.mckinsey.com/insights/high_tech_telecoms_internet/the_perils_of_ignoring_
   software_development

4.3.2 Silos inside IT

Silos can also show up within a department—let's call them *lower-level silos*. Lower-level silos are an organizational anti-pattern. They may be disbanded by reorganizing along business outcomes. For instance, IT-B itself may be set up in the form of verticals like architecture, database, UX, development, QA, release management, etc. These verticals often end up behaving like lower-level silos.

> An *IT silo* results when a specialized competency is localized in such a way that it drastically increases the cost of handoffs in a delivery value stream.

Here are some signs of these silos:

- Takes forever to get things done
- Not enough collaboration between teams or departments
- A culture of "play it safe"—everyone worried about protecting themselves from blame
- A culture of one-upmanship—department heads trying to highlight their team's achievement without much regard for overall business outcomes

Silos may result from a variety of factors. These factors never operate in isolation; they are contributory. Some common factors are listed below:

- Multiple teams per business outcome
- Multiple power centers per business outcome (e.g., matrix organization)
- High-friction communication protocols
- Silo-inducing tooling

The first two factors listed above are common in big organizations. They are a side effect of organizing for cost-efficiency or making simplistic attempts at scaling. We address them in detail in Chapters 5 and 6. Communication is addressed in Chapter 14 and tooling in Chapter 11.

4.3.3 Higher-Order Silos

Even when organizational units are designed to be aligned with particular business outcomes, they may be misaligned with higher-order, overarching business outcomes. These higher-order silos are somewhat tolerable if they at least deliver on individual business missions (e.g., two products that do not play well together but do well individually). On the other hand, if synergy matters more than individual success, then they need to be combined into a single organizational unit.

In this book, we are more concerned with business units and departments that aren't even created around a business outcome (e.g., departments created around activities like development and testing). Where they are outcome oriented, we are concerned about silo-inducing internal structures that limit their performance. We first aim to get rid of the lower-level silos.

Once a unit proves itself, it is appropriate to think about and address second-order problems that inhibit synergies and consistencies. It is a kind of premature design optimization to address second-order issues before the unit proves itself. This is somewhat analogous to how lean start-ups invest in technology and infrastructure. They first focus on proving the product in the market (success of the first order). Once long-term funding is secured, the architecture can be refactored for scalability, lower cost per transaction, etc. (success of the second order).

Whatever way we organize, the unit of organization is a team, and any team can turn into a silo if it acts in an insular manner. Therefore, in a sense, we can't eliminate silos but only try to design around their side effects. By designing teams around critical first-order business outcomes, we shield primary outcomes from the side effects of silos. Secondary outcomes (e.g., integration between products, bundled offerings) will still be exposed to the side effects of silos and will need different coping mechanisms.

Before concluding that you don't have a problem because all your silos are higher order, check to see whether what you call a higher-order silo is really an outcome-oriented unit. That is, before asking how I can make my current set of teams work better together, ask whether they are the right configuration of teams.

We don't deal with higher-order silos here as they are about dysfunctions of a higher order rather than business-IT ineffectiveness. Here, we are concerned with the state of business-IT ineffectiveness where first-order success itself is a challenge. To deal with higher-order silos, Lencioni[5] advocates the use of overarching goals, objectives, and metrics to get silos to cooperate. Aaker[6] discusses silo-spanning solutions for effective marketing.

4.4 Summary of Insights

- An outcome (or suboutcome) is something that is independently valuable to the business.
- Activities serve outcomes. Having teams responsible for activities puts the business outcome at risk of activity-level optimization. By contrast, outcome-oriented teams can be allowed greater autonomy.

5. (Lencioni 2006)
6. (Aaker 2008)

- An organization design geared toward autonomy has to be somewhat decentralized.

- Although organization design by itself cannot eliminate silos, it can help avoid silos that come in the way of business success of the first order (primary outcomes).

4.5 Summary of Actions

- Before asking how I can make my current set of teams work better together, ask whether they are the right configuration of teams.

- Decentralize along lines of business, product lines, or regions rather than along functional specialization. This retains greater alignment with business outcomes and improves prospects for outcome realization.

- Form teams around business outcomes rather than activities. Although it may be necessary to split high-level business outcomes into suboutcomes, the process can be kept in check by using the testable, valuable, independent, and negotiable (TVIN) test. Failure of the test indicates that the suboutcome is not really a business outcome but a contributory activity.

- For each outcome-oriented team, designate one person as the outcome owner. This is a full-time role.

- Make sure that your outcomes (or suboutcomes) are independently achievable and valuable before forming teams around them.

- Product lines (or LOBs) need to be individually successful. This is success of the first order. Exploiting cross-product synergies, offering bundles, and achieving cross-product standardization for marketing are examples of higher-order success. Do not organize for higher-order success before first-order success is achieved. Doing so puts the cart before the horse.

Chapter 5

Team Design

The first four chapters were short and introductory. The water gets deeper from here on. This chapter describes how various multiteam configurations, including the matrix organization, reduce organizational agility and how having fewer outcome-oriented, cross-functional teams can help. It explains why activity-oriented teams cannot work with small batch sizes required for lower cycle time. It covers why testing and maintenance are not separate activities and how certain configurations of outsourcing work better than others do. In terms of the key themes laid out in Chapter 3, the discussion in this chapter expands on organizing for responsiveness over cost-efficiency.

5.1 Framing the Problem

Why do business-IT organizations end up in situations where multiple teams are collectively responsible for a single business outcome? Here are some typical reasons:

- The scale of the problem is such that a single team would be unwieldy.
- Organizational boundaries
- Functional (activity-oriented teams)
- Regional (distributed teams)
- Business (product teams)
- Contractual (e.g., outsourcing)
- Shared support services (e.g., IT helpdesk, product support)

Whatever the reason for multiple teams serving a single outcome, once they are in place; it reduces the effectiveness with which the larger outcome may be realized. Why? Because collaboration within a team can be continuous, but collaboration between teams is always discontinuous (discrete). Meetings, for instance, are a great indicator of discontinuous collaboration. Continuous delivery needs continuous (and unscripted) collaboration. Effective collaboration on any given task between two individuals X and Y on two different teams depends on the following:

- Their individual dispositions to collaborate
- Their history of working together (relationship)
- The prevailing interteam communication protocol
- Whether the task has the same level of importance and urgency for both teams

The last two points can be affected by organization design. Can two individuals, X and Y, simply meet with each other, agree on what is required, and go back and do the work? Do they have to involve their respective managers in the process? Do the managers have to sanction the time for it? Does it all have to be via some system of record? The more process and indirection there is, the greater the friction for effective collaboration.

By contrast, people within a team don't have to schedule meetings to collaborate with each other. They collaborate continuously and get into huddles (informal, ad hoc meetings—virtual or face to face) on demand. But given that multiple teams are unavoidable and that it reduces effectiveness, how can we design teams so that the most important outcomes are affected the least? This is the basis for the rest of our discussion in this chapter.

5.2 Activity-oriented Teams

Sales, marketing, product development, support, recruitment, and finance are all examples of specialized competencies. It is quite conventional to have a separate team per competency of this sort. Often called *specialist teams,* we call them *activity-oriented teams* to convey that they are formed around activities rather than outcomes (Section 4.1). Activity-oriented teams are a form of functional organization. In terms of traditional staff and line terminology,[1] all staff and line functions are activity-oriented teams when they are organized separately by function.

---

1. http://en.wikipedia.org/wiki/Staff_and_line

For example, it is common to organize by specialization for a given line of products and assign a manager (full or part time) per line item below:

- Inside sales
- Field sales
- Sales engineers (pre sales)
- Marketing—content
- Marketing—advertising, social media
- Marketing—SEO, product web site
- Marketing—strategy
- Product management
- Product development
- Architecture
- UX
- Analysis
- Development
- QA
- Release management
- IT operations
- Product support
- Product solutions (custom installations, add-ons)
- Product training and certification

This effectively results in a dozen activity-oriented teams per product. Organizing teams like this isn't the best way to serve the business outcome—that is, a successful product. It results in multiple, high-latency handoffs across teams to get anything done, whether it be developing a new feature, launching a marketing campaign for a product release, fixing a bug identified by a customer, or closing a new deal. Yet, it is what happens when IT-B is organized as a matrix.

5.2.1 Hamstrung by High-Latency Handoffs

As defined in Section 2.4.3, a value stream is a series of activities required to deliver an outcome. N activities require N − 1 handoffs for a work item (or batch) to pass through the value stream. Handoffs are simply a result of activity specialization. However, when a value stream is serviced by a series of activity-oriented teams (functional organization), each handoff is a handoff between teams. This makes it slower and more expensive.

Consider the case where this work item is a software build. If the testing team is separate from the development team, they will not accept builds on a continuous basis but rather have their own schedule by which to take new builds. This means that each new build accepted by QA will have a lot more changes (large batch size) than in the case where new builds from development are automatically deployed into a QA environment on an ongoing basis.

Expensive handoffs encourage large batch sizes to reduce the total number of handoffs. A separate database team will not entertain piecemeal requests for query optimization. They'd rather own the data model and enforce indexing conventions across the board. They won't review or help with unit-level database migration scripts. They'd rather review the whole set of migrations when the application is ready for UAT or some other similar state of maturity. On the other hand, a database specialist embedded in a development team will be much more responsive to piecemeal requests.

Large batch sizes lengthen cycle times. Items in the batch have to wait their turn for processing and, after processing, have to wait until all other items are processed before the batch can be handed over to the next stage. Even when all items are taken up for processing at once, the cycle time of the batch is at least equal to the cycle time of its slowest item. Long cycle times won't do. There is mounting pressure to bring new capabilities to the market faster than ever.

> In any system of work, the theoretical ideal is single-piece flow, which maximizes throughput and minimizes variance. You get there by continually reducing batch sizes.
> —The Phoenix Project[2]

Short cycles require small batch sizes. Reinertsen[3] argues that reducing batch size helps reduce cycle time, prevent scope creep, reduce risk, and increase team motivation. Reducing batch size is impractical when handoffs are expensive. Recall that a value stream with N activities requires $N - 1$ handoffs per batch. Halving batch size doubles the total number of handoffs needed. This is only feasible when handoffs are inexpensive; that is, when we move away from using multiple activity-oriented teams to service a value stream. Figure 5-1 summarizes the discussion thus far in this section.

2. (Kim, Behr, and Spafford 2013)
3. (Reinertsen 2009)

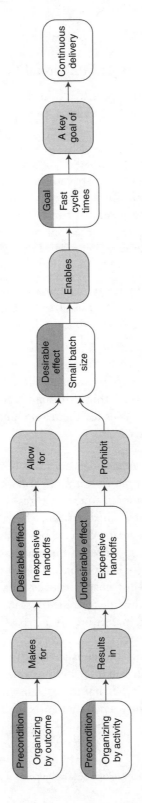

Figure 5-1 *Team design influences batch size.*

5.2.2 The Traditional Lure of Functional Organization

Why has functional organization persisted over the years despite the drawbacks described above? The traditional motivation for specialized teams can be traced to a legitimate desire for:

- Efficient utilization of specialist resources across a line of products: Rather than dedicate, say, two specialists to each of four products with an average specialist utilization of say 60%, it is more efficient to create a shared activity-oriented team of five (since 2 * 4 * 0.6 = 4.8) people available on demand to any of the four products. This is also an attractive option in a situation where supply of the said specialty in the market is scarce.

- Standardization: As members of a single specialty team, say, a marketing content team, it is easier to standardize templates and formats, achieve consistent messaging across product lines, and coordinate product releases.

- Nurturing the competency by localizing it: When people of a common specialization sit together, it is easier to share knowledge and help each other with troubleshooting, think through a solution, review each other's work, etc. It is also easier for the team manager to ask for a training budget and other resources.

The traditional model has come under question because of the increasingly shorter time *to market* and time *in market*.[4] Software products have a very short window available to monetize new features or capabilities. We can no longer take for granted an entrenched customer base; it is likely their patience will wear out unless they see a steady delivery of valuable capability. Even in the case of enterprise IT, being responsive to the business is more important than minimizing cost per function (or story) point. The traditional model of activity-oriented teams may be good for cost-efficiency, but it is bad for end-to-end cycle time. It is therefore worthwhile to trade off some efficiency for the sake of responsiveness. As we will see in Section 5.4, a cross-functional team is a good way to achieve this tradeoff.

Just enough standardization and consistency can still be achieved without being part of the same team. It is harder but possible, as we will see later from the Spotify example. On the other hand, specialist teams have a tendency to adhere to a mindless uniformity across all sorts of unnecessary things in the name of consistency across the product line.

---

4. http://www.thoughtworks.com/insights/blog/rise-serial-innovator

As for nurturing competencies, it is important, but not at the expense of the business outcome. Organization design ought to cater to first things first. There are other ways of nurturing competencies like cultivating communities of practice. More on this in Section 5.7.

5.2.3 When Is It OK to Have Activity-oriented Teams?

What about departments like HR, admin, legal, and finance? Are they organized around outcomes or activities? If we go by how we distinguish between outcomes and activities in Section 4.1, it is clear that these support functions don't own independently valuable business outcomes. Therefore, they are activity-oriented teams. Does it then mean they automatically become silos and therefore candidates for being disbanded?

Some activities are closer to the outcome than others. For example, UX is closer than admin to the outcome of product success. Ask whether the realization of the outcome is dependent on repeated successful iterations through some core value stream. If yes, then the activities belonging to this value stream should not be conducted in separate activity-oriented teams. Activities that aren't an integral part of a business outcome's core value stream may be spun off into separate teams without much risk.

Even where they are not part of a value stream, activity-oriented teams tend to standardize their operations over time. Their appetite for offering custom solutions begins to diminish. Complaints begin to surface—"They threw the rule book at us," "What bureaucracy!" and so on. However, as long as they don't directly affect business outcomes, they are allowed to exist.

For example, it is an anti-pattern to maintain a long-lived knowledge management (KM) team. It is an activity-oriented team for what is meant to be a collective activity. Disband it after initial rollout of the KM system. KM is everyone's responsibility. Knowledge is documented via recorded conversations, videos, blog posts, proposals, and reports. Let the relevant community of practice (Section 5.7) curate its content on the KM system. It is generally so specialized that it doesn't help to hire a generalist technical writer or content curator.

5.2.4 Independent Testing, Verification, and Validation

Independent testing is the notion that the team that tests should be different and separate from the team that develops in order to achieve greater rigor in testing. Many IT services vendors offer independent testing services. Doesn't this justify a separate activity-oriented team for testing? In my experience, there is no loss of rigor or conflict of interest in including developers and testers on the same team. Any deficiency in testing is bound to show up in UAT or production and reflect poorly on the team or the vendor. Given the cost of acquiring new clients, IT suppliers are generally extremely keen to land and expand, that is, cultivate long-term relationships and grow accounts.

On the contrary, independent testing wrecks the flow of work through the development value stream. It discourages collaboration between developers and testers and leads to all sorts of suboptimization by both teams to protect their reputations. The chapter on metrics (Chapter 12) describes a number of scenarios of suboptimization resulting from independent testing.

Hiving off testing for lack of in-house skills is a different matter altogether. For example, it is common to engage a third party for testing security—vulnerability assessments, penetration testing, etc. However, this doesn't come in the way of the development value stream as much because it is somewhat removed from the functionality being built.

Then there are those who argue that verification and validation activity should be conducted at arm's length from each other. But the traditional distinction between software verification and validation[5] is old school. One distinction is that validation is akin to field tests while verification is closer to lab tests. In case of pure software, A/B tests[6] and beta customer programs come close to field tests whereas tests of functionality and simulated performance tests are closer to lab tests. Although the distinction makes sense, it is no reason to separate the people that perform field and lab tests from each other and from the rest of the development team. A second oft-quoted distinction also makes sense in this light but is rarely applied correctly. It is said that verification checks whether we have *built the thing right,* and validation checks whether we have *built the right thing.* However, in practice, we frequently find no provision for field tests and so-called validation teams are responsible only for end-to-end lab tests, while verification teams are limited to component-level lab tests.

5.3 Shared Services

Shared services are similar to activity-oriented teams except that they are usually shared across unrelated business outcomes. All shared services are activity-oriented teams, but all activity-oriented teams aren't shared services. For example, if a product development team is split into a team of developers and a team of testers with a manager per team, they are activity-oriented teams but not shared services. Typical examples of shared services include IT helpdesk,

---

5. http://en.wikipedia.org/wiki/Verification_and_validation_%28software%29
6. http://en.wikipedia.org/wiki/A/B_testing

software product level-2 support (single team serving multiple products), internal private cloud team, and call centers. Although they play a crucial supporting role in the realization of business outcomes, they are often treated and managed purely as cost centers. Shared services cannot be totally avoided, but they shouldn't be encouraged as a way to do more with less. It is usually counterproductive to have enterprise architecture, UX, software testing, IT operations (e.g., for a SaaS product) or even product marketing and sales as shared services. Ethar Alali has written a great two-part article explaining the drawbacks of shared services and activity-oriented teams with a non-IT example.[7]

5.3.1 Shared Services Lose Purpose

When several teams of developers share a common team of testers, what is the purpose with which the testers identify? The developer teams each have a product to develop; their purpose is a successful product or at least a successful release. The shared testing team's purpose often degenerates to that of being an efficient provider of testing services with allegiance to no particular product.

It is important to recognize this aspect of shared services. By definition, shared services are used by teams responsible for different business outcomes. The shared team itself isn't responsible for those outcomes. It is no surprise then that we sometimes get the feeling of dealing with mercenaries when interacting with a shared service team. They don't seem to have their skin in the game.

Shared services struggle to find purpose. An organization design that aims for conditions of autonomy, mastery, and purpose should strive to minimize shared services and eliminate them from mission-critical value streams.

5.3.2 Reducing Friction in Shared Service Interfaces

Interteam collaboration typically requires following a communication protocol enforced by a work tracking tool or a single point of contact. It means meetings between team representatives with documented minutes of meetings. Feedback loops lengthen, reducing our ability to fail-fast (Section 2.4.1). Team managers try to showcase their team's performance with team-level metrics. Incoming work gets queued and prioritized based on some centrally conceived criteria. Dependent teams get frustrated with turnaround times and attempt priority escalations.

Here is an example of how a communication protocol designed for cost-efficiency ends up affecting responsiveness. It is typical for IT support to use ticketing systems. It helps the IT support manager track the workload. Some

---

7. http://goadingtheitgeek.blogspot.co.uk/2014/07/the-drawback-of-shared-services.html

employees who are friends with the engineers in IT support tend to request help directly via chat. This is understandably discouraged because it flies under the manager's radar and does not leave an audit trail. Once a ticket is assigned to an engineer, she is expected to carry out the task and put the ticket in the state of "completed subject to customer confirmation." Sometimes, the ticket lacks some information or it needs troubleshooting on the requestor's computer. Depending on the nature of the ticket, she may choose to:

- Reply to the ticket asking for more information and put the ticket in a state of "awaiting customer response" or

- Get in touch with the requester via phone/chat, obtain the needed information, carry out the task, and close the ticket.

The first option is probably more efficient from an IT support perspective. She doesn't have to look up the requestor's phone number and there is no wasted communication effort if the requestor is not available at that moment. Besides, everything is written down and recorded. The second option is more responsive from the requestor's perspective. It feels less like dealing with a bureaucracy.

The first option can get worse for the requestor if the ticket is reassigned to a different engineer every time the requestor responds. We experience this first-hand when trying to sort out a nontrivial problem with our bank or telecom provider's call center. We are expected to explain the whole problem all over again to a new agent. Being able to switch agents freely on a ticket helps maximize agent utilization. Unfortunately, it also maximizes customer frustration.

Designers of the system may argue that the history of the ticket is recorded, and so the customer should not have to repeat it. However, the recorded history is seldom self-explanatory. Besides, an agent new to a ticket would much rather hear it again first-hand than having to read through and assimilate the record.

What if the situation is level-3 commercial product support for external customers? Getting in touch with the requestor might be unrealistic, but we could at least have the same person responding until the ticket is resolved. What if, in order to provide 24×7 support, level-3 people are located in different time zones? Now we can't help agent switching, can we? Well, at least we can avoid agent switching within a time zone on a given ticket.

5.4 Cross-functional Teams

A cross-functional team (also called multifunctional, poly-skilled, or interdisciplinary) is one whose members belong to different specializations and work together toward a common outcome. They are a necessary consequence of organizing for business outcomes rather than activities. The realization of any outcome is bound to involve many different activities. This calls for people with widely different skills to be part of the same team. For example, a cross-functional product team may consist of people with all the skills listed in Section 5.2.

The top half of Figure 5-2 shows a conventional stratified IT organization. The product owner is quite removed from daily development. The term development team is only applied to a minimally cross-functional team of developers, testers, database, and UX people. Sometimes it is worse—development team just refers to developers. In either case, the team is not equipped to own a business outcome.

The lower half of the figure depicts what it would take to own an outcome. The inner box represents a well-equipped cross-functional product development team. Architects, business analysts, deployment engineers, and product owners join the team. Some parts of IT operations, marketing, and sales are also folded in. For example, Operations-A provide a virtualized platform that Operations-B uses for test and production deployments. Field sales and inside sales (Sales-A) may sit outside, but sales engineers (pre-sales) could very well be part of the team. Similarly advertising, SEO, promotions, and pricing (Marketing-A) may sit outside, but social media and content (Marketing-B) would do well to be part of the team.

Cross-functional teams aren't a new idea. Only the proposed extent of cross-functionality is new. Agile software development teams have always been

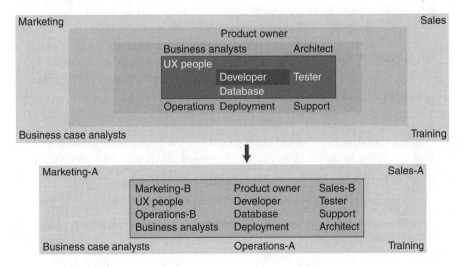

Figure 5-2 *Moving from a stratified setup to a cross-functional setup*

cross-functional with respect to architects, analysts, developers, and testers. With DevOps, cross-functionality expands to include deployment and some IT operations people. At this point, the cross-functional team is capable of agility in delivery. For full IT and business agility, the circle needs to expand further to include dedicated product owners, UX people, sales, marketing, and support.

5.4.1 DevOps = Cross-functional Dev + IT Ops Team

The DevOps movement advocates a merger of development and related IT operations. It makes a team cross-functional with respect to development and IT operations. Unfortunately, this aspect is often ignored in comparison with the technical aspects of DevOps. From an IT point of view, we broadly have three departments in a typical setup—business, development, and IT operations. There may be many more subdepartments, but this picture is enough to understand what DevOps is not.

In a typical case, once the VP of IT operations is convinced about DevOps, she decides that her team should now acquire so called DevOps capability. Accordingly, they evaluate and buy some product claiming to be a DevOps enabler, do a bit of research on virtualization and infrastructure automation tools, start version controlling their deployment scripts, and then rename their department to DevOps. Is it really DevOps? Well, it isn't DevOps if you don't have IT operations people as part of your development organization. The whole point of DevOps is to locate development and operations skills within a single team. The VP of IT operations is not to blame though. Effecting a DevOps reorg is usually beyond her pay grade and fraught with implications for her future role.

5.4.2 Organizing for Responsiveness

It Works!

@Apple

Apple uses cross-functional teams as part of its Apple New Product process (ANP). Cross-functional teams are used for product discovery and definition, product development, and even to define the ANP.[8]

---

8. http://www.roundtable.com/download/db8e1af0cb3aca1ae2d0018624204529/9778d5d219c50
   80b9a6a17bef029331c

> ## @Spotify
>
> Spotify is a streaming music Internet business with 40 million+ users and 1,200+ employees.[9] They are a popular case study for cross-functional organization with 30 teams spread over 3 cities. Their basic unit of organization is a cross-functional team called a squad. Each squad has a long-term mission such as building, running, and improving the Android client, creating the Spotify radio experience, scaling the backend systems, or providing payment solutions.[10] Each squad has a product owner and manages its releases. Related squads are grouped into tribes and physically co-located in the office to promote collaboration. Different specialists (e.g., testing, development) within a tribe have their own chapters to nurture their competency. Chapters are similar to communities of practice except that the chapter lead is line manager for her chapter members and yet part of a squad and involved in day-to-day work.
>
> > "This matches the *professor and entrepreneur* model recommended by Mary and Tom Poppendieck. The PO is the entrepreneur or product champion, focusing on delivering a great product, while the chapter lead is the professor or competency leader, focusing on technical excellence. There is a healthy tension between these roles, as the entrepreneur tends to want to speed up and cut corners, while the professor tends to want to slow down and build things properly. Both aspects are needed, that's why it is a *healthy* tension."[10]

Cross-functional teams fold the entire software delivery value stream into a single team rather than let it span across multiple activity-oriented teams. This reduces the cost of handoffs, allows reduction in batch size, and thereby decreases cycle time (improving responsiveness). Cross-functional teams aligned to outcomes can get meaningful things done within the bounds of the team. In this respect, they are much more autonomous units than activity-oriented teams. They are also more fun to be since autonomy is an intrinsic motivator.

Cross-functional teams aren't anti-specialization. These teams still consist of specialists. Specialization isn't the problem; organizing along the lines of specialization is. Functional organization makes for slower and more expensive handoffs.

---

9. http://en.wikipedia.org/wiki/Spotify
10. https://dl.dropbox.com/u/1018963/Articles/SpotifyScaling.pdf

5.4.3 Utilization

Will specialists dedicated to product teams be underutilized? Probably yes. This is where the rubber meets the road in terms of trading off cost-efficiency for the sake of responsiveness. Beyond a certain threshold of utilization, responsiveness decreases as utilization increases. This is a well-known effect from queuing theory. Without some slack, we can't have responsiveness. A fully utilized highway is a parking lot.[11]

Besides, as a side effect of being part of a cross-functional team, specialists usually start to acquire adjacent skills. So developers pick up infrastructure skills while product analysts pick up testing skills. This lets them contribute to adjacent areas during lean intervals and jump back to core areas as soon as something comes up. Pure specialists start morphing into generalizing specialists.[12] Their skill profile changes shape from the letter I (all depth) to the letter T (some breadth).

5.4.4 T-shaped People

Pure specialists are all depth and very little breadth. Although they may be brought together in a cross-functional team, they might face challenges in interacting with their team members from other specializations. For effective cross-functional collaboration, we need some breadth as well as good depth. Breadth provides perspective and empathy. Hard-core specialists are susceptible to caring only about their part of the work. T-shaped people[13] can relate to and build upon ideas coming from outside their domain with greater ease.

5.4.5 Team Size

Common recommendations for development team size range from three to nine.[14,15] Another idea called the two-pizza team (number of people that two pizzas will suffice for) comes from Amazon. As long as the architecture is modular (via services or otherwise), these are reasonable heuristics for team size of a single module or service. However, highly cross-functional, outcome-oriented teams, as in Figure 5-2, are likely to be much bigger if the outcome (or suboutcome) requires it. It doesn't mean humungous standup meetings or that everyone communicates regularly with each other. The cause of responsiveness is

---

11. Tweet by Paul Sutton, @FragileAgile.
12. http://www.agilemodeling.com/essays/generalizingSpecialists.htm
13. http://en.wikipedia.org/wiki/T-shaped_skills
14. https://www.scrum.org/Forums/aft/680
15. http://www.infoq.com/news/2009/04/agile-optimal-team-size

served by having a single, dedicated outcome owner for the whole team of teams. The cause of autonomy and purpose is served by having a team big and capable enough to own a business outcome (or suboutcome).

5.5 Cross-functionality in Other Domains

The notion of cross-functional organization is also pertinent to disciplines other than IT. It is only fair to indulge in a few interdisciplinary analogies while on the topic of interdisciplinary (cross-functional) teams.

5.5.1 Hospital Pod Teams

A study[16] conducted at the emergency department (ED) of a city hospital corroborates the advantages of moving from an activity-oriented team design to a cross-functional one. Their initial design had three activity-oriented teams of nurses, residents, and attending physicians servicing a value stream that consisted of the following activities:

- Triage incoming patients
- Begin patient care work (nurse)
- Order tests, make decisions about diagnosis, treatment, and disposition (resident)
- Approve or change the orders and decisions (attending physician)

The study notes that back-and-forth discussion was not enabled by this design. Responsiveness was poor—an average of 10% of patients left without being seen because of delays. As a redesign, the ED teams were divided into pods (cross-functional teams). Each pod had the personnel and equipment necessary to treat any type of ED patient; that is, it had the ability to service the entire value stream above. The study found that the pod system delivered a 40% reduction in cycle time (in this case, cycle time is the average amount of time a patient spends in ED) without any significant difference in any other aspect of the quality of care. Note that the rest of the hospital functions can continue with an activity-oriented organization, as they are not directly part of the patient-care value stream.

---

16. Valentine, M. A., and A. C. Edmondson. 2014. *Team scaffolds: How meso-level structures support role-based coordination in temporary groups.* Cambridge: Harvard Business School.

5.5.2 A Cross-functional Museum Layout

The Rijksmuseum in Amsterdam is a good example of the power of cross-functional organization. Traditionally, museum galleries have a functional organization—one gallery for sculpture, another for ceramics, a third one for paintings, and so on. Each gallery is managed by a specialist curator—the museum analogue of our function lead. But the new Rijksmuseum has opted for a more integrated or, shall we say, *cross-functional* organization. Each section in now devoted to a different century, and within that section you will find all the artifacts from that period arranged in an integrated holistic display that effectively conveys the story of the age.

An article about the reopening of the museum in *The Guardian*[17] describes the new layout. A Rembrandt gallery, for example, displays some of his early work alongside period-piece furniture, glass and silver artifacts made by people he knew, and a portrait by an art-patron friend. Rijksmuseum's director of collections, Taco Dibbits, says, "You get a sense of the world in which Rembrandt was producing his art." This is similar to how a product analyst gets a sense of the world into which the product is deployed by working in a cross-functional team that includes deployment specialists.

A cross-functional layout is arguably more work for the curators to manage and maintain. It may also nettle expert visitors who may be interested, for example, in sculpture but not ceramics. But from the point of view of majority generalist visitors to the museum (the outcome that matters), a cross-functional layout is probably more meaningful.

5.5.3 Taskonomy

Design guru Dan Norman talks about taxonomy versus taskonomy in the context of human-centered design.[18] Imagine how much less usable a word processor or spreadsheet might be if it only supported main menus, that is, no support for context-sensitive (right-click/pop-up menu) actions. As exemplified by Figure 5-3, the main header menu of an application is taxonomy whereas its myriad context-sensitive menus are taskonomies. Taxonomy is a functional classification or arrangement whereas a taskonomy is a cross-functional arrangement based on the needs of the task at hand. Taxonomies provide navigability—they offer a map of available functionality. Taskonomies provide ease of use and responsiveness—they are responsive to the needs of the user in context. In a user interface, both have their place. In organization design, the

---

17. http://www.theguardian.com/culture/2013/apr/05/rijksmuseum-reopens-long-refurbishment-rethink
18. http://www.jnd.org/dn.mss/logic_versus_usage_.html

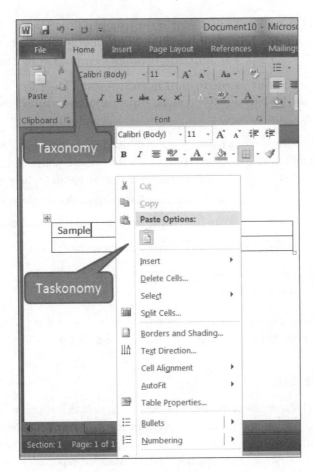

Figure 5-3 *Taxonomy is to taskonomy as functional arrangement is to cross-functional arrangement.*

org chart provides enough taxonomy. For responsive day-to-day work, we need taskonomies, which is what cross-functional teams are.

5.6 Migrating to Cross-functional Teams

It is quite disruptive to move from an IT-B matrix organization (or other functional organization) to self-sufficient, cross-functional teams. Here is one method of doing it gradually:

1. Identify products/capabilities that differentiate the business. You will need as many cross-functional teams as the number of differentiating business products/capabilities.

2. Identify a product/capability for piloting the transition. Ideally, the candidate won't have too many dependencies with other products/capabilities. Make sure there is a full-time outcome owner (Section 4.1.2) available.

3. Have the product owner come up with an initial product roadmap and backlog.

4. Identify people from existing activity teams that will make up the pilot team. Explain to them the rationale for the pilot. Use the penny game[19] to drive home how small batches and inexpensive handoffs help reduce cycle time.

5. Make sure the pilot team has all the skills required to be self-sufficient.

6. Let the new team start working through the backlog.

7. See how it goes for about three months before deciding to spin up another cross-functional team.

This only addresses the structural aspects of migration. Operational, cultural, and political aspects are addressed in the following chapters.

5.6.1 Separation of Duties

Sometimes, IT governance people say that cross-functional teams are not permitted by accounting and investor protection regulations such as SOX and payment regulations such as Payment Card Industry Data Security Standard (PCI-DSS). In particular, they speak of a control called *separation of duties*.[20] In effect, it aims to separate authorization for making changes to an application/system from authorization to release those changes into production. Traditionally, this hasn't been a problem because the production deployment team was different from the development team. However, even if separation of duties requires that the same person not have both authorizations, it does not prohibit two people with the combination of authorizations from working together on the same team.[21]

---

19. http://www.leansimulations.org/2014/04/variations-of-lean-penny-game.html
20. http://en.wikipedia.org/wiki/Separation_of_duties
21. http://continuousdelivery.com/2012/07/pci-dss-and-continuous-deployment-at-etsy/

5.7 Communities of Practice

We saw earlier that a cross-functional team encourages its members to morph from pure specialists to generalizing specialists. This does not have to come at the cost of mastery in their specialization. A community of practice (CoP) is an alternative solution to nurturing a competency in the absence of a functional organization. A CoP does not require its members to be all part of the same team. It functions like a loose, professional association of specialists with mechanisms for online and offline interaction and knowledge sharing.

A lead is usually elected, nominated, or appointed per CoP. The lead comes from the same specialist background and is someone with people and organizing skills. The CoP lead is by no means a full-time role—she continues to work as a first-class member of some product team while devoting maybe 20% of her time to CoP work. CoP leads sponsor brown bag sessions, training programs, internal conferences, and sponsor members to participate in external conferences. They weigh in on tools and modes of collaboration within the community. They are accountable for the health of the community.

In addition, mastery in IT specialist areas may be sustained by getting involved in groups and activities outside one's organization. Specialist user groups and conferences are thriving in many cities. The Internet has many great resources for specialist skill enhancement. Even just following relevant Twitter hashtags goes a long way toward staying up to date. After all, individual mastery is at least as much the individual's responsibility as the organization's.

5.8 Maintenance Teams

Cross-functional product teams own their product—they shape it, build it, maintain it, and run it. However, many organizations retain separate teams for maintenance (bug fixes and minor enhancements) and IT operations.

Figure 5-4 shows a traditional cycle. Maintenance and IT operations work on what is released while development works on the next release. To cater to users who cannot upgrade to newer releases promptly, there is usually a support window of current minus N releases (N = 1 in Figure 5-4).

There is common but flawed notion in enterprise IT circles that maintenance work requires less skill than full-scale development. As a result, project sponsors looking to reduce cost opt for a different team of lower-cost people for maintenance work. This is false economy. It hurts the larger business outcome

			Time
Development team	R2	R3	R4
Maintenance team	R1	R2, R1	R3, R2
Operations team	R1	R2, R1	R3, R2

Figure 5-4 *Typical software release cycle*

and reduces IT agility. When the same product team does development and maintenance, there is no handoff at release time. It is easier to merge bug fixes from release branch to trunk because the team is familiar with the ongoing changes in trunk. What's more, trunk-based development[22]—a branchless technique that is gaining adoption—is nearly impossible with separate development and maintenance teams.

End-of-life support is one situation where a maintenance team might make sense. This team keeps an old app/product running while a new replacement is built. Other than that, it is all about tearing down potential silos such as separate maintenance teams. Even in case of end-of-life support, a capability-oriented IT organization may choose to have the old and new coexist in a single capability team (Section 8.2). A separate maintenance team is a dinosaur in an age of continuous delivery and DevOps.

5.9 Outsourcing

When IT-B work is outsourced, we need to take care that the resulting team design does not violate the conditions of responsiveness, autonomy, mastery, and purpose discussed previously. Otherwise, business outcomes may be at risk. For example, the CapEx-OpEx distinction results in separate contracts/teams/vendors for development and maintenance. Some organizations go a step further and outsource even IT operations to a different team/vendor under a separate contract. The rationale is to stick to core business competency and outsource everything else (let vendors compete with each other for our slice of IT). Depending on how critical an application is for revenue generation, this strategy of "divide-and-conquer IT" can be frustrating at best and suicidal at worst. Internet businesses and ISVs typically outsource little to none of their IT-B. This is simply because having to orchestrate between three teams/vendors for every new feature is a huge drag on the ability to go to market quickly.

---

22. http://paulhammant.com/2013/04/05/what-is-trunk-based-development/

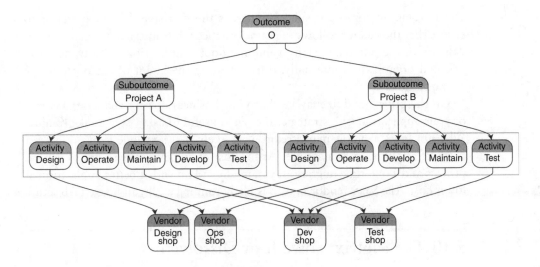

Figure 5-5 *Avoid activity-oriented outsourcing.*

Equally important, the feedback loop is badly constricted at contractual boundaries. Designing formal, service-level agreement (SLA)-driven protocols of communication between business, development, IT operations, and maintenance is a recipe for bureaucracy and indifference.

Outsourcing along outcomes is better than outsourcing along activity lines—that is, consider outsourcing application A to vendor X, B to vendor Y, and C to vendor Z (Figure 5-6) rather than handing development of A, B, and C to vendor X, IT operations to vendor Y, and maintenance to vendor Z (Figure 5-5).

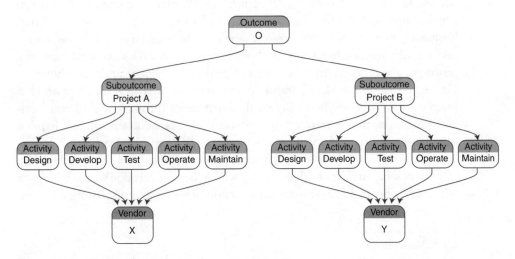

Figure 5-6 *Adopt outcome-oriented outsourcing.*

Outsourcing outcomes (or suboutcomes) is the first step. The next step is to ensure that the vendor follows the same practice while internally organizing for delivery of the outcome. Many vendors adopt a utilization-friendly, activity-oriented organization internally, thus defeating the intent of the outsourcing configuration.

On the other hand, it may be that your business doesn't change that often or your application isn't strategic. If so, it is useful to ask, "Why make (build)? Why not buy?" SaaS is mainstream. It is likely that someone is offering your bespoke application as a service. At the cost of some tweaks to your business process and a one-time migration, you might end up with a better application at lower cost. The SaaS vendor in turn is likely running a fully in-house IT-B setup.

5.10 The Matrix: Solve It or Dissolve It

> Half the world is so used to matrix management as to take the scheme for granted.
> The other half just thinks it's bizarre.
> —Tom DeMarco in *Slack*,[23] p. 15

A matrix structure is one whose members have two bosses—typically a project manager for day-to-day work and a longer-term function lead for performance appraisals and training. In case of IT-B, the project managers work with product owners who either come from the business or liaise with people from the business. Function leads in IT-B have titles like head/VP/director of architecture, development, UX, database, testing, or release management. Function leads own "resources" (e.g., developers, testers) who get assigned to projects as needed. Given that IT is itself a "function," an IT-matrix represents a functional organization within a functional organization—a near guarantee of pain. From business's point of view, they are the verticals (lines of business) in the matrix and the different IT functions are horizontals. From IT-B's point of view, the functions are verticals and the different projects are horizontals. As shown in Figure 5-7, we use the latter frame for our discussion. The verticals in an IT-B matrix are activity oriented whereas the horizontals (projects) are outcome oriented. As work moves through the software delivery value stream, it is handed over from one vertical to the other in the IT-B matrix. As explained in Section 5.2.1, these handoffs present a structural impediment for short cycle times.

Matrix structures are probably okay where the verticals don't have to engage with each other in a fast-moving value stream; for example, a sales organization

---

23. (DeMarco 2002)

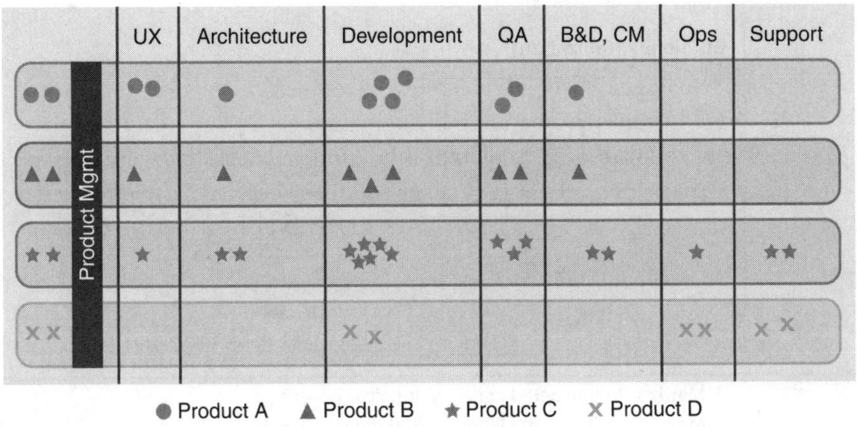

		UX	Architecture	Development	QA	B&D, CM	Ops	Support
●●	Product Mgmt	●●	●	●●●	●●	●		
▲▲		▲	▲	▲▲▲	▲▲	▲		
★★		★	★★	★★★★★	★★★	★★	★	★★
××				××			××	××

● Product A   ▲ Product B   ★ Product C   × Product D

Figure 5-7 *Typical IT-B matrix*

may be set up as a matrix with verticals for different product lines and horizontals for different regions. However, a matrix is inappropriate for an IT-B organization that aims for continuous delivery. Continuous delivery requires continuous collaboration—a lot of it unscripted. It is something with which the verticals in a matrix simply can't cope.

While no matrix structure is suitable for continuous delivery, some are worse than others. In the following section, we'll explore different types of matrices and contrast them with cross-functional teams.

A handoff between two verticals in a matrix can be represented as a queue; for example, development does its work and puts it in the queue of the testing team. A vertical may have a single queue for all incoming work or one queue per project. In the latter case, specific people may be assigned to handle a given project's queue or it might just be a capacity allocation without fixed people assignment. The relative merits of various configurations are illustrated in Figure 5-8 and discussed below. Modern business by necessity trades cost-efficiency for responsiveness because business agility is a critical success factor.

5.10.1 Matrix of Shared Services

A matrix of shared services allocates both capacity and people just in time i.e. all projects share a single queue for a given function. There is no certainty of available capacity for projects. Wait times are indefinite but resource utilization is maximal. This is the worst possible matrix configuration for continuous delivery.

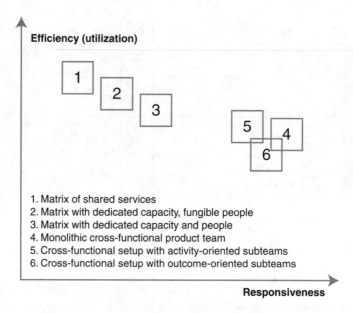

Figure 5-8 *Performance characteristics of various team designs*

5.10.2 Matrix with Dedicated Capacity and Fungible People

In this case, every project gets its own queue and a certain number of full-time equivalents (FTEs) to service the queue, but the actual people who make up the FTEs aren't fixed. Although this makes for flexible work assignment, there is drastic loss of context as people switch tasks.

5.10.3 Matrix with Dedicated Capacity and People

Here, we assign a fixed set of people to a product for an agreed-upon period of time. Product owners still have a tough time getting their work done through the different layers from left to right. Occasional power struggles break out between outcome owners and function leads. It is still bad in the sense that there are too many handoffs. There is a tendency for batch size to go up. It does not encourage continuous collaboration, and hence, we see a lot of meetings taking place.

In my experience, a matrix organization can achieve monthly releases at best. But release interval is not the same as cycle time. Monthly releases imply a minimum cycle time of a month, very likely much higher; for example, it might take six months for a new feature to move through all the verticals of a matrix before it is released.

5.10.4 Monolithic Cross-functional Product Team

Figure 5-9 shows self-sufficient cross-functional product teams. The product team is fully accountable for the success of the product. It is almost like a different business unit except that they still depend on external shared verticals such as finance, admin, legal, and HR. Each product team has one person in charge as the outcome owner.

5.10.5 Cross-functional Setup with Activity-oriented Subteams

A single monolithic team may be unworkable after a certain size. At that point, the outcome owner may choose to assign an additional manager to the largest groups of specialists, for example, a manager for the developers or the inside salespeople.

5.10.6 Cross-functional Setup with Outcome-oriented Subteams

It is better to scale big product teams by creating teams that own suboutcomes rather than activities. Apart from the advantage of responsiveness, this also

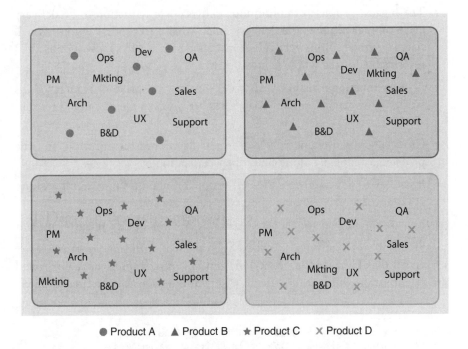

● Product A   ▲ Product B   ★ Product C   ✕ Product D

Figure 5-9 *Monolithic cross-functional product teams*

promotes modular software architecture. Conway's law[24] states that the design of a system is likely to reflect the communication structure of its team. Accordingly, monolithic teams tend toward monolithic architectures, layered teams (separate teams for front end, business logic, persistence, etc.) tend toward layered architectures, and teams that own different product modules will tend toward a modular architecture. The *ThoughtWorks* Technology Radar called it the "Inverse Conway Maneuver."[25]

5.11 Summary of Insights

- Collaboration within teams tends to be unscripted—on demand, just in time, and continuous. Collaboration across teams tends to be discontinuous and discrete (e.g., via meetings). This can be factored into team design by locating all roles that require continuous collaboration within a single team.

- Handoffs are mostly a result of specialization. Organization design cannot reduce these handoffs, but it can make them faster and cheaper by making them occur inside a single team.

- The biggest promise of continuous delivery is a reduction in IT delivery cycle time. It requires the delivery value stream to process work in small batches, which ultimately calls for a single team (or as few as possible) responsible for the whole value stream.

- A cross-functional team consists of people with different primary skills working toward a common goal. They are an example of valuing responsiveness over cost-efficiency.

- Cross-functional teams aren't anti-specialization. Specialization isn't the problem; organizing along lines of specialization is.

- It is okay to have activity-oriented teams for activities that aren't an integral part of a business outcome's core value stream.

- Release interval is not the same as cycle time. Monthly releases imply a minimum cycle time of a month, very likely much higher.

- Given that IT is itself a "function," an IT-matrix represents a functional organization within a functional organization—a near guarantee of pain.

---

24. http://www.thoughtworks.com/insights/blog/demystifying-conways-law
25. http://www.thoughtworks.com/radar/techniques/inverse-conway-maneuver

5.12 Summary of Actions

- Shift from activity-oriented organization to outcome-oriented cross-functional teams. They tend to be self-sufficient (autonomy) and business goal–directed (purpose).

- Communities of practice complement outcome-oriented organization. In the absence of a functional organization, they provide the necessary umbrella to nurture specialist competencies.

- If needed, divide work among multiple teams by splitting the outcome into suboutcomes (e.g., modules of an application or different applications) rather than activities (development, testing, etc.). The same applies for geographic distribution and outsourcing.

- Don't encourage creation of shared services that service critical value streams. They tend to lose the sense of business purpose and this hurts responsiveness.

- Don't commission separate teams for maintenance. It is an example of unnecessary handoff created by team design. Besides, rarely is anything in a pure maintenance mode. It always coexists with forward-looking development. A separate maintenance team is a dinosaur in an age of continuous delivery and DevOps.

- Move away from an IT-B matrix to outcome-oriented teams aligned with business verticals.

Chapter 6

Accountability

If the last two chapters felt like a power-to-the-teams manifesto, then this and the next chapter provide the balancing act. Accountability helps people use their autonomy judiciously. Clear accountability helps clarify decision rights and input rights. It helps avoid decision stalemates and improves responsiveness—one of the three key themes described in Chapter 3. It helps us learn quickly after failing-fast (Section 2.4.1). Otherwise, we might just keep failing for the same reasons.

We'll see how to clarify accountability, how power struggles may result from a suboptimal assignment of authority and accountability, how to drive accountability not only for results but also for the decisions along the way, and how to address the skewing of accountability that results from the separation of planning from execution.

6.1 Power and Hierarchy

Some of us may not be comfortable with the use of the word power in the context of an IT organization. We may believe that power is out-of-date and influence is what matters. Unfortunately, this is usually untrue, especially in large organizations. In particularly bad cases, influence is only exerted by those in positions of power. In the slightly better ones, formal authority or power isn't required in theory but is highly desirable and expedient in practice. This isn't surprising. Through the ages, we humans have developed a taste for exercising control over our environment or domain. Acknowledging this desire for power is the first step toward designing to contain it. Sweeping it under the carpet is what makes for the difference between reality and what is said on the "Our Work Culture" page of the company web site.

This book recommends limiting hierarchy but it isn't anti-hierarchy. Some hierarchy is essential for the effective functioning of an organization. Eliminating hierarchy has the frequent side effect of slowing down decision making and diffusing accountability. For example, an engineering team without a clear leader may have trouble settling down on a solution design. A distributed sales team without a clear leader may lose a big lead for want of someone to ensure concerted effort.

Some mature, self-organizing teams may be able to function effectively without a named leader. They consist of people with a rare combination of qualities—competence, emotional intelligence, and integrity. Even these teams often choose to be situationally hierarchical; that is, a member with specific skills is allowed to take charge in a given situation. For most teams, though, some structure is required to prevent dysfunction.

Besides, informal hierarchies arise in the absence of formal ones. Aristotle may have been incorrect in observing that nature abhors a vacuum,[1] but we can safely observe that in an organization, hierarchy abhors a vacuum—hence, the term *power vacuum* in politics. In an influential essay called "The tyranny of structurelessness,"[2] author Jo Freeman argues that the idea of structurelessness only prevents formal structures, not informal ones. Informal structures are harmful because:

> As long as the structure of the group is informal, the rules of how decisions are made are known only to a few and awareness of power is limited to those who know the rules. Those who do not know the rules and are not chosen for initiation must remain in confusion, or suffer from paranoid delusions that something is happening of which they are not quite aware.

Therefore, some formal hierarchy is necessary, but its dysfunctions can be mitigated with due care. For example, hierarchies are self-propagating when left unchecked. New positions are created in order to hire hot talent, to retain or reward high performers, to pacify good performers who feel left out, and to quarantine (or kick upstairs) pesky people who have powerful protectors. No matter why, the resulting rank becomes a status symbol. We begin to guard

---

1. http://science.howstuffworks.com/question200.htm
2. http://www.jofreeman.com/joreen/tyranny.htm

it by ring fencing our teams from external influence, by trying to increase the size of the team (empire building), and by securing ever-increasing budget and resources. We begin to highlight our team's achievements, sometimes disproportionately to the overall business value of the achievement. This is the road to local optima and silos.

The real problem is abuse of power, not power itself. It is great to use one's power to realize business outcomes. It is not so great when we act primarily with an eye on personal gain and without regard for the big picture. To discourage this, we need clear accountability for outcomes.

6.2 Balance Autonomy with Accountability

Although we have set out to go about organization design with a view to fostering autonomy, it has to be balanced with accountability in order to secure alignment with business goals. In an organization context, autonomy also needs authority—freedom to act needs to be supported with the power to act.

Table 6-1 captures different levels of devolution of authority and accountability and the resulting autonomy. In all cases, the boss has minimal responsibility for execution while the sub (subordinate) has full responsibility. A delegating style makes sense for Agile cultures (collaboration or cultivation; refer to Section 2.3). By default, the subordinate has decision-making authority commensurate with accountability with the proviso that it may be overridden by the boss. A good boss would rarely need to exercise this right. A delegating style provides subordinates with much-needed autonomy while letting their bosses override decisions when necessary to ensure alignment.

Table 6-1 *Effects of Different Management Styles*

Style	Authoritarian		Federal		Delegation	
	Boss	Subordinate	Boss	Subordinate	Boss	Subordinate
Authority	Full	Minimal	Minimal	Full	Override	Default
Accountability	Full	Minimal	Nominal	Full	Full	Full
Responsibility	Minimal	Full	Minimal	Full	Minimal	Full
Resulting Autonomy for Subordinate	NA	None	NA	Yes	NA	Yes. Boss gets to override sub's decisions.

6.3 Assign Accountability

On October 1, 2013, the US HealthCare.gov web site had a terrible launch that threatened the credibility of the second-term Obama administration. A rescue effort was initiated after a few weeks of misery. A *TIME* magazine article[3] reports the observations of Mike Abbott, who was brought in to oversee the rescue. Abbott saw a lack of ownership and a collaboration deficit among government contractors (IT suppliers). It was nearly impossible to figure out who was even *supposed to be* in charge of the launch. In other words, there was a complete absence of accountability.

In order to cultivate a culture of accountability, first it is essential to assign it clearly. People ought to clearly know what they are accountable for before they can be held to it. This goes beyond assigning key responsibility areas (KRAs). To be accountable for an outcome, we need authority for making decisions, not just responsibility for execution. It is tempting to refrain from the tricky exercise of explicitly assigning accountability. Executives often hope that their reports will figure it out. Unfortunately, this is easier said than done.

6.3.1 Who Owns the Outcome?

> **Scenario 6-1 A Stalemate**
>
> Mary and John are mad at each other. Mary is the product manager of a product that hasn't been selling well recently. John is the head of sales of the entire product line of which Mary's product is but one. Mary thinks that the sales approach that works for other products isn't working for hers. She wants John's team to gain in-depth knowledge of the product. She has observed that her product's prospective customers are often actual users and not checklist-driven decision makers from procurement. They ask in-depth questions about usage scenarios and find the sales engineers out of their depth. John thinks this is so because the product is hard to figure out. He'd rather have Mary improve the usability and documentation of her product. He is quietly furious with Mary for pointing a finger at his team.
>
> They have a common boss who isn't inclined to intervene and would rather have them sort it out among themselves. The impasse could be

---

3. http://time.com/10228/obamas-trauma-team/

> resolved by doing a field survey to find what the real problem is. However, as things stand, both Mary and John are convinced that the problem is with the other person. Neither of them wants to commission a truth-finding survey out of his or her budget. Besides, each feels that the other would reject his or her survey.

In the above scenario, who is the first person to be held to account for product sales? We may say that it's John, but given the situation above, he's simply going to point out that the other products are selling well, implying that the problem is not with the sales team. Being the joint responsibility of both Mary and John, it is a case of collective ownership gone awry. Mary controls resources for product development, John for sales. There is one overarching business outcome with two centers of power and no single outcome owner (Section 4.1.2). Mary has to bother about just her product while John is responsible for a product line. Mary has complete accountability and incomplete authority for her product. John has partial authority and partial accountability for each product. Their boss doesn't have enough context, bandwidth, or will to step in and break the impasse. And neither John nor Mary could override the other. The impasse prolongs for want of a decision. Real-world situations are often further complicated by the presence of a director of product management to whom Mary would report. Usually, the product hobbles along in these situations until the board or investors start asking uncomfortable questions or until there are personnel changes.

Thus, a business outcome risks becoming dependent on multiple competing power centers in the absence of a single, full-time dedicated outcome owner (Section 4.1.2) accountable for realization of the outcome and having control over budget and team(s). However, this might involve changes to the org chart, and that is not always practical. The next section suggests a way to clarify decision rights without redrawing the org chart.

6.3.2 Accountability Maps

Most organizations suffering from business-IT ineffectiveness would dread the following activity. Let's call it accountability mapping. It is a map of who is accountable for what outcomes. As shown in Figure 6-1, we draw an organization chart and a business outcome tree and then map boxes in the org chart to outcomes in the tree. Where multiple people or teams are accountable for the same outcome, the executive leadership rank orders them to get a clear line of

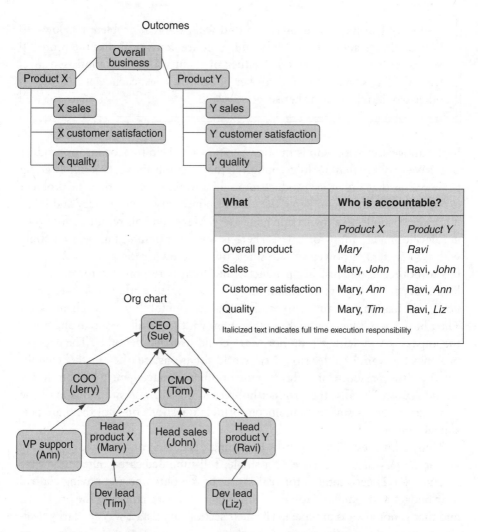

Figure 6-1 *Accountability mapping*

accountability. Bosses are always nominally accountable for the work of their teams. The mapping table only captures names of people dedicated full-time to the outcome. The first person in a line of accountability has the right to override the decisions of the second or third person. This corresponds to the delegating style in Table 6-1. One would imagine that it would be great to have a map like Figure 6-1 on paper for everyone to see. It greatly clarifies who is accountable for what. It could aid in resolving decision-making deadlocks and speed up decisions. Yet we never encounter this information radiator in an otherwise Agile organization. It is not because of effective collective ownership. The average well-performing business professional is not equipped to navigate the ambiguous waters of self-organization and collective ownership at the level of business outcomes. A research report called "Challenges and Strategies of Matrix Organizations"[4] found that 87% of middle managers cited *unclear roles* as a major issue but only 23% of execs thought them to be so. No wonder things get stuck in the middle. The report finds that assignment of accountability for business objectives is basic to achieving clarity of roles.

In the absence of clear assignment of accountability, we often get collective owning of authority and collective disowning of accountability. Collective ownership works better within a team, and the most common example is collective code ownership in development teams. However, there is clear accountability even in the context of collective code ownership. The question "Who broke the build?" fixes accountability unambiguously when version control and continuous integration are in use. Besides, even within Agile development teams, things aren't so egalitarian. The tech lead has ultimate authority and accountability (ownership) for technical design decisions. The product owner has ultimate authority and accountability for what goes into a feature. Collective ownership of business outcomes across teams is an order of magnitude more difficult to achieve. Kudos to those who can pull it off. For the rest, clarifying ownership is a first step to improving organizational agility.

It is the job of top leadership to clarify ownership along these lines. It is a tough job. You can't please everybody but unless such a map is in place, shared, and commonly understood, decision making is likely to slow down. In the absence of clear owners, disagreements may fester and routinely get escalated for someone higher up to break the deadlock. Unfortunately, some leaders seem to want exactly this—they prefer that all decisions are referred to them rather than settled at a lower level. It seems to give them visibility and control. However, it makes for a political climate. A clear accountability map can serve as an antidote against an unhealthy decision-making climate.

Meeting and e-mail overload[5] is a frequent symptom of unclear roles and broken accountability. When decision ownership is unclear, everyone is invited to all meetings and cc'ed on all e-mails. The recipients are also unsure what to attend and what to skip and so they try to attend all the ones that their bosses are likely to attend in order to maintain "visibility." Inclusiveness and consensus making are usually offered as reasons for meeting and e-mail overload. This is in name only. Most parties to the meeting or e-mail chain are mute spectators with no real say. No doubt, it is necessary to keep relevant people in the loop.

---

4. Thanks to Nicolay Worren (@NicolayWorren) for pointing me to this study:
   http://www.boozallen.com/media/file/HRPS_Challenges_Strategies_Matrix_Orgs.pdf
5. http://www.economist.com/news/business/21610237-businesses-must-fight-relentless-battle-against-bureaucracy-decluttering-company

But when roles are unclear, we don't know who is relevant to what discussion and therefore we keep tens of people in the loop for just about everything.

Accountability maps are good for sorting out confusion with overlapping roles. However, where possible, it is better to define roles such that there is minimal overlap of ownership. This is the topic of the next section.

6.4 Minimize Power Struggles

Teams and departments within an organization are social systems. Their people dynamics cannot be ignored if the organization is to function effectively. One such dynamic exists between heads of line functions and heads of lines of product/business. Functional specializations such as product management, design, engineering or development, QA, operations, and support are activities whereas products (or lines of business) are outcomes. Function leads (specialist leads)—for example, VP of sales, head of marketing, director of engineering—lead activities that serve outcomes. It is necessary to designate someone as an outcome owner to avoid stalemates of the kind described in Section 6.3.1.

6.4.1 Matrix Paralysis

Matrix organizations are organized by specialization as described in Section 5.10. Having function leads control resources needed by outcome owners as in Figure 6-2 sets the stage for power struggles. The function leads are minimally accountable for outcomes, but they control specialist resources for engineering, support, operations, etc. As discussed in the previous chapter, digital transformation and continuous delivery need cross-functional teams. However, a matrix org with many function heads cannot deliver effective cross-functional teams. It

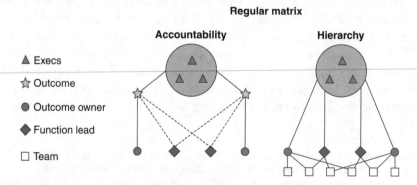

Figure 6-2 *Configuration #1: a regular matrix*

has too much potential for territorial power struggles. It's not just in sales that territory acts as an indicator of status, just that it is explicit in sales. Inside an organization, territory may be marked by function, project, or team. For example, a threat-perceiving, territorial marketing manager might say to a development manager: "Could you please bother about shipping on time and leave the marketing to me?" (marking territory by function).

6.4.2 Absolute Hierarchies

Subordinating all function leads to the outcome owner (Figure 6-3) is one way to prevent territorial behavior from compromising the outcome. However, it robs function leads of their autonomy (and motivation). It also requires more function leads than the matrix since each lead is now dedicated to one business outcome. It is conceivable to start with configuration #2 (e.g., while setting up a new product team) if we have a strong poly-skilled outcome owner who can also provide leadership over functions like marketing and sales. However, it is nearly impossible to migrate from configuration #1 to #2 without people quitting the organization.

6.4.3 Professor-Entrepreneur

So how do we let function leads retain autonomy and yet avoid setting it up for a power struggle? We start by recognizing that, although we need leadership across multiple functions/specializations, that's more about the ability to wield influence than power. Influence is about affecting people's thoughts and actions. People wield influence based on perceived competence, reputation, interpersonal skills, or vested authority. Only the last of these is about power. In our context, power is about exercising authority. Power requires control over

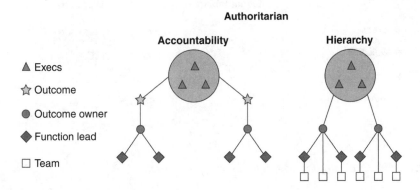

Figure 6-3 *Configuration #2: an authoritarian setup*

resources. In IT, these resources are budget and people. With power comes the responsibility to resolve impasses in one's domain, to take decisions that involve hard tradeoffs, and to remain accountable for them.

Trouble is, the way most organizations are set up, it is not possible to wield influence on a regular basis without also being in a position of power. To remedy this, the configuration suggested in Figure 6-4 places positions of influence and position of power on an equal footing in the hierarchy. This arrangement is just another take on the professor and entrepreneur model of the Poppendiecks,[6] and it is described briefly in the Spotify story (Section 5.4). The outcome owner is the entrepreneur, and the function leads are professors.

Function leads now have autonomy without control over resources. They still decide how the work occurs in their area. But nobody reports to them. They don't control anyone's time. This eliminates small fiefdoms. Function leads now work like how an Agile coach would work—by going to the teams—not by owning a team. They are free to make decisions, but their decisions may be overridden by outcome owners. To compensate for reduction in their authority, they are second in the line of accountability for the outcome. Outcome owners are first. This helps avoid stalemates for want of decisive action.

Function leads don't report to outcome owners. They are still on the same level in the hierarchy. They can highlight to the execs any disagreements with outcome owners. They get treated on par with outcome owners; for example, they get invited to company off-sites and other meetings to which outcome owners get invited. After all, hierarchy also manifests in things like who gets to sit at what tables. The arrangement needs outcome owners who can respect autonomy for function leads. If outcome owners abuse the situation and disregard function leads, the outcomes will likely suffer in a short while.

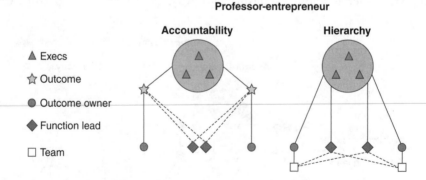

Figure 6-4 *Configuration #3: professor-entrepreneur setup*

---

6. http://www.youtube.com/watch?v=ypEMdjslEOI#t=3855

Even though specialists don't report to them in this model, function leads have a greater say in the performance review of specialists in their function. This gives some leverage to exert their influence on teams that aren't otherwise under their control.

6.5 Decide on an Outcome Owner

In configuration #3, there is a single power center for the business outcome. This single power center is someone *dedicated full time* to achieving the business outcome (unlike Mary and John's boss in Scenario 5-1). We put one person in charge. This person is fully empowered and accountable for product leadership (quality, innovation, and relevance), market leadership (revenue, mindshare), operations, and customer satisfaction (support, training).

So far, so good. But who should this person be? Should she be from products (domain or design SME), marketing and sales, or people/general management? Depending on the situation, she could be from any of these disciplines. If she comes from products, she'd be supported by a sales function lead and vice versa. In addition, she could be supported by a people/general manager who reports to her.

McKinsey's three-horizons framework[7] can aid this decision. The first horizon (H1) represents mature lines of business where the emphasis is on sustaining/improving market performance to maximize remaining value. Products in this horizon could benefit from an alpha-salesy, rainmaker-type outcome owner. The second horizon (H2) represents emerging lines of businesses with greatest potential for growth. Products in the second horizon need a product-savvy outcome owner. The third horizon is more of an incubator for new ideas and experiments and not as relevant for this discussion. All that said, given the increasing pace of business change, ISVs and Internet businesses rarely have the opportunity to inhabit the first horizon for more than a couple of quarters. The product is never mature; it is always maturing until it is finally obsolete. The digital wave promises to extend this dynamic to other businesses as well.

Thus, in the situation with Mary and John described earlier, John should be the outcome owner if the product is H1 category. He should hear out Mary's concerns with the sales approach and make changes if it makes sense to him. If not, he can ask Mary to improve product usability and documentation. In either case, he remains accountable for product success. Since Mary doesn't report to John, she can make her case with execs about why she disagrees with John although she is doing what he wants.

---

7. http://www.mckinsey.com/insights/strategy/enduring_ideas_the_three_horizons_of_growth

On the other hand, if the product is H2 category, then Mary should be the outcome owner. John would continue to drive sales efforts for different product lines. However, if Mary is convinced that her product needs a different sales approach, she can override John and ask for changes. The very existence of her right to override discourages John from ignoring her concerns about the sales approach. On the other hand, by virtue of being at the same rank in the hierarchy, John gets to put his views in front of the execs, thus ensuring that Mary isn't the only source of truth when it comes to sales.

6.6 Migration

Migration from configuration #1 (matrix) to #3 (professor-entrepreneur) can be a difficult exercise. Some function leads will resent the loss of power. On the other hand, professorial types will welcome the opportunity to focus 100% on their area of expertise without having to spend time on administrative overhead tasks that come with power over budget and people. Hiring new function leads into this configuration is also entirely feasible.

Another option is to pair up function leads with outcome owners—depending on interest and ability. An outcome owner role like product head usually has a wide scope—product vision, pulse of market, interfacing with sales and marketing, keeping in touch with customers, prioritizing features and providing direction to the development teams, keeping a tab on support. There is more than enough scope of work for a two-in-a-box setup.

What about other managers, such as development managers, delivery managers, iteration managers, or Scrum masters within the product team? Well, since the function leads no longer own budget or team, all other managers report to the outcome owner directly or indirectly.

6.7 Decision Accountability

Making people clearly accountable for results and giving them the authority to go about it as they choose provides autonomy and purpose to organizational subunits. It doesn't, however, guarantee results. When results disappoint, people are called to account. Explanations are offered, and sometimes mistakes are acknowledged. The point of spotting mistakes is to learn, not to shame or discredit. Ackoff[8] points out there are two types of mistakes: *errors of*

---

8. (Ackoff 1999)

commission, doing something that should not have been done; and *errors of omission,* not doing something that should have been done.

Errors of commission are easier to spot than errors of omission, and heroic rescue acts are easier to applaud than quiet acts of foresight that nip problems in the bud before they grow to need a rescue. Errors of omission are often failures to anticipate problems or to seize opportunities. For example, an application outage might occur because of an unauthorized change in production (error of commission) or because of an air-conditioning failure in the data center leading servers to overheat and automatically shut down. The latter is potentially an error of omission—an omission to perform preventive maintenance of the air-conditioning system. Could the person in charge of the data center have anticipated that bringing up more servers is likely to overload the air-conditioning system? Could it be that the potential for failure was brought up by an engineer and not heeded by the person in charge?

It is easy to learn from honest mistakes. Unfortunately, we also tend to make mistakes of the not-so-honest kind. For example, we do not pay enough attention to signals from our peers or subordinates or people outside our line of command.

Scenario 6-2 Unrecoverable Disaster

Sellmore Inc. provides a white-labeled e-commerce platform as a service to brick-and-mortar retailer clients. It saves them the effort of developing and running their own platform and lets them focus on their business. Recently, PetaMart, a big retailer, evaluated Sellmore and decided not to use them because they did not have an automatic failover disaster recovery (DR) solution for their data center. Sellmore's CEO held her CTO responsible for this.

The CTO was a post-technical IT manager and mainly business facing. Under pressure, he held a brief discussion with his infrastructure lead Ivan and went back to the CEO and announced that they'd be ready with a solution in three months. Ivan was shocked to hear this—he had clearly pointed out that the infrastructure landscape changed every day as new applications or releases were rolled out. He had said that it would take three months just to rollout a one-time snapshot DR solution against the current landscape, but it would be out of date the moment it rolled out. An always-up-to-date solution would need a lot more work. The CTO just brushed off his concerns saying they just needed to show something to get PetaMart's business. They could roll out full dynamic DR later.

(continues)

> Three months later, PetaMart was informed that Sellmore was DR ready. Could Sellmore please have their business? PetaMart coolly replied that they'd like an independent DR capability report from an external consultant/auditor of their choice. When Ivan confirmed that an independent report would expose them, the CTO started acting furious as if it was news to him. He told Ivan, "First you make a false promise and now you have the gall to say I told you so?"

6.7.1 Decision Record

Decisions made in the manner described above are called HiPPO[9] (highest paid person's opinion) decisions. How can organization design address accountability in the above situations? More importantly, can we put mechanisms in place that *deter* cavalier behavior of the sort exhibited by Sellmore's CTO? E-mail trails may help fix accountability and prevent plausible deniability.[10] However, this is after the fact. How can we discourage decision makers from ignoring signals provided by stakeholders? In the professor-entrepreneur setup described in Section 6.4.3, how do we ensure that entrepreneurs don't develop a habit of overriding professors? How do we discourage people with decision rights from disregarding the input rights of their colleagues?

We could draw inspiration from an engineering practice called *continuous integration*. It is a way of ensuring the integrity of a build and fixing accountability when the integrity is compromised. A continuous integration server keeps a record of builds—who initiated a build, at what time, with what change set, and with what result. "Who broke the build?" is the question that is asked and easily answered when the integrity of the build is compromised.

For decisions that have the potential to make or break business outcomes, it makes sense to have a system that continuously records and integrates inputs towards a decision. A decision record system provides a way of soliciting input on proposed decisions, weighing in on decisions that one isn't accountable for, documenting context and reasons for decisions, and clarifying ownership of decisions. It allows for collaborative, distributed, offline decision making and minimizes the need for meetings—physical or virtual. It is much better than an e-mail trail in that it is visible to a larger group and accessible outside of private inboxes.

---

9. http://www.forbes.com/sites/derosetichy/2013/04/15/what-happens-when-a-hippo-runs-your-company/

10. http://en.wikipedia.org/wiki/Plausible_deniability

This is not about democratizing decision making. Once we have account-ability maps in place, it is relatively easy to agree on the owner of a decision. If still unclear, the outcome owner can nominate a decision owner on a case-by-case basis. Decision rights vest with decision owners—decision records just nudge them toward giving a serious thought to others' input. On the contrary, the usual practice of calling a meeting to discuss an issue often ends with lots of discussion but no decision. Decisions are then made offline and presented as an outcome of the meeting, but no one is accountable for it. To maintain account-ability, meeting agendas should specify what decisions are to be taken and who their owners are.

6.7.2 Tools

Existing free and open source software such as Loomio[11] may be used to host a decision record. The following description is less an endorsement of a particu-lar tool and more a description of what's possible with such tools. Figure 6-5 illustrates the steps in a decision-making process with a relatively trivial example:

1. Context is shared. Issue under discussion is described. People start commenting and someone proposes a solution.

2. Others weigh in on the proposal.

3. The first proposal is discarded (closed) in view of the inputs, and a second solution is proposed.

4. The second proposal finds wide acceptance, and the final decision is documented.

It Works!

An article about Loomio in *Wired* magazine[12] describes how a tourism company with many local partners located around the world has suc-cessfully adopted the tool for consultative decision making. Input for important decisions come from employees and a selection of success-ful partners. Although they did not do it with the intention of driving accountability, it is a happy side effect of maintaining a decision record.

---

11. www.loomio.org
12. http://www.wired.com/2014/04/loomio/

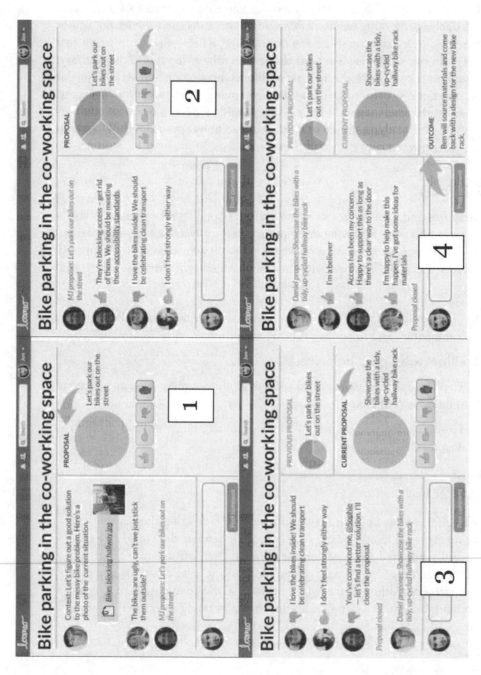

Figure 6-5 *Using Loomio (www.loomio.org) as a decision record system*

6.7.3 Scope

Not all decisions need be recorded like this. HR and sensitive business decisions could be left out or shared with much smaller groups. Product-level decisions could be shared with the whole product team. Business-as-usual decisions in contentious areas are a good candidate for this. For example:

- Decisions on marketing and sales strategy

- Decisions that change or tweak the business model

- Decisions to start/stop a project or initiative

- Decisions to build or buy some software

- Decisions on adopting technology standards

- High-level architectural or design decisions

- Decisions that shape a product roadmap

- In a professor-entrepreneur setup, decisions by outcome owners to override recommendations of function leads

- Decisions to go ahead with development based on estimates from someone outside the development team

6.7.4 Resistance

Of course, there is bound to be a lot of resistance to adopting such a system. Table 6-2 lists some expected objections and clarifications. As noted above, it greatly helps to formally know at the start of a discussion who the ultimate decision makers (decision owners) are. Accountability maps help determine them. There are always one or more decision owners for every decision, but there is usually no official way to find who they are.

Truth is, many leaders are hesitant to state their positions in writing for fear of being proven wrong later. They'd rather make decisions unilaterally in private and present it as a collective team decision. Career-progression wise, this strategy preserves upside reward while minimizing downside risk. But it makes a mockery of accountability. It goes against the idea of fail-fast to learn quickly. But it doesn't have to be so. There ought to be no downside risk for decisions that seem wrong only in hindsight. All we can ask is that decisions are taken on the back of well-sought-out information. Executive leadership can help ensure this with the aid of a decision record.

Finally, it is worth noting that the decision record system proposed here is somewhat similar to what Ackoff proposes as part of a more comprehensive organizational learning, adaptation, and management support system.[13]

---

13. (Ackoff 1999)

Table 6-2 *Resistance to Decision Records*

Objection	Clarification
This will slow down decision making.	No, it need not. Assuming it takes three meetings over ten days to arrive at a decision today, it should take no longer provided the decision owner posts a tentative, proposed decision into the system after the first meeting.
Decision owners lose their authority if they have to seek consensus.	First, a system like this makes it mandatory to call out owner(s) for each decision, and often that is half the battle. Second, there is no need to drive consensus. The decision owner is free to make a decision that runs contrary to some inputs and stay accountable for it.
It will be a huge distraction for people who are not meant to be a party to the decision.	As if people are short of distractions otherwise. Time management is individual responsibility. Only involve people who have decision rights or input rights. Besides, this system saves time as it saves meetings where everyone has to be invited even if they don't have any input just so that they don't feel left out.
The system will have a poor signal-to-noise ratio. Decision makers will waste time sifting through unsolicited, mediocre input.	Decision makers are free to ignore input that they consider useless. Sorting by upvote count could help highlight notable input. Community action could help deal with spurious input.
It is a waste of time documenting the context, pros, and cons for each and every decision.	There is bound to be some overhead, but the idea is that it will pay off in terms of greater transparency and fewer errors of omission. Each team can decide what level of decisions they want to document.

6.8 Planning and Execution

Sometimes, unaccountability stems from the separation of planning and execution roles. In an IT-B context, execution is closest to the goal of actual software delivery and business outcome realization; planning is at least one level removed. Middle managers, IT governors, and above are uber-planners in that all their direct reports are also planners. Except for some meetings, they almost never work directly with executors or serve customers.

Execution includes activities such as fleshing out stories, creating promotional material, organizing events, conducting customer health checks, responding to support tickets, making sales calls, coding, testing, writing documentation, building, deploying, performing system administration, and so on. Planning includes activities like providing an architecture or a design, making and evaluating business cases, approving funds, scheduling work, staffing teams, selecting vendors, release planning, tracking progress, creating status reports, negotiating scope, collating estimates, conducting retrospectives, and coming up with conventions, policies, and metrics. In most IT organizations, job roles are defined such that they are all planning or all execution. This separation of roles is undesirable as explained below.

Scenario 6-3 Is Execution Beneath a Planner's Pay Grade?

Ava is a project manager. All day she interacts with her team and project stakeholders and works with project planning and tracking tools, e-mail, status reports, estimates, risk spreadsheets, and burnup charts. She used to be a good tester, but she doesn't test anymore. For one, she is too busy with project management to have the time to test. But she is also schooled to think that she has grown past testing. The norms of the organization and the marketplace say that testing is an activity below her pay grade, and her time is too valuable to be spent testing. She has thus transitioned from a role that was primarily execution oriented to a role that is mainly planning oriented.

6.8.1 Disadvantages of Separation

To organize at scale, we need a hierarchy. Some division of labor is also required. Both hierarchy and division of labor have their problematic aspects. By default, hierarchy tends to centralize decision making at the top. This erodes the autonomy—an intrinsic motivator—of the execution roles. Separation of planning from execution aggravates the erosion of autonomy.

Separation of planning from execution isn't good old division of labor. Good old division of labor is along skill boundaries (e.g., a visual design expert does not have a developer's coding skills and vice versa). Separation of planning from execution is division of labor along hierarchical boundaries. It tends to acquire the patronizing overtones of the relation between management and labor. In the example above, Ava has testing skills but she doesn't do it anymore because of division of labor along hierarchical boundaries. When organization design prescribes a clear separation of planning from execution, moving up the hierarchy means moving to planning-dominated roles. This is problematic on several fronts:

- **Ability:** Not everyone is equally good at planning and execution. But if there is no other option to move up career-wise, all executors will aspire to planning roles, whether they are good at it or not. This also results in the loss of good execution talent.

- **Respect:** Some places have equal pay but unequal respect; for example, hands-on people can grow as specialists, they get pay raises, etc., but their performance reviewer is always a planner, sometimes junior to them in rank. On the other hand, they are never called upon to review the performance of another planner. Since performance reviews can never be completely objective, this dynamic sets up an asymmetric power equation between planners and executors.

- **Credibility:** Increasingly, team members respect their managers based on their ability to perform hands-on work if needed. Otherwise, they can only demand respect, not command it. Staying hands-on helps managers understand, for instance, why actual effort is much more than estimated. They could do it themselves and see. If they are able to do it better, perhaps they have something to teach the team.

- **Accountability:** Decisions are made by people without corresponding responsibility or bandwidth to execute (e.g., the ivory tower architect only ever designs on the whiteboard or in his diagramming tool, never in code). When these designs run into problems in execution, the default reaction is to blame it on poor execution. Rarely do retrospectives wonder whether better decisions could have been made. Why don't the executors point out that flawed decisions are the root cause of some problems? Because centralizing decision making also centralizes power. The project manager/product manager/lead architect not only has decision-making power for day-to-day project operation, they also have performance review power over the team. For all the talk of 360-degree feedback, weightage attached to feedback follows the chain of hierarchy. Questioning decisions beyond a point could prove to be career limiting for executors. Their lot is to rant and gripe in private.

Of course, many planners aren't autocratic decision makers. They do consult the team. However, there is no institutional mechanism to make consultative decision making the norm. Decisions don't have to be democratic or even consensual, but the executors do need to be consulted. A common objection to any suggestion of more inclusive decision making is that it will slow things down and paralyze the organization. This need not be so as explained in the previous section. A clear understanding of authority and accountability helps avoid potential deadlocks. Those with accountability need to have authority to take a final call on decisions. Often, authority is clear or made clear but accountability is diffuse. Separation of planning from execution confers authority differently from accountability.

How is accountability fixed in a setup where there is a separation of planning from execution? This is usually only relevant when things go wrong. Sometimes, there is a clear lapse in execution and accountability is easily fixed. Sometimes, planners finger point that the executors didn't fully obey them—they went their own way and botched things up. This breeds a culture of unquestioning obedience. On the other hand, when execution stands up to scrutiny, there is no institutional mechanism to question decisions. On the rare occasion that a decision is questioned, decision makers are able to get away citing external factors outside their control.

6.8.2 The Forest and the Trees

Instead of having the people close to the situation look for ways to make things better, the people close to the situation are generating reports in the hope that people removed from the situation will make it better. It yields no constructive insight into the problems at hand.
—Ross Petit[14]

A consequence of separating planning from execution is that the executors do not get to make decisions outside of execution; they only get to provide input to planners. This is cited as good practice because, apparently, the executors are likely to miss the forest for the trees. However, extending the analogy, planners are likely to only notice the emergent and canopy layers of the forest and miss the understory and forest floor.[15] Except for people with exceptional levels of empathetic comprehension, it requires the *same person* to step back from the details in order to see both the forest and the trees clearly. Separation doesn't help.

For example, inside sales and field salespeople have the pulse of the target segment. Sales engineers get to know what prospective end users want. Support engineers are in touch with how well the product is serving the needs of users. Developers know that slightly different ways of realizing the same functionality can have very different effort estimates. IT operations engineers know what might bring down a server. People on the product management team are often acutely aware of long-pending feature requests, capabilities of the competition, and industry trends. Rather than just having them provide input for decisions and taking decisions on their behalf, planners would do well to have them take a call and play a supporting, vetting role in the process. This is how we scale by true delegation.

---

14. http://www.rosspettit.com/2012/04/shorten-results-cycle-not-reporting.html
15. http://en.wikipedia.org/wiki/Rainforest#Layers

6.8.3 Overlapping

To bridge the divide between planning and execution, overlap them. It is possible to design an organization where planners are required to spend, say, 20% of their time in execution. An architect could spend some time writing code or performance tests or simply trying to address technical debt in some area of the codebase. This will also give her a feel for how easy or hard it is in practice. A director/VP/head of engineering/development could spend some time contributing to deployment scripts or to the build infrastructure that allows for continuous integration. A program manager could spend some time manually testing an application. An IT finance analyst (business case maker) could do the same or help in writing/reviewing acceptance criteria for user stories.

Even better, they could just pair up with a hands-on team member for one day a week. Pairing eases context switching. It avoids the need for carving out a small piece of work that can fit into 20% time (also see Section 10.3.4). It doesn't help to do this piecemeal in the form of 2 hours a day. One day a week is ideal but not always practical. At a minimum, planners should aim to perform execution work by pairing for 4 days a month.

What are the benefits of overlapping? It's one way of gaining credibility with the team. Demonstrating one's competence at execution and leading by example works better than leading by speech and authority with plans, charts, and metrics. Regular bouts of execution help us stay in touch with ground reality and help planning. Too many hierarchies lose their credibility in the eyes of those at the bottom just because they are out of tune with ground reality. Another benefit is that we gain new perspective by putting ourselves in the shoes of less powerful people. This leads to better-informed decisions. Generally, these benefits more than compensate for the 20% loss of planner bandwidth.

6.8.4 Dealing with Opposition

Unfortunately, the opposition to being hands-on often comes from the planners themselves and not from executive sponsors. Especially if they haven't been hands-on in a while, they may fear that their rusty skills will be exposed. This needs soft handling. One solution is to immerse a group of planners into a week-long back-to-hands-on workshop where they aren't judged by their teams. They also need to be reassured that they aren't being nudged down the hierarchy.

Then there are the planners who have a directing style of leadership and are used to pulling up their subordinates for output that falls short of plans. They fear that once their subordinates find that they themselves are no superhumans at executing, they'll lose their control on the team. These planners have to be helped out of a directing style to a more supporting or coaching style of leadership.

In some cases, planners are so overloaded with work that any talk of execution seems laughable. A context-specific approach is required to deal with this. Sections 8.6 (introducing project assistants) and 10.3.4 (avoiding part-time assignments) provide some options.

So much for changing the habits of tenured planners. However, it is easy and powerful to set an expectation of 20% execution with people right at the time that they are promoted from an execution role to a planning role. Encouraging them never to leave a toehold from execution is a good way to gradually institutionalize this norm.

6.9 Org Chart Debt

This and the last two chapters ventured into reorganization. Moving to outcome-oriented, cross-functional teams, moving away from the matrix, and adopting a professor-entrepreneur model are all examples of structural reorganization. Drawing up lines of accountability, nominating outcome owners, encouraging decision records, and overlapping planning with execution are all examples of operational reorganization. This type of deliberate reorganization is in contrast to reactive rejigs.

Usually, corporate reorganization is a reaction to events like promotions, new hires, or mergers and acquisitions or is an attempt to retain top talent. While they are unavoidable, it is essential to step back occasionally and examine whether the reorgs have gone against the principles explained so far. Have we unwittingly created positions with unbalanced autonomy and accountability? Have we diffused outcome ownership or compromised the authority of outcome owners? Have we created activity-oriented teams? If yes, then, we have taken on org chart debt. We need a round of deliberate reorganization to repay this debt.

This is similar to how we deal with technical debt[16] in software. In the run up to a release, developers sometimes take a quick and dirty approach to getting the functionality out of the door. If left unattended, the codebase atrophies over time and turns into a liability. Therefore, good tech leads always buy time from product owners to refactor code and repay technical debt as soon as possible. The refactoring process is informed by sound principles of good design. Org chart debt needs to be dealt with similarly. Deliberate reorgs help repay org chart debt. Going back to basics, they review whether people are accountable for activities or outcomes. Are the outcomes any good? Are they independently valuable and achievable? (See Section 4.1.) Just like software, org chart debt

---

16. http://martinfowler.com/bliki/TechnicalDebt.html

that is not repaid gradually turns into a liability for the organization in the form of silos, politics, and turf wars.

6.10 Summary of Insights

- Agile software development favors collective ownership of code. However, collective ownership of business outcomes across multiple teams is a different matter altogether.

- Informal structures of power are worse than formal ones. They crop up when an organization kids itself about collective ownership of business outcomes.

- Clear accountability helps clarify decision rights and avoids decision stalemates.

- Every business outcome or suboutcome needs a full-time dedicated outcome owner having authority commensurate with accountability for achieving the outcome.

- Separation of planning from execution isn't good old division of labor. Some problems of unaccountability arise from this separation.

6.11 Summary of Actions

- As far as possible, refactor the organization to transition from multiple power centers per outcome to a single one.

- Publish accountability maps to clarify the line of accountability for outcomes with multiple owners. They are just another example of information radiators.

- Try the professor-entrepreneur model. Create function lead roles having autonomy but not authority. This helps avoid territorial struggles.

- Push for transparent decision records. They provide accountability for decisions and help avoid errors of omission.

- Avoid complete separation of planning from execution by instituting, say, 20% execution content for all planning roles.

- Periodically repay org chart debt using the principles described in this and the last two chapters.

Chapter 7

Alignment

We have been making the case for autonomous teams, and it is natural to worry that this will erode alignment with IT and business strategy. In this short chapter, we see ways to retain alignment. We also look at how to improve cooperation between IT and business. This topic ties back indirectly to the theme of designing for autonomy laid out in Chapter 3. Ensuring alignment lets us design for autonomy without worrying about runaway autonomy, which is a common cause of silos.

7.1 Articulate Strategy for General Alignment

Strategy is ineffective if it cannot be articulated in terms of day-to-day tradeoffs. For example:

- In enterprise architecture, it isn't so useful just to say that teams should design for high availability. It's much more useful to say that teams should value availability over consistency.

- Articulating the pros and cons of make-versus-buy and providing guidelines for making a choice in the context of one's IT landscape helps avoid sad postmortems of distressed change programs.

Tradeoffs exist at different levels of IT and business. The more they are consciously acknowledged and articulated, the easier it is for everyone to be aligned with strategy.

7.1.1 Operational Excellence, Product Leadership, Customer Intimacy

In a competitive landscape, it makes sense to play to one's strengths. It's not just about choosing what markets and segments to play in. It is also about the *style* of play. *The Discipline of Market Leaders*[1] argued that in order to do well in the 21st century, a company could choose to stake its market reputation on *only one of three* value disciplines: operational excellence, product leadership, or customer intimacy.

Roughly speaking, operational excellence is about offering a good-enough product or service at a great price (e.g., low-cost airlines), so cost control is all-important. Product leadership is about innovation and quality (Apple's products, to use a popular example). Customer intimacy is about having an intimate understanding of client needs. It is generally applicable to service industries. It means offering clients a *total solution* even if it requires putting together parts of the solution from outside of one's own offerings.

When we think of companies we admire through the lens of this framework, we find that they predominantly exhibit one of these three characteristics. Operational excellence is the mindset that values cost-efficiency more than other attributes. On the other hand, the credo of responsiveness over cost-efficiency described in Section 3.3 is more relevant for an organization driven by product leadership or customer intimacy. Once an organization decides its style of play (value discipline) and communicates it far and wide internally, it becomes a useful, practical guide for making tradeoffs. All the previous arguments against activity-oriented teams and shared services in Chapter 5 make even more sense in this light. Reiterating the value discipline helps managers balance their natural urge to maximize utilization or productivity (operational excellence) with some thought toward responsiveness.

Even for businesses driven by operational excellence, their IT-B organizations tend to be more about R&D than operations. Operational excellence applies to operations. IT-B is strategic product or business capability development, not operations. For instance, an e-commerce company aims for operational excellence in its operations. What about IT-B? It depends on whether the e-commerce platform is built or bought. If it is built, it had better be a differentiator and, in that case, it is better run as a unit driven by product leadership.

---

1. (Treacy and Wiersema 1995)

Scenario 7-1 One Company, Two Faces

Koparati Inc. is an IT company that offers custom build services (appdev and systems integration) as well as a suite of software products. Services and products are run as two different business units. However, in order to provide employees with a diversity of experience and opportunities for growth, they are allowed to move from the products division to the services division and vice versa. Besides, it allows Koparati to share a common recruitment and staffing team between the two units. For the most part, skills are transferrable between IT product development and IT appdev services, but there are some differences in desired orientation.

A linear revenue business like IT services requires very high customer orientation, whereas a nonlinear revenue business like products requires a high product or customer-segment orientation. For example, in IT services, you are expected to find tailor-made solutions for your client's situation whereas, in the case of products, the solution is not tailor made to any one customer but rather to a market segment. While providing customer support, product support teams are encouraged to improve product documentation rather than spend lots of time handholding users who raise support tickets. There is emphasis on developing a community of users who can help each other out.

The leadership at Koparati recognizes this. The value discipline for the services division is customer intimacy whereas it is product leadership for the products division. Recognizing this provides a basis for describing the difference in desired behaviors and in orienting employees accordingly. In the products division, employees are able to balance the tradeoff between spending time attending to a single customer and attending to the product.

7.2 Aligning IT with Business

Business strategy comes first. IT can be aligned with business provided that business strategy is commonly understood and accepted. Sometimes, this first step itself is a hurdle. Business strategy may exist in the heads of the execs but it may not be articulated or shared beyond vision, mission, and a plan for the year. Believe it or not, this may be the case because:

- They just haven't gotten around to putting it on paper.
- They are themselves not very sure and don't want to commit to a strategy on paper.
- A published strategy might indicate that a certain line of business is less important than others. In order to avoid resentment, the execs refrain from making it explicit.

A different sort of challenge arises when IT assumes without concurrence of business that it co-owns the business strategy. Under this impression, IT may fund initiatives for which business doesn't see justification. While there is no question that IT is strategic to a digital business, it is an empty platitude unless business comes around to acknowledging it. The starting sentence in the first chapter of Joseph Topinka's 2014 book, *IT Business Partnerships*,[2] corroborates this:

> Forrester Research, a global business research and advisory firm, estimates that less than one-third of businesses involve IT in their strategic planning efforts.

Given this state of affairs, it isn't uncommon to come across situations like the one described in Scenario 7-2.

Scenario 7-2 Business-IT Divide in Unbundling

At an e-commerce platform vendor, it was common knowledge that they had to unbundle their monolithic platform to increase sales. However, business and IT had implicit and different ideas about what unbundling meant. As depicted in Figure 7-1, business (commercial managers) thought that a core platform + add-ons approach would be good for sales. For example, they wanted to sell European language capability as an add-on to the base English package.

Platform architecture leadership (IT-B), on the other hand, thought that unbundling capabilities like catalog, cart, and invoicing would help potential buyers mix and match their existing solutions with relevant pieces of the unbundled platform. Accordingly, they started using the architecture budget to achieve unbundling along capability boundaries.

---

2. (Topinka 2014)

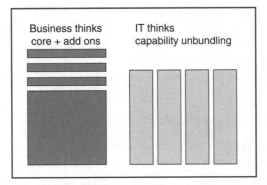

Figure 7-1 *Two views of unbundling*

When I pointed out (as an external consultant) that business didn't exactly care about this type of unbundling, they basically said that business had no clue how to monetize the platform, and it was up to IT to do it and show. Meanwhile, the commercial managers' requests for configurable add-on features also started getting built under business project funding.

Whatever be the reason for nonalignment, it is the responsibility of the execs to ensure that business strategy is articulated, shared, and accepted. Once strategy is in place, business needs to be sure that IT is using funds in line with their priorities. How do we ensure that IT's priorities are continuously aligned with business? Whether it is money spent on business features or enterprise architecture and infrastructure, an explicit mapping helps bring out the alignment for everyone to see and achieve shared understanding. Let's explore different ways of doing this.

7.2.1 MIT's Operating Models

Operating models are described in the book *Enterprise Architecture as Strategy*,[3] which is based on research work at MIT Sloan School of Management's Center for Information Systems Research. Operating models provide a high-level orientation to IT strategy. First, business context is mapped along two IT dimensions—integration and standardization. This requires active participation from senior management. Integration needs are determined to be high if the daily functioning of business units relies on data from other units. Standardization needs are determined to be high if there is significant upside to

---

3. (Ross, Weill, and Robertson 2006)

standardizing operations across units. However, uncalled-for standardization that doesn't align with business needs is usually counterproductive. Determination of integration and standardization needs leads to determination of an operating model from one of four integration-standardization quadrants. Enterprise architecture then takes its cue from a commonly understood operating model.

7.2.2 Pace-Layered Application Strategy

The pace-layered application strategy developed by Gartner[4] classifies IT systems based on how much they change, the level of change control needed, and the clarity of requirements. The classification is then used to guide selection, investment, planning, and management of systems in each category. Systems of record (e.g., payroll and HR) are like utilities (electricity, water, etc.). Although they are essential, they need to be cost-efficient. Systems of differentiation (e.g., a commercial SaaS offering) provide competitive advantage. Systems of innovation are built to try new ideas and graduate the ones that perform well to systems of differentiation.

This classification correlates with the pace of change experienced by the systems. Systems of record tend to be (and need to be) most stable and long lived whereas systems of innovation are ephemeral. The act of classification brings about a basic alignment of IT with business. Category-specific approaches can now be used to deal with these systems.

Stewart Brand introduced the concept of pace layering in his book *How Buildings Learn*[5] to describe how outer layers of a building such as interior layout, wiring, and plumbing change faster than inner layers such as walls, beams, and the foundation. In another book called *The Clock of the Long Now*,[6] he extended the concept to social systems such as cities and to civilization as a whole. He notes that while the outer layers get all the attention, they rest on and are powered by the inner layers. In other words, robust systems of record provide the necessary foundation for systems of differentiation and innovation.

7.2.3 Alignment Maps

Alignment maps (somewhat reminiscent of impact maps[7]) are simple information radiators that bring out the relationship between business imperatives and ongoing work. We use a simple mapping: business imperative → area of

4. https://www.gartner.com/doc/1635516/gartners-pacelayered-application-strategy-governance
5. Brand, S. 1994. *How buildings learn: What happens after they're built.* New York: Viking Adult.
6. Brand, S. 1999. *The clock of the long now: Time and responsibility.* New York: Basic Books.
7. Adzic, G. 2012. *Impact mapping: Making a big impact with software products and projects.* Surry, UK: Provoking Thoughts.

architecture → tech story; that is, what architectural objective does a tech story contribute to, and how is that architectural objective relevant to the business. As shown in Figure 7-2:

a. Different areas of architecture are mapped to business imperatives, and ongoing architecture work under each area is called out. For example, a business imperative of unbundling a solution may lead to an architectural action item of achieving data isolation, which is then executed as a series of technical stories. Not all teams engage in all ongoing architecture work at any given point in time, so it is useful to create team-level maps with active areas highlighted.

b. Team A's map depicts how their current work (auto-deploy to test environment) is meant to help with continuous delivery, which in turn is meant to reduce cycle time.

c. Team B's map depicts how their current work (extract customer DB) is meant to help with the architectural objective of data isolation, which in turn is meant to help the business goal of unbundling the solution they take to market.

d. Finally, this map may be used in periodic sync-up meetings between business and IT. The map helps business understand how the various streams of work are aligned with business objectives. It may be used to capture business satisfaction with progress on various fronts. This can now be used as an input to prioritize work for the next cycle.

When all teams consistently use this map as an information radiator, it serves to achieve shared understanding of how architecture work is aligned with business imperatives. It is also useful to use such maps to bring out the alignment between business projects and business objectives (business imperative → program of work → project).

7.3 Structural Alignment

Aligning IT-B teams with business units provides a foundation upon which alignment of ongoing work may be pursued. For example, an insurance business may have separate departments for new business (customer acquisition), policy administration, and claims administration. IT-B teams could be organized along similar lines. Each such team is then responsible for all the IT-B needs of its business counterpart—be it maintaining existing systems or building and migrating to newer ones.

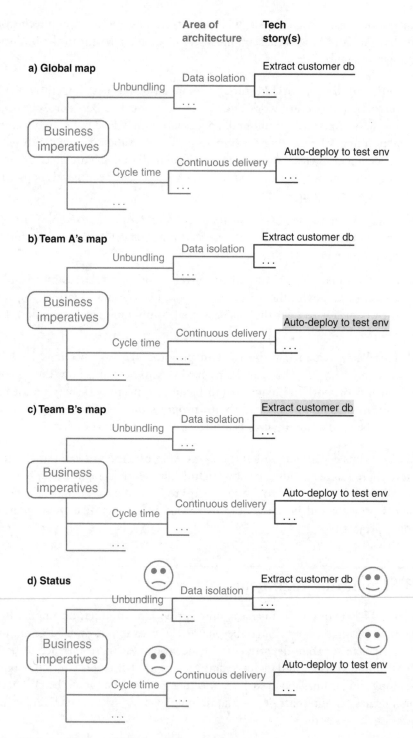

Figure 7-2 *Architecture-business alignment map*

Structural alignment of this sort takes us very close to the ideal of embedding IT into business units and eliminating the business-IT divide (Section 1.2). However, it is hard to effect this sort of restructuring if the IT-B organization is viewed as merely a big pool of IT resources to be assigned indiscriminately to whatever projects are funded. It needs a capability-oriented rather than a project-oriented vision for IT. This topic is explored in Section 8.2.

7.4 Making Business Play Its Part

IT is commonly blamed for failing to meet the expectations of business. However, business also has a big role to play in the success of IT efforts. As much as IT needs to align with business, business needs to align with IT-B's execution model. This assumes that IT-B owns the execution model, which unfortunately isn't always the case.

When product owners come from business, they have to understand that one-off interactions with the product development team aren't enough. If they cannot free themselves up for greater availability, they need to nominate someone from IT to act and decide on their behalf. Business stakeholders have to understand that demanding predictability is counterproductive, and they can get better results by learning to be value driven rather than plan driven (Chapter 8). They have to realize the value of iterative development and the concept of a minimum viable/ marketable product that can be iterated upon toward greater sophistication. They can be helped in this journey by a business-savvy IT role called an IT business partner.

7.4.1 IT Business Partner—A New Role

Topinka[8] makes the case for regularizing the role of IT business partners. These are people who help:

- Align IT with business
- Align business with IT's execution model
- Champion the value of IT to business and ultimately obtain for IT a seat at the business strategy table

He points out that several companies already have people in this capacity with varying titles such as business relationship manager, IT liaison, client executive manager, or even senior business analyst. They report to IT leadership and function at a higher level than story-writing business analysts. Their chief job[9] is

---

8. (Topinka 2014)
9. http://blog.hellersearch.com/Blog/bid/194081/IT-Business-Partner-Job-Description

translation—translating business objectives, context, and concerns to IT and translating IT ideas and achievements to business.

7.5 Summary of Insights

- Strategy is ineffective if it cannot be articulated in terms of day-to-day tradeoffs.
- Structural alignment provides a foundation for work alignment.
- As much as IT needs to align with business, business needs to align with IT's execution model.

7.6 Summary of Actions

- Articulate the organization's value discipline in order to help inform day-to-day tradeoffs.
- Clarify business strategy first, and then seek alignment of IT with business.
- Secure high-level alignment with frameworks like operating models and pace layering.
- Use alignment maps to link ongoing work to strategic goals. They serve as useful information radiators and as a visual aid for assessing impact of various projects on business objectives.
- Consider having the role of an IT business partner in order to help business and IT understand each other on an ongoing basis.

Chapter 8

Projects

The avant-garde of the software community has already moved beyond traditional projects. A popular example is that of Spotify, as described in Section 5.4.2. But even a survey conducted by Forrester[1] in 2009 showed that leaders in application development were selectively moving from a project-centric model of execution to a product-centric model. In this chapter, we will explore the reasons behind this shift and how they apply to enterprise IT as well. In terms of the key themes laid out in Chapter 3, this chapter expands on chasing value instead of chasing predictability. It argues for organizing IT along business capabilities and funding capability teams instead of project teams. This chapter is best read along with the next two short chapters on finance and staffing. The topics are closely interrelated.

8.1 What Is Wrong with Plan-driven Software Projects?

A project is a temporary organization that is needed to produce a unique and predefined outcome or result at a prespecified time using predetermined resources.[2] With three occurrences of the prefix "pre," it is a definition predicated on predictability. Although there are other definitions, the one quoted largely captures the mindset of a community brought up on a diet of PMP, PRINCE2, etc. Even when they manage so-called Agile projects using Scrum,

---

1. https://www.forrester.com/product-centric/fulltext/-/E-RES55099
2. CCTA. 1999. *Managing successful projects with PRINCE2.* p 22. Stationery Office Books.

project managers are strongly guided by a project or release plan rather than just a prioritized backlog. A release plan represents an elaborate prediction of scope, budget, and schedule—a prediction that rarely materializes, as reported in Section 3.1.

This plan-driven mindset is also a reflection of the demands made by people who sponsor the projects. They in turn are perhaps influenced by the Wall Street model of expecting predictable quarterly results. We can't do much about Wall Street behavior (although Dell went private[3] for this reason), but we can certainly choose to behave differently inside the organization.

A change in behavior is needed because whatever the reasons for the expectations of predictability, the results have always fallen short, as highlighted in Section 3.1. It is because software development is a design process and is, therefore, hard to predict. It is better to aim for valuable output rather than predictable output; for example, a team reliably delivers something relevant and useful by an expected date but exactly what is delivered (internal scope) can't be predicted even a month in advance. The oft-heard "When will we be done?" or "How long will it take?" needs to be revised to "What can we do by the end of the week/month?" It's a shift in focus from being on-plan to delivering value. It's great to have both, but value is more important than predictability. Given the history of the pursuit of predictability, going after both value and predictability at the outset feels like the plot for a heroic Greek tragedy.

Plan-driven projects are a consequence of traditional ways of commissioning and funding IT-B work. We need to decouple project funding from IT budgeting cycles. Another problematic aspect is that a project team is a temporary team that lasts only as long as the project, although it ends up creating something that is meant to last much longer. Many sections of the industry, especially new-generation ISVs, have recognized the limitations of plan-driven projects and moved toward a value-driven model. To appreciate this model, we need to understand the difference between a projects approach and a capabilities approach to IT-B execution. We also need to understand how plan-driven projects are first conceived as business cases and what's wrong with it. The next three sections deal with these aspects.

8.2 Budget for Capacity, Not for Projects

The conventional IT budgeting process plans expenditure by estimating upcoming projects. High-level scope is fixed upfront for the sake of estimation. Given

---

3. https://www.linkedin.com/pulse/20141209034750-25383300-going-private-is-paying-off-for-dell

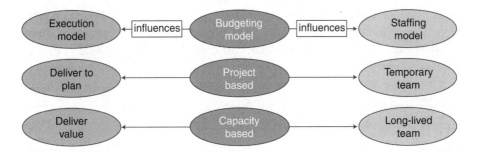

Figure 8-1 *Impact of budgeting approach*

the vagaries of software development described in Section 3.1, plans against fixed scope usually run into trouble. Things work better when there is freedom to alter (reduce) internal scope given fixed buckets of time and budget. However, in the world of conventional budgeting, reducing internal scope while retaining budget is viewed as cheating. Budgeting for a design process (rather than a production process) requires a shift in thinking because the budgeting model has a big impact on IT-B's execution model and staffing model (Figure 8-1). A program/project-based budgeting approach enforces a "projects" model of execution with an emphasis on delivering to plan. Projects also imply temporary teams, which isn't the best way of growing business-centric IT capability. By moving to a team-capacity-based budgeting approach (described below), execution can be reoriented toward delivering value with a stable, long-lived, outcome-oriented, cross-functional team.

In a capacity-based budgeting approach, instead of approving budget for lined-up projects, we approve budget for a desired team capacity based on a strategic assessment of the needs of different business-IT capabilities (described in the next section). This is practical since the bulk of IT-B cost is wages. Therefore, we plan (budget) cost against capacity and incur cost against features developed by a capability team. An outcome owner releases sanctioned funds by approving the use of team capacity for a specific piece of work. Instead of assigning resources (people) to planned projects, we assign scope (or a roadmap, or a set of problem statements) to long-lived teams. The Scaled Agile Framework describes a variation of this approach.[4]

Budgeting for capacity does away with the tracking of project-level cost variance because project cost is no longer considered at the time of budgeting. Outcome owners secure budget for team capacity and allocate it just in time based

---

4. Lean|Agile budgeting with the scaled Agile framework: Beyond project cost accounting. http://scaledagileframework.com/new-leanagile-budgeting-with-the-scaled-agile-framework-beyond-project-cost-accounting/.

on delivery of value. Outcome-oriented metrics in the form of key (business) performance indicators (KPIs) help drive accountability over the use of funds. This approach steers clear of project-centric thinking. The resulting budgeting process is a drastically simplified version of the project-based budgeting process.

8.3 Business-capability-centric IT

By definition, a project represents a temporary organization (team). It is typically executed by a team drawn from a global pool of IT resources. They finish the project and return to the pool. The pool may consist of employees, contractors, or complete teams from IT suppliers (outsourcing/offshoring). This is a poor model of capability development. Capability here does not refer to engineering capability; it refers to an understanding of the business as codified in its IT assets. This understanding can only reside in people's minds, although it might be aided by external artifacts of documentation. It is best achieved with a stable, long-lived, cross-functional team. The team (and the systems it owns) constitutes the capability. For effective decision-making and accountability, each capability is assigned a capability owner.

Capabilities align well with business. Capability teams are organized around business capability boundaries and not along architectural boundaries such as API or front end. For example, an e-commerce business has capabilities such as buying and merchandizing, catalogue, marketing, customer service, order management, and fulfillment. An insurance business has capabilities such as policy administration, claims administration, and new business. A telecom business has capabilities such as network management, service provisioning and assurance, billing, and revenue management. A platform of capabilities is all the more important for digital transformation efforts (as explained in Section 1.4). As illustrated in Figure 8-2, multiple software applications, APIs, or products may constitute a capability. They may come and go, but the capability lives forever (or as long as the business doesn't undergo radical change). As Table 8-1 points out, product/application/API teams last longer than project teams but shorter than capability teams. In enterprise IT, a capability team owns all systems relevant to the capability. They may be systems of record, differentiation, or innovation. In the spirit of DevOps, they are built and run by the capability team.

ISVs have long understood this. Product development teams do not work in terms of projects. Their reasons apply to enterprise IT as well. Once we have long-lived capability teams that own their products (internal or external), APIs, and applications, we find that the need for commissioning new projects goes down. After all, most projects are enhancements to existing capabilities, so they can be treated as new items on the capability roadmap. The business may

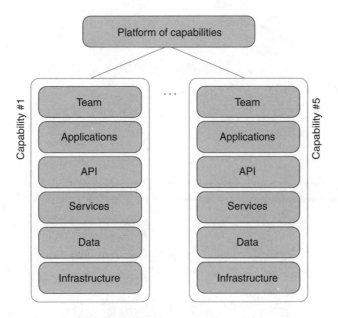

Figure 8-2 *What's in a capability?*

Table 8-1 *Long Live the Capability Team*

Unit of Organization	Life Span	Effectiveness
IT-B project teams	Short-term vehicles of asset creation	Unsuitable life span for team
Product, API, or application teams	Medium-term IT assets	Second best to maintain teams around products, APIs, and applications
Capability-centric teams	Long-term organizational assets	Best to maintain teams around business capabilities

continue to approve the use of funds from the capability budget for each item. Figure 8-3 illustrates the difference between the two approaches to IT execution. The projects approach ramps up and ramps down short-lived teams from a free pool of IT resources. Project teams finish development and move on, leaving an operations team and sometimes a maintenance team to deal with their offspring. By contrast, the capabilities approach features a stable long-lived team for all relevant, coarse-grained business capabilities. Capability teams have their own roadmap and budget. Only cross-capability streams of work need be funded and managed separately as projects, but they still don't

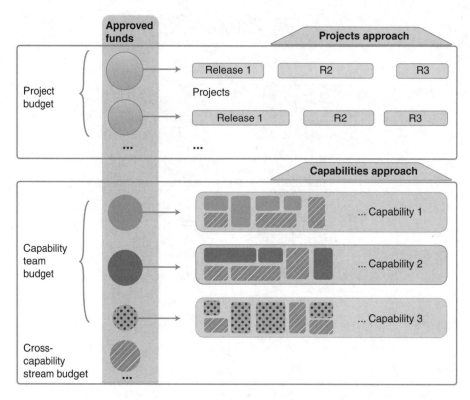

Figure 8-3 *Project teams versus capability teams*

call for separate teams. The overall scope is broken down into features/epics/ stories as appropriate and distributed to relevant capability teams. A project outcome owner interfaces with capability owners to influence prioritization and coordinate dependencies.

What about when IT-B is outsourced? Can we afford to have long-lived capability teams when they are outsourced? Section 10.2 in the chapter on staffing describes how this can be achieved without an increase in cost. A projects model of intermittent ramp-ups and ramp-downs is not going to help build a capability. Systems of differentiation better not be outsourced this way.

What about sudden unplanned projects? Don't we need a project team if the capability teams cannot spare capacity? No, it isn't advisable to enhance a capability through a new temporary team that is separate from the capability team. It leads to loss of knowledge and problems in maintenance. It is better to bolster the capacity of the capability team temporarily and have them take on the additional unplanned work. Doing so will slow down the ongoing efforts of the capability team, but this is to be tolerated in favor of doing something separately and then have the capability team take care of it.

It will take some serious relationship management skills to roll out this model in a place where business is used to demanding predictability (and not getting it), fixing scope, and setting deadlines. Creating the role of an IT business partner, as described in Section 7.5.1, might help. Chapter 10 deals with some other common reservations against stable, long-lived teams.

8.4 Project Business Cases

IT-B work is usually meant to create or enhance an IT asset. It needs approval of funds from executive sponsors and finance. They may look for a financial justification in terms of a cost-benefit analysis called a *business case*. A business case may show that the cost of not upgrading some system or that the benefit of developing a new system is sufficiently higher than the funds required for the effort. During the process of capital budgeting, funds are allocated to a subset of competing investment proposals based on, among other factors, the relative strength of their business cases. Other less-acknowledged factors include the strength of interpersonal relationships and the need to keep important people happy.

A lot of assumptions and adjustments are involved in developing a financial business case.[5] Assumptions include multiyear projections of costs of running old systems versus new systems, cash flow estimation for developing a new system, usage projections, and cost of capital. Adjustments include project risk adjustments, inflation, tax, discounting cash flows, and asset depreciation. Using numbers based on these assumptions and adjustments, a business case is presented in terms of metrics like net present value (NPV), internal rate of return (IRR), payback period, profitability index, return on investment (ROI), or total cost of ownership (TCO). Given the number of variables involved, business cases can't help being somewhat speculative and often widely miss the mark in terms of actual benefits. It's similar to how a country justifies capital expenditure for hosting the Olympics.

Once funds are sanctioned and IT-B work begins, IT-finance personnel track actual expenditure against budgeted (planned) expenditure (based on the projected cash flows in the business case). However, plan-driven IT-B projects have long lead times between incurring cost and delivering benefit. It is easy to track incurred cost, but there is no benefit delivered while development is in progress. Because this phase could be several months long, IT managers settle for tracking delivery per the plan. When something takes longer than planned to

---

5. For a detailed explanation, see (Blackstaff 2012).

develop, it translates into higher than projected costs and calls for a revision to the business case calculations. At a certain threshold of overruns, the calculations may indicate that the business case ceases to exist—that is, the projected benefits are no longer sufficiently higher than costs. Cold reason would suggest that this is the time to stop the effort and write off the investment. However, any admission of failure would mean a loss of face for IT managers and others that backed the business case. Therefore, the business case is commonly recast with greater projected benefits and tweaks to various assumptions and adjustments (rationalized as based on newly available information) that bring it back into viable territory.

None of this has anything to do with real benefits. They only accrue after software goes into production. Real benefits are very hard to track in plandriven projects and they seldom are tracked. This is unfortunate because it is important to validate business case assumptions and recalibrate adjustments using data from real benefits. This ought to inform the next round of investments.

In the absence of benefits validation, the whole exercise of the business case turns out to have the sole purpose of securing commitment for funding.[6] To this end, benefits are commonly overstated.[7] Even when there is no overstatement, intangible items may be overlooked. Denning and Christensen[8] point out how Dell relied too much on IRR and ROI analyses in deciding what to outsource to ASUSTeK. Dell ended up losing its expertise and created a formidable competitor in ASUSTeK. Clearly, their business case for outsourcing overlooked the cost of loss of in-house know-how and the cost of inability to innovate in the future.

8.4.1 Benefits Validation Powered by Continuous Delivery and Analytics

It is possible to track the impact of new features by leveraging usage analytics from production and releasing features in small increments. Usage analytics are introduced to first baseline usage patterns. Each incremental release into production is analyzed for deviations from the baseline. Stable deviations are used to re-baseline. This allows for fine-grained validation of business cases. Better yet, the fast feedback and the relatively low cost of a few incremental releases

---

6. Ward, J. 2006. Delivering value from information systems and technology investments. Cranfield, UK: Cranfield School of Management, Information Systems Research Centre.

7. http://www.rosspettit.com/2012/01/business-cases-simplicity-over.html

8. http://www.forbes.com/sites/stevedenning/2014/05/26/clayton-christensen-do-we-need-a-revolution-in-management/

allow experimenting with new ideas without constructing elaborate business cases. This is also referred to as the build-measure-learn feedback loop in *The Lean Startup*[9] approach.

8.4.2 Deemphasize Financial Business Cases

Once we have fast validation of actual benefits in place as described above, we can reduce the emphasis on big upfront financial business cases. There is a notion in many organizations that we'll be laughed out of the room if we ask for funding without a financial business case. But we'll be laughed out of the market if we proceed on the basis of dubious business cases. And as explained above, most IT-B financial business cases are dubious.

Whether powered by usage analytics or not, a mindset of adaptability requires fast feedback about actual benefits. A mindset of predictability uses a big upfront financial business as a soft pillow to dream up castles in the air. Physical domains like civil construction are nowhere as malleable as software; they have little choice but to play a high-stakes game (e.g., debt-financed mega construction projects for mega sporting events) with big upfront business cases. The software opportunity is ours to lose.

Make no mistake, upfront deliberation is definitely invaluable before committing funds. The argument here is only against insisting on a seemingly objective, hard-nosed quantitative evaluation of cost and benefit. Will the absence of upfront cash flow projections lead to fiscal imprudence? Not if the outcome owner is made to share the results of actual benefits validation every month or quarter.

8.5 Value-driven Projects

Value-driven projects differ from plan-driven projects in that they aim for valuable rather than predictable results. They focus on solving problems and delivering value rather than on delivering to a plan. In value-driven projects, Product/Solution/Outcome owners play a more important role than project/delivery/development managers. To highlight the differences, it is enough to take the case of a plan-driven project executed by a single capability team, one that isn't part of a larger program of work. Let's assume that the releases made by this team can directly go into production and reach end users. Table 8-2 summarizes the differences.

---

9. (Ries 2011)

Table 8-2 *Plan-driven Projects versus Value-driven Projects*

	Plan-driven Project	Value-driven Project
Funds	IT-B budgeting is based on upcoming projects. Funding is obtained from annual budgets that are approved based on elaborate business cases.	IT-B budgeting ends up allocating stable team capacity. Funding is obtained from preapproved team capacity budgets. Where short feedback loops are in place, a simple qualitative business case is enough.
Scope	High-level scope is determined prior to funding.	Only the problem to be solved, desired outcome, and possible levels of outcome are determined based on a round of solution discovery. Scope is usually much smaller (e.g., one feature at a time) than in a plan-driven project, where the drawn-out funding process discourages small projects.
Team	Work is done by a team put in place for the project.	Work is done by one or more preexisting product/capability teams.
Dependencies	Careful release planning is required to navigate a minefield of dependencies.	Internal dependencies aren't treated very differently from external ones (third-party APIs, frameworks, etc.). Loosely coupled architectures as well as loosely constrained and backwards-compatible API ensure that frequent releases aren't held back by dependencies. Coarse-grained capability teams own other proximate systems, so most dependencies are under the control of a single outcome owner.
Cost	Project cost is estimated based on high-level scope.	Costs are estimated for varying levels of solution.

Table 8-2 *Continued*

	Plan-driven Project	Value-driven Project
Time	A release plan indicates what scope is to be delivered by what time (i.e., predetermined scope is to be delivered by a predetermined date).	There is no release planning as such. Instead, some initial scope is determined, and the stories are added into the team's backlog and prioritized. After this is developed and released, the next round of scope is determined. Usually this results in many more releases than a plan-driven project. By default, there is no deadline. If external factors dictate a tight deadline, the approach is to work toward delivering something relevant and useful by that time even if it is not necessarily the best solution for the problem. The best solution is arrived at iteratively.

8.6 Project Managers

We can't talk about projects and leave out their managers, can we? Managers of plan-driven projects have unenviable jobs. They are responsible for ensuring that a fundamentally unpredictable process delivers to plan. Given this onerous mission, considerations of value take a backseat.

Many project managers operate in a content-free mode, concerned only with burnup charts; progress reports; risks, assumptions, issues, and dependencies (RAID) reports; staffing plans; and so on. They only have a superficial understanding of what is being developed and why. They might know that feature X is 70% done and feature Y is 25% done, but they might not know why feature Y is more important. They might not know that there is a way to ship a minimal but workable feature Y with roughly a week's worth of effort. They may not even be able to demonstrate key user journeys through the application, let alone test it on their own.

Sometimes, this is because of the separation of planning roles from execution roles (Section 6.8). But often, it is because manager roles carry too much administrative overhead: requesting seats, ID cards, access, licenses, etc. for new members; following up and approving timesheets and expenses; scheduling meetings; making travel/visa requests; arranging team outings; etc. This is not servant leadership. Servant leadership is mainly about deep listening and stewardship, not about carrying water for the team. We can easily free up 20% of managers' time for execution (Section 6.8.3) by offloading administrative overhead to a new junior role called project assistant. This is somewhat similar to the role of executive assistants with two crucial differences. First, the project assistant helps the whole team (or potentially multiple teams) with administrative tasks that project managers would otherwise attend to. Second, we need to take care that allocation of a project assistant does not become a status symbol for the manager and that they aren't tasked with protecting anyone's calendar from so-called unwanted appointments.

When the execution model shifts from being plan driven to being value driven, the focus shifts from counting value to creating value.[10] Products and solutions are emphasized over projects. Project managers would do well to embrace this change and directly participate in value addition.

8.7 Governance

The legislature, the judiciary, and the executive are the three branches of a democratic government. In IT, governance is to management what legislature is to the executive in a democracy. In terms of the discussion in Section 6.8, governance people (e.g., GRC teams, most PMOs, enterprise architecture boards, many portfolio and program managers) are uber-planners whereas most managers (e.g., project managers, product managers, development and release managers) are vanilla planners.

Governance teams legislate on matters of frameworks/standards, tools, metrics, methodologies, risk, and compliance. When governance teams are out of touch with ground reality, they may get overly prescriptive and thorough about procedures and controls and thus erode the autonomy and responsiveness of execution teams. However, legislatures in democracies tend to have decent feedback loops. There is provision for public consultation before laws are made. People protest against troublesome laws or enforcement. Media

10. https://hbr.org/2013/08/tests-of-a-leadership-transiti/

hold the government accountable. Unpopular lawmakers even get voted out of power. An IT organization has none of this. To allow for first-hand feedback, it is very important not to have full-time governance roles. Usually, the function leads (as described in Sections 6.4 and 6.8.3) take up some governance responsibilities.

Although essential, governance is an activity, not an outcome. This makes it risky to grant autonomy to a pure governance team. Instead, it is better to constitute each area of governance as a community of practice (Section 5.7) consisting of practitioners from various capability teams.

8.8 Change Programs and Initiatives

Large programs and projects are sometimes the result of high-profile change programs or initiatives. The typical script goes something like this: A transformation expert is hired and given a big budget to run a change program. In an attempt to roll out changes quickly, the expert uses the budget to build a new IT-B unit separate from the existing organization. This new unit is allowed to decide how to integrate and navigate dependencies with existing systems. Sometimes, in the rush to get going, the knowledge and concerns of the incumbent custodians are set aside. Many such programs flounder and lose their way after a quarter or two. A few survive through to launch and even manage a couple of releases after launch. The expert is quick to proclaim victory and move on to greater assignments, taking along some of his team before the transformation has been fully delivered. However, problems surface in operations, migrations, and decommissioning of older systems that the change program promised to get rid of. The operations team feels frustrated in having to deal with incomplete, high-tech systems delivered by the change program.

The CHAOS Manifesto report referenced in Section 3.1 comes down heavily on large projects. It reports that they generally fare worse than small projects. It observes that large projects are also about status, visibility, power, and empire building—this is partly why, despite a dismal track record, they continue to get funded. It advocates doing large projects as a series of small projects with independently valuable outcomes—thereby differentiating the approach from a breakdown into milestones and phases. However, it cautions that it is difficult to make this shift under a conventional funding and tracking regime in which the associated overhead discourages small projects. This is where a clean break from a projects approach to a capabilities approach helps (Section 8.2). When we fund fixed team capacity rather than projects, there is little extra overhead in allotting approved funds one feature or epic at a time.

8.8.1 Digital Transformation Programs

The preceding discussion applies to digital transformation initiatives (Section 1.4) as well. Running these programs in isolation is a recipe for short-term success and medium-term failure. For example, it is easy to set up a new team for a mobile channel, but it is only a matter of time before this team finds that it needs deep integration with existing systems managed by other teams. What's more, cross-channel transactions such as buy-online-and-pickup-at-store are better handled by teams organized along business capabilities (e.g., catalog, order, fulfillment) than those organized along channels (e.g., web, mobile, store).

8.8.2 Limit Work in Progress

In large IT-B organizations, it is common to find hundreds of in-flight projects. When projects are started at a greater rate than they are finished, it results in a buildup of unfinished work waiting to progress and losing market relevance in the process. Just like traffic congestion on the road, project congestion is a symptom of overburdened capacity. The solution isn't always wider roads or flyovers. On the contrary, adding more people to a late project makes it later (Brooks's law[11]), and hiring more people to start more projects usually results in more unfinished work. Instead, it is more effective to put less important projects on hold while the more important ones run through to completion. In Kanban, this is called limiting work in progress (WIP). The Phoenix Project[12] describes how this is effective for IT-I projects.[13]

With long-lived capability teams, two different WIP limits can be set—one on the number of in-flight projects (features) inside a capability and the other on the number of in-flight projects that span capabilities. The second limit is ideally just one or two per capability. How do we determine a reasonable limit for the first? The upper bound is constrained by various factors:

- Team capacity.
- The feature mix—how much do they overlap in the code base?
- The ability to release increments to one feature at a time while keeping the enhancements to other in-flight features switched off.[14] This is essential to

11. http://en.wikipedia.org/wiki/Brooks's_law
12. (Kim, Behr, and Spafford 2013)
13. http://itrevolution.com/resource-guide-for-the-phoenix-project-kanbans-part-2/
14. http://martinfowler.com/bliki/FeatureToggle.html

the extent outcome owners wish to validate the business case for specific features using a build-measure-learn feedback loop (Section 8.4).

- The first three points relate to planning for an upper bound. When work is in progress, it is clear that the upper bound is reached when queue size grows too much at any stage of the development value stream.

The lower bound is constrained by the need to build a feature iteratively, having each iteration use the feedback (preferably from production) from the last iteration. This constrains us from throwing all available capacity at a feature because too much of it will be built too soon without feedback. Having too few in-flight features increases parallel work on a single feature and reduces opportunities for feedback-based learning.

It helps to maintain a portfolio Kanban board—a story-card-wall-like information radiator for planned and in-progress projects within the organization. Each card represents a project and captures its purpose, outcome owner, intranet home page, and team location. This information is generally available to portfolio managers and above, but there is no reason to restrict it to that group.

8.9 Summary of Insights

- Aiming for predictable software development hasn't yielded satisfactory results over the years. It is time to stop chasing predictability and chase value instead.

- Projects imply transient teams. Transient teams aren't good for developing business-IT capability. It calls for stable, long-lived project teams. The team is the capability.

- Traditional business cases have mainly served as a mechanism to secure funding. Projected benefits are rarely validated post-implementation.

8.10 Summary of Actions

- Switch to value-driven projects. A value-driven project is a logical construct compared with a plan-driven project that has its own team. It works with existing capability teams, defines the problem but not necessarily the full solution at the outset, and works on an ongoing basis of "What problems can we solve by this date?" rather than "We've got to do this by this date."

- Achieve reliable benefits validation with the combination of continuous delivery, usage analytics, and value-driven projects.

- Instead of approving budget for lined-up projects, approve budget for a desired team capacity per capability based on a strategic assessment of the needs of different business-IT capabilities.

- Shift to long-lived stable teams with capacity-based budgeting. This takes project planning out of the budgeting process, lets IT-B managers and outcome owners make funding decisions just in time, and better facilitates capability development within teams.

- Introduce project assistants in order to free up managers from administrative work and help them achieve 20% execution.

- Limit work-in-progress (WIP) at a portfolio level just as you would at a project level.

- Maintain a portfolio Kanban board as an information radiator.

- Execute large projects as a series of small projects with independently valuable outcomes.

- To allow for first-hand feedback, encourage people in governance roles to participate part-time in execution work.

Chapter 9

Finance

In the last chapter, we saw that the prevalent plan-driven projects model is, to some extent, a consequence of how IT-B work is funded. This chapter further explains how considerations of accounting, budgeting, and project finance affect the funding, formation, and functioning of software teams. It highlights the harmful side effects of some accounting and budgeting practices and suggests alternative approaches without attempting a deep dive into finance and accounting. In terms of the three themes laid out in Chapter 3, this is a discussion of a financing model tuned for valuable rather than predictable returns.

9.1 Relevance

Why talk about budgeting and accounting in a book about IT organization design? One may be excused for thinking that agilists have a problem with everything. At first, it was the development organization, then the product management and delivery governance organizations, later IT operations, and now finance. Actually, it is the theory of constraints[1] that is really at work here.

The throughput of a system is constrained by exactly one bottleneck at a time (i.e., the weakest link in the chain). When we elevate the current bottleneck, the next one becomes the limiting factor. The Agile software community has had good success with bottleneck elevators such as user stories, test/behavior-driven

---

1. http://en.wikipedia.org/wiki/Theory_of_constraints

development, refactoring, continuous integration, and DevOps. In some situations, though, the accounting or budgeting approach turns out to be the bottleneck. Thus, we encounter objections like, "We can't do DevOps because we need to separate CapEx work from OpEx work," or "We can't have long-lived teams because our funding is project based and our projects are short-lived."

Therefore, let's explore the bottlenecks created by traditional models of IT finance.

9.2 Cost Center or Profit Center

A cost center is an organizational unit that is financially only accountable for its cost. Traditionally, cost centers are the first to have their budgets cut when there is a financial crunch. Profit centers are the parts of an organization that bring in revenue. Although profit centers generally cannot function without the support of one or more cost centers, they are considered more valuable and often accorded greater respect than cost centers. These notions originated in mass production and found their way to IT organizations.

IT never directly generates revenue. IT-B (Section 1.1) is close to revenue in case of ISVs and Internet businesses but quite removed in case of enterprise IT. In case of ISVs (e.g., SaaS companies) and small Internet businesses, IT-B is often embedded with business and so the question of cost or profit center does not arise. In case of enterprise IT, the default is to classify all of IT as a cost center. It gets worse when a cost-center classification is applied to each arm of a functionally divided IT-B organization. It gives rise to local optima hell with testing, development, UX, and architecture each trying to protect its turf against cost imposed from the outside.

The projects model of funding IT-B work is in some ways a result of viewing IT-B as a cost center. IT-B is treated as a workshop to which jobs (projects) are assigned with strict parameters of scope, cost, and time. Given that software development is not a production process (Section 3.1), the project model proves to be a lost opportunity for business to *co-create* value along with IT-B.

9.3 Chargebacks

Chargebacks are a way of apportioning costs of shared resources and services among users to encourage judicious usage. IT-I costs (e.g., infrastructure, licenses, ticket servicing) are routinely charged back to business units using a simple pro-rata mechanism or a more sophisticated metered usage mechanism called *activity-based costing*[2] (ABC). Some CIOs have even tried to turn IT-I into a profit center by claiming revenue against services provided through such a system of internal chargebacks.

IT-B is usually free from chargebacks because it is capitalized and reported as a corporate expense. Chargebacks usually kick in when internal users start using what IT-B has built.

While ABC mechanisms may ensure fair allocation of costs, they are expensive to deploy and run, and they have side effects. The moment there is a rate card for everything, team members may find they cannot simply requisition resources and services as and when needed. Cost-conscious business unit leads may frown on requests not in the plan or may introduce approval gates even for small costs. Thus, fine-grained chargebacks tend to encourage cost-efficiency over responsiveness. Coarse-grained, post-facto chargebacks work better in this regard, even though they tend to apportion incurred costs less accurately.

9.4 CapEx and OpEx

In the chapter on team design (Sections 5.8 and 5.9), we discussed how, in an attempt to reduce costs (among other reasons), operations and maintenance teams are kept separate from development teams. Cost and accounting considerations are usually offered as reasons against having a single long-lived, cross-functional team for prototyping, development, operations, support, and maintenance. The cost objection, as discussed in Section 5.8, is false economy. Let's understand the accounting objection.

Conventional accounting wisdom has it that development is investment (i.e., CapEx) and maintenance or operations are cost (i.e., OpEx). Wages paid to IT-B personnel usually come under CapEx, whereas those paid to IT-I personnel come under OpEx. Any software or hardware purchase is CapEx, whereas leases and subscriptions (e.g., SaaS, cloud) are OpEx. DevOps mixes development's CapEx with operations' OpEx, and the accountants don't like it.

A long-lived, outcome-oriented, cross-functional, DevOps team performs asset creation work (CapEx) alongside operational work (OpEx). We can't simply capitalize the wages paid out to the team members. We could expense everything and keep the auditors happy. However, the accountants may still not like it because it has a negative impact on the income statement. As a result, the company may appear less attractive to investors. Besides, the OpEx budget may

---

2. http://www.apptio.com/blog/activity-based-costing-best-allocation-methodology

not allow for expensing everything. On the other hand, depending on the business situation, it may be more tax efficient to expense the cost at one go.

Capitalizing development costs creates an asset on the balance sheet and takes 80% to 100% of the cost off the income statement for the current year. The reality, though, is that investors are savvy enough to spot dubious assets on the balance sheet. However, sometimes it is a desire to protect bonuses (which are based on P&L, i.e., income statement) that becomes an unstated reason for capitalizing costs.

Given these considerations, we cannot simply capitalize or expense everything. In order to run a true DevOps team, we have to keep track of time spent on operational activities and capitalize the rest, or vice versa. The next section describes one way of doing it.

9.4.1 CapEx, OpEx Accounting without Timesheets

Timesheets are usually a poor source of information for deriving CapEx and OpEx. Nobody likes to fill timesheets, and the more fine-grained we get, the more the mistakes in entry. Besides, timesheets are out of band with respect to the daily rhythm of work. Instead, Agile project management tools are a better source of information—assuming activity status is promptly updated by the team.

Once we get into the habit of tagging each story card as asset creation or operational, we can derive a report of the total time spent on asset creation versus operational work in a given reporting period. This report will not filter out time spent in meetings, etc., but that's okay. We could apply a factor. For example, a team of ten people incurs 400 hours of wage cost per week. Say the card activity reports 300 hours of asset creation work. The rest is OpEx. Assuming 10% of team time is taken up by meetings; we subtract it from asset creation and add it to operations. Thus, we now have 270 hours of asset creation and 130 hours of operational work.

A couple of things have to be kept in mind. The card activity report has to be designed such that:

- It only includes time for the given reporting period—not the lifetime of the story card.
- It excludes any wait/idle time (e.g., time spent by the card awaiting development, testing).

The second condition cannot be met with a minimal story card wall that just has three lanes—open, in-progress, and done—because it does allow us to track idle time for a card. Typical story card walls have more lanes (e.g., analysis,

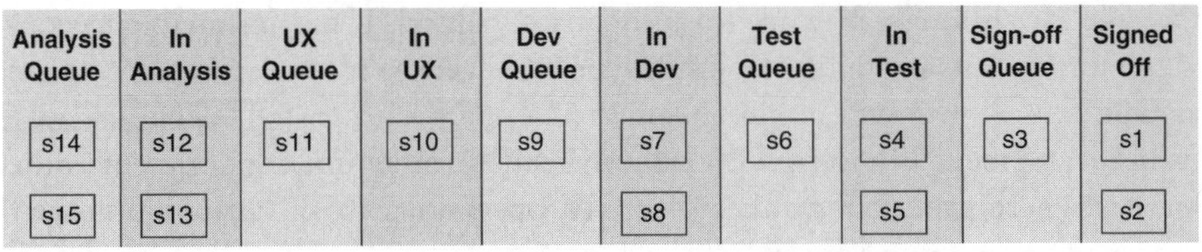

Analysis Queue	In Analysis	UX Queue	In UX	Dev Queue	In Dev	Test Queue	In Test	Sign-off Queue	Signed Off
s14	s12	s11	s10	s9	s7	s6	s4	s3	s1
s15	s13				s8		s5		s2

Figure 9-1 *Story card wall with alternating work centers and queues*

development, testing, and done) but even here, wait time is not distinguishable from active time. A card in the testing lane could mean it is ready for testing or actually undergoing testing. In case of physical card walls, teams figure this out by checking whether someone's name is tagged against the card. To get an accurate activity report from a software card wall, we need different lanes for when a card is idle versus when it is actively being worked on (e.g., awaiting analysis, in analysis, awaiting development, in development). In Lean terminology, the waiting lanes are called *queues* and the active lanes are called *work centers*. Work centers alternate with queues in a development value stream as shown in the card wall in Figure 9-1. Once a team gets into the habit of promptly moving cards to correct lanes, the card activity report can be easily made to exclude wait time. Next, let's see how to decide whether a card is CapEx or OpEx.

9.4.2 Activity Classification

All work on business features is of an asset-creating nature, whether it is analysis, design, development, UX, deployment, or testing. Operational work, on the other hand, includes activities such as monitoring servers, upgrading software, maintaining and upgrading infrastructure, setting up automated backups, etc. Any development spikes or tool evaluation is also to be expensed. Time spent by L1 and L2 support teams is also considered OpEx.

Bug-fixing effort has traditionally been treated as OpEx for bugs reported after shipping or going live. This logic is flawed because software maintenance is not similar to servicing a car when we accept software development as a design process (Section 3.1). A bug fix is an improvement to the design. A new deployment is required to roll the fix out to production. It improves all future production, not just a single instance of a product—which is what maintenance generally means.

This is all the more reason why people who fix production bugs should be part of the development team. The conventional accounting practice of expensing bug fixes while capitalizing development is wrong in this light. The same applies to work on technical debt or build and deployment infrastructure. Therefore, there is a case to be made for being able to capitalize costs under these heads although they are traditionally expensed. If we are unable to convince accountants or auditors of this, then we revert to traditional classification as OpEx.

If development is a design process, then the production environment is the factory where production takes place. IT operations work keeps the factory running by managing servers, networks, storage, etc. This is properly expensed.

9.5 Conventional Budgeting

As discussed in Section 8.3, budgeting has the greatest impact on how work is staffed and executed in IT-B. Budgeting is an exercise in planning expenditure. Budget plans are weighed against expected revenue or investment. When done well, the budgeting exercise helps optimally allocate limited funds to competing needs. But it has a flip side.

The practice of modern budgeting originated[3] in the school of highly centralized management. People in charge of approving budgets are still referred to as *controllers*. Controllers usually go about their jobs by holding people to approved plans. They are known to frown upon changes to plan or deviations from plan even when the plans in question are several months old. This control mentality is antithetical to Agile IT where the mantra is "embrace change," not control change.

At a minimum, the process has to be participative. Participative budgeting mitigates the aspect of centralized control somewhat by asking the people in charge of expenditure to come up with a proposed budget rather than impose, say, a 5% markup over last year's budget or actual spend. More than the output, the process is invaluable—plans are useless, planning is priceless.[4] It makes line managers think about what is likely to happen on different fronts in their part of the organization and share their insights with the custodians of money, who can then make appropriate provision.

9.5.1 Targets

It is common practice to assign cost/profit targets based on approved budgets. Financial incentives are tied to the achievement of these targets. For example, an IT-I organization may have an approved budget based on an expectation of 5% cost savings. The CIO may stand to earn a fixed bonus upon meeting the

---

3. McKinsey, J. O. 1923. *Budgetary control.* New York: The Ronald Press Company.
4. Variants of this line are attributed to Winston Churchill and Dwight D. Eisenhower.

expectation and an additional variable bonus of 1% of any further savings. This is monitored against service levels to ensure that the savings don't result in degradation of service.

However, this practice can be risky for the IT-B organization. Value addition here is difficult to measure, and there may just be too much at stake for the business to let IT-B optimize for its own targets. On the other hand, this ceases to be a consideration when IT-B isn't a separate organization but rather is embedded with the business. This is the model adopted by new-generation ISVs and many Internet businesses that have a tech-savvy business organization.

Even though targets are discouraged for IT-B, enterprise IT cannot continue to function under the impression that they have a captive internal customer base. Shadow IT[5]—instances of business bypassing in-house IT by hiring IT contractors and leveraging the cloud—is on the rise. It is an indication that business is growing impatient and willing to take matters into its own hands. Nimble, empowered portfolio management is needed to address shadow IT.

9.5.2 Budgeteering

Here is how things play out in a typical enterprise IT situation. IT portfolio managers are asked to come up with detailed expenditure plans for the next year. This requires them to draw up plans for various projects with very limited visibility. They submit prematurely detailed plans with talked-up benefits[6] in order to secure funding. When things don't go as planned, they go through an approval process for more funds or for reallocation of existing funds. And they scurry to spend it all by the year-end so that next year's funding isn't cut. Budgeting gains notoriety and is spoken of as *budgeteering*.

The good news is that alternative solutions are already available. An overview is presented here. Common to all the alternatives is the recognition that line managers need the ability to respond to changes in outlook by making range-bound adjustments to plans without having to wait for central approval. In other words, we need a regime that supports responsiveness—one that is aligned with the Agile manifesto principle of *responding to change over following a plan*. Instead of a central finance function tracking if funds are utilized as per plan, we have outcome owners accountable for realizing value out of preapproved funds tied to outcomes rather than plans.

---

5. Krigsman, M. 2013. Rogue IT: Sad truths and unfortunate stories. http://www.zdnet.com/rogue-it-sad-truths-and-unfortunate-stories-7000023779/

6. Ward, J. 2006. Delivering value from information systems and technology investments. Cranfield, UK: Cranfield School of Management, Information Systems Research Centre.

9.6 Agile Budgeting

An Agile approach to budgeting recognizes the need for frequent course correction by outcome owners. It recognizes that outcome owners can be most responsive to the business or to the market when they have a degree of autonomy in the use of funds. It relies on accountability mechanisms rather than expenditure tracking mechanisms to ensure appropriate use of funds. It is the mentality of designing road intersections with roundabouts rather than traffic lights.[7] Roundabouts demand cooperation; traffic lights demand rule compliance.

It Works!

The budgeting recommendations discussed here may seem new and radical. Far from it—they have been successfully implemented at a 142-year-old Swedish bank called Svenska Handelsbanken[8] since 1970! With profits of over two billion and a track record of never needing government bailouts, its public annual report for 2013[9] states:

> "We work without budgets, central sales targets, or broad, traditional marketing. Instead, we apply a highly decentralised working model, where each branch has a high degree of autonomy on its local market. Consequently, it is our branch managers who take the majority of important business decisions in the Bank."

In other words, the branch manager functions as an *outcome owner* with corresponding autonomy and accountability. Handelsbanken is one of over 25 members of a research network called the Beyond Budgeting Round Table[10] established in 1998 in response to growing dissatisfaction with traditional budgeting.

9.6.1 Rolling with Agility

One good practice is to take a monthly or quarterly rolling approach to budgeting. For example, near the end of every quarter, managers update their plans for

---

7. http://www.agilealliance.org/resources/learning-center/keynote-beyond-budgeting-agile-management-model-new-business-and-people-realities-statoil-implementation-journey

8. Libby, T., and Lindsay, M. R., Svenska Handelsbanken: Accomplishing radical decentralization through "beyond budgeting," 31 July 2006. http://www.researchgate.net/publication/256068797

9. http://www.handelsbanken.co.uk/shb/inet/icentrb.nsf/vlookuppics/handelsbankenrb_aboutthe-group_annual_report_and_sustainability_report_2013/$file/annual_report_and_sustainability_report.pdf

10. http://www.bbrt.org

the next four quarters. This bakes in a regular process for updating plans. Quarterly updates allow for better projections over shorter horizons. However, this is only useful if significant new information becomes available in time for the quarterly update; that is, it is no use for the planning horizon to be shorter than the feedback horizon. Short planning cycles need shorter feedback cycles. This is exactly what Agile methods give us—fast feedback. In the era of sequential development, feedback cycles could be several quarters long, so quarterly budget updates didn't make sense. With Agile methods, it is normal to expect delivery/demonstration of value every two weeks. Freezing budget plans over several months has disadvantages similar to freezing requirements for several months of development—it comes in the way of learning from feedback and other new information.

9.6.2 Collaborative Budgeting

To improve cross-departmental collaboration, try creating a small discretionary budget made up of funds from several departments. Involve a representative from each in the allocation process, with decision-making and stakeholding in proportion to their contribution. Make the projects you are allocating funds to things that will benefit the organization as a whole. You will be amazed at everyone's ability to raise their thinking up to the big-picture level, to recognize necessary tradeoffs, and to work together to use resources in the most effective way.[11]

The above suggestion is from an article describing efforts at collaborative budgeting at Enspiral[12]—a decentralized network of social entrepreneurs. Sharing insights from their journey, it says[11]:

- "Management time has been greatly reduced and the cognitive load of deciding what to do and where to spend our energy is spread across the whole network."

- "Real transparency isn't about the numbers being technically available—it's about proactively making the information accessible in a way people can understand and engage with meaningfully....People actually have their heads around the numbers now."

- "Supporting one thing means saying no to something else, and the process has led everyone to think not in terms of their personal perspective, but in terms of how they can support the collective goals by their individual choices and contributions."

---

11. http://www.mixprize.org/story/collaborative-funding-dissolve-authority-empower-everyone-and-crowdsource-smarter-transparent
12. http://www.enspiral.com

- "We have been able to connect our budgeting and funding process directly to our strategy…"

- "Collaborative technology creates transformative possibilities for structuring an organization, specifically when it comes to deciding how money, information and control are distributed."

- "Collaborative funding has allowed us to really 'walk the talk' of collective ownership combined with empowerment and autonomy….[However, collaborative funding] is not a budgeting panacea. All the problems every organization faces are still right there. The difference is they are transparent, and collectively owned."

Enspiral is working on a free and open source tool called Cobudget[13] to help with this process.

9.6.3 Venture Funding Enterprise IT

In some places, enterprise budgeting has begun to reinvent itself in the image of startup funding. Think of IT-B portfolio managers as venture capitalists, financial controllers and business sponsors as venture fund investors, product managers (or outcome owners) as entrepreneurs, and the myriad projects (or capability teams) as start-ups at various stages of funding. It is now up to the portfolio managers to release subsequent rounds of funding based on performance since the last round of funding. It gives them the flexibility to hold funds in reserve, run short experiments, shutdown projects that don't seem like they are going anywhere, and support the good ones with steady funding. Once financial controllers approve the budget outlay for a year, the center of gravity for funding shifts to portfolio managers.

9.7 Summary of Insights

- Cost/profit center mindset cannot coexist with IT and business agility.

- CapEx/OpEx accounting considerations need not influence team design or time reporting.

- Agile project management tools, when used as suggested, may be used to derive time spent on CapEx versus OpEx activities without the use of separate timesheets.

---

13. http://cobudget.co/

- When Agile software development provides fast feedback of value delivered, it allows for correspondingly shorter budgeting cycles.
- Agile budgeting helps managers focus on delivering value over conforming to a budget plan.

9.8 Summary of Actions

- Use accountability mechanisms rather than expenditure tracking mechanisms to ensure appropriate use of funds. Instead of a central finance function tracking if funds are utilized per the plan, have outcome owners accountable for realizing value out of preapproved funds tied to outcomes rather than plans.
- Be wary of fine-grained chargeback mechanisms as they tend to encourage cost-efficiency over responsiveness.
- Consider the use of collaborative budgeting tools such as Cobudget.
- Consider moving to a venture funding model that allows portfolio managers and outcome owners more discretion in the use of funds.

Chapter 10

Staffing

Chapters 7 and 8 explored the financial and governance aspects of alternatives to plan-driven projects. This chapter explores the people aspect. Having the right team in place makes a huge difference to the outcome. People aren't fungible in a software development effort—whether on the IT side or on the business side of the table. Putting together a good team requires intelligent staffing. In this chapter, we examine challenges and opportunities for better staffing.

10.1 Dealing with the Talent Crunch

An organization design tuned for intrinsic motivators still depends on the availability of people who can rise to the opportunity and make the most of it—people who have the required aptitude, attitude, and integrity. Unfortunately, the industry has grown so fast since the nineties that demand for good IT skills far outstrips supply. The rapid growth has also meant that IT people are used to moving up the ranks at a steady pace—often, they don't stay at a rank long enough to master a skill or to transfer it to newcomers.

To a limited extent, this shortage can be addressed by training and outsourcing. However, good trainers are either very hard to find or too expensive for extended assignments. Besides, training is a slow process. Attempts to scale it by training the trainers with a one-week course mostly fail because the newly minted trainers cannot pass it on effectively without real-world experience.

Outsourcing is no panacea either. At an industry level, outsourcing does not reduce the demand for good IT skills. It merely shifts the problem of finding talent to IT vendors who then try to staff projects with as much *leverage* as possible. Leverage here refers to the practice of staffing teams with a few competent and experienced hands and many rookies. It lets a vendor execute the maximum number of projects for a given staff mix. This approach is risky when the extent of leverage is decided by uber-planners (Section 6.8) rather than specialist leads on the team. However, one of the consolations of a leveraged team is that there aren't too many strong opinions on how to engineer a solution. The rookies are eager to learn and prove themselves, and there aren't too many ego clashes. In this respect at least, work progresses without stalling or meandering.

Is it possible to narrow the demand-supply gap for good talent from the demand side of the equation? One option is for the industry to shift more toward buying software from ISVs rather than custom building it. This is already happening. For IT systems that aren't considered strategic, the conventional wisdom around build-versus-buy (or make-versus-buy) is to buy as far as possible and build only as a last resort. Organizations where IT is a key enabler for business choose to build systems (in-house or outsourced) that they believe to be critical to revenue growth or competitive advantage (systems of differentiation). This is fine if there is some certainty of long-term access to good IT talent. Otherwise, it becomes a high-stakes gamble for the business.

10.1.1 Limit Scope and Sophistication

It is not always possible to choose buy over build. This is the case when the bulk of the work involves integrating existing systems. Or when there simply isn't a readymade solution in the market—as in the case of most Internet businesses. While it may be necessary to build custom solutions in these cases, it is still possible to limit the scope and sophistication of the proposed solution. Often, IT has an inherent bias for the latest technology, and business has a bias for making scope as comprehensive as possible. Put the two together and we get situations where the original needs are blown out of proportion. Instead of a modest solution capable of being built by a middle-of-the-pyramid workforce, we end with an ambitious solution that calls for scarce top-of-the-pyramid talent. In situations of talent scarcity, IT and business need to learn to pare scope and sophistication towards a just-enough solution without succumbing to delusions of grandeur.

Electronic voting machines used in general elections in India and Brazil[1] are an example of using just enough technology in situations of limited resources and limiting ambition for a 100% solution. The variant in use there

---

1. http://en.wikipedia.org/wiki/Electronic_voting#Direct-recording_electronic_.28DRE.29_
   voting_system

is a paperless system called a direct-recording system. It is technologically and logistically simpler than systems based on optical scanning of paper ballots. But it is less tactile and a marked change for those used to paper ballots. However, neither has voter turnout been affected nor has there been an increase in the number of invalid votes.

The suggestion to limit scope and sophistication does not run counter to the aim of developing systems of differentiation. The differentiation lies in the overall utility of the solution and its user experience, not necessarily in the breadth of features or in the use of latest technologies.

10.1.2 Let Org Design Help with Retention

The talent crunch is as much about talent retention as it is about finding talent. It is said that people leave their bosses, not so much their organizations. However, in many cases, the bosses are the way they are because of the organization culture or, more generally, the organization design. Therefore, refactoring the organization toward greater responsiveness, autonomy, mastery, and purpose as suggested in this book will not only help IT and business agility but is also likely to help with people retention in the long term.

10.2 Go Beyond Project Teams

IT organizations are rife with stories of systems that are unmanageable. Typically, these stories have a common thread—the team that originally built the system is long gone and the business-as-usual (BAU) team has no one from the original development team. They have moved on to other projects, they were contractors who are long gone, or it was built by another vendor. This is a problem with projects. Project teams are short-lived compared to the life span of what they build. Considering that these systems were important enough to be built (rather than bought), it is a shame that they inevitably languish and acquire legacy status in less than two years.

The truth about software is that no amount of documentation, handover, and knowledge transfer can make up for a 100% churn in team. Yet this is exactly what a project model brings about. IT capability does not reside in maturity models, process templates, documentation, code, or the IT infrastructure. It resides and grows in a team. Teams take time to develop capability. Tuckman's theory of group development[2] asserts that a team goes through a

---

2. Tuckman, B. W. 1965. Developmental sequence in small groups. *Psychological Bulletin* 63:384–99.

series of suboptimal phases (forming, storming, and norming) before it finds its groove in the *performing* phase. A project model of staffing may disband teams just as they come out of their group gestation period. In my experience, it takes a freshly constituted team about four to six months to sort out interpersonal dynamics and gel together. There is a good article by Allan Kelly at InfoQ[3] on this topic.

Previously, the argument used to be that project teams are a natural consequence of project-based budgeting. With team-capacity-based budgeting (Section 8.2), we can move from short-lived project teams to long-lived product or capability teams. Capabilities have even longer lives than products because products may have to be overhauled once they get outdated. A long-lived team is one that lasts at least for a year, frequently three to four years or more. Capability teams may last as long as the business capability they serve. Long-lived teams reduce the need for temp hiring—a side effect of planning for ramp-ups and ramp-downs. Otherwise, the intermittent entry and exit of contract workers weakens team capability. In situations where temp hiring is required for other reasons (e.g., there's a freeze on permanent headcount), it is important to have long-term contracts.

10.2.1 Cost

Long-lived teams don't incur more cost than project teams. As shown in Figure 10-1, the team is maintained at a steady medium size instead of being subject to the highs and lows of project ramp-up and ramp-down. The steady size can be arrived at by working backward from the budget so that total personnel cost for the year is the same. Instead of sizing the team based on planned work, we now plan work based on a fixed team capacity.

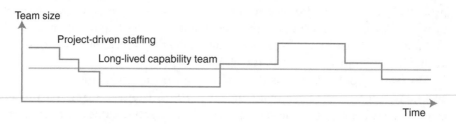

Figure 10-1 *Team stability*

---

3. http://www.infoq.com/articles/kelly-beyond-projects

10.2.2 Challenges

There are challenges to having a long-lived team from the team side of the equation as well. Some people don't like to stick around in the same team for long; they crave variety, get bored, and begin to look for other opportunities. This is okay—a team can tolerate an exit or two occasionally. Capability loss is minimal as long as there is a tenured majority ready to absorb a newcomer replacement. By contrast, a project ramp-down is far more invasive and rapid. A typical ramp-down and handover period is three months. Team composition changes by 80% or more in three months.

On the other hand, teams that find their groove tend to bond well and live long. They tend to socialize outside of work and perform much better than the average team.

10.2.3 Other Objections

What if there isn't enough work for a stable long-lived team? This is usually more of a worry for an application team, not for a capability team that owns a set of systems as illustrated in Figure 8-2. In contrast to project teams that wax and wane, a medium-sized capability team (as illustrated in Figure 10-1) can steadily work through an evolving capability roadmap. Besides, it is okay to allow some downtime. The team could use it for skill development or pet projects.

Isn't there a risk that a stable long-lived team will grow insular with time? Won't it stop innovating as it grows too familiar with the idiosyncrasies of the systems it owns? Well, given the career mobility of IT people, there is bound to be some natural churn that will bring in new brains occasionally. Besides, as described in the next section, a good mix of competency profiles and personalities will ensure continued vitality.

10.3 Better Staffing

10.3.1 Staff by Skills, Not by Roles

A cross-functional team may begin life as an assortment of specialists working together. The effectiveness of these teams improves further when its members have the flexibility to wear different hats at different times. For example, Ravi may wear a tester hat one day, an analyst hat on a second, and a pre-sales engineer hat on a third.

Over time, the specialists gain adjacent skills and become T-shaped people (as explained in Section 5.4.4). It now becomes a *team of cross-functional (poly-skilled) people* rather than just a cross-functional team of specialists. This transition is desirable for a number of reasons:

- Specialists can better go about their work in a given stage of the value stream when they have some first-hand knowledge of other stages.
- A team of poly-skilled people can exhibit greater responsiveness than a poly-skilled team of specialists.
- Utilization of specialists improve when they are able to do other things.

Organizations with many T-shaped people can benefit from staffing based on skills rather than roles. T-shaped people are versatile. Pigeonholing them into developer, tester, UXer, etc. for the purpose of staffing doesn't do justice to their versatility. Instead, by maintaining a skills inventory, we can staff teams by skills rather than by role as illustrated in Table 10-1. Note that the skills are defined at a higher level of abstraction than specific tools and technologies like Solr and Ruby. A is no longer just a developer but someone with good development and testing skills and fair support skills. E is no longer just a tester but

Table 10-1 *Staffing by Roles versus Skills*

Staffing by Role		Staffing by Skill		
Role	*People*	*Skill*	*First Line*	*Second Line*
Developer	A, B, C	Development	A, B, C	D, F
Tester	D, E	Testing	D, E, A	C, L
UX	F, G	UX	F, G	I, M
Manager	H	Delivery mgmt.	H	B
Analyst	I	Stakeholder mgmt.	H	E
Support	K	Analysis	I	E
Performance engineer	L	Support	K	A, D
Technical writer	M	Performance engineering	L	C, D
Build and deploy	N	Technical writing	M	B, H
Infrastructure	O	Build and deployment	N, C	L
		Infrastructure	O	K

someone who is good at testing and good enough at analysis and stakeholder management. In recognizing a second line of skills, staffing by skills improves team capability and responsiveness as a whole. This often happens informally, but it is more effective to institutionalize it within the organization and keep the skills inventory updated with second-line skills.

It is easier to aim for a team of cross-functional people when the team is staffed by permanent employees than when it is staffed by temporary contractors/consultants. This is because the market pays higher for temps with specialist skills than those with generalist skills. Temporary workers care more about maintaining a marketable resume and resist moving from hard-core specialists to generalizing specialists—a necessary transition in moving from a cross-functional team of specialists to a team of cross-functional people.

The shift from staffing by role to staffing by skills naturally follows the shift from a specialist workforce to a workforce of T-shaped people. It has implications for people's titles and designations.

10.3.2 Job Titles

T-shaped people have very good skills in one or two areas and good-enough skills in another set of areas. They may end up playing widely different roles on different assignments or at different times within the same year. Fixed, specialty-oriented titles like engineer, manager, designer, QA, analyst, or architect aren't suitable for the dynamic scenario presented by skill-based staffing. One option is to use specialty-agnostic titles like senior/lead/principal/distinguished member of staff. The other option is to eschew titles internally and use paygrades where required. A variety of business cards bearing short-lived, role-specific titles may be issued for external use.

In my experience, specialty-oriented titles have subtle side effects. For example, when someone is labeled a manager, anything she says outside her labeled area of competency automatically assumes less credibility. We end up discounting the credibility of people in domains outside their specialty-oriented titles. Soon people start buying into their labels. Developers refuse to test. If you can communicate well, you are suspect as a developer. Managers shy away from writing code or (shudder) gaining even basic user-level technical competence. They go about saying, "I can't handle technology," as if it were a feather in their cap. We become ever more entrenched in the silos created by our labels. Truly ploy-skilled people get disheartened in the process. A person with a title of analyst may have a great aptitude for domain modeling, but her inputs may be sidelined by developers. After a while, she either starts believing in her alleged limitations or starts looking for another job where her skills are more broadly appreciated.

10.3.3 Profiling Skills

Development in particular is a big skill category. It is useful to know whether we have the right mix of subskills within development. By the very nature of code, development work tends to be more closely knit than other areas. It is where the effort of upstream activities like analysis and UX come together, where we practice continuous integration to bring together the work of all developers. It is a process of synthesis that requires more than just programming skills. For example, a typical developer will have strengths in one or two of the following dimensions:

- Programming languages and algorithms: This dimension is the domain of computer science. People with these strengths are proficient in multiple languages. Sometimes referred to as *language geeks,* they are good at applying appropriate algorithms to solve nontrivial problems.

- Technology: Knowledge of a wide variety of tools. Constant experimentation. People with a nose for technology. They never complain about being out of work. They usually have some side projects going on out of personal interest.

- Communication: Being articulate about design, architecture, communicating status of development work, and articulating risks, issues, and dependencies. Being able to write readable code.

- Delivery: Being able to put one's head down and get it done. They may not be the most knowledgeable people around, but they are great at getting it done with what they know. They are also not picky about the tasks they take up.

A good mix for a team of developers is about 60% to 80% delivery and 20% to 40% other dimensions. An overweight delivery team may end up moving heaven and earth with wrong technique. A team lopsided the other way may spend its time trying to solve all problems with bleeding-edge technology or going around in circles arguing about design or choice or tools.

People with real-world experience of staffing projects may think all this talk of the right mix is unrealistic given how difficult it is to get hold of even a half-decent person for the job. However, this is partly due to the practice of temporary project teams. Frequent ramp-ups and ramp-downs are more difficult to staff properly. Long-lived product teams make fewer staffing requests. Maintaining skill profiles as shown in Figure 10-2 helps send the message that various dimensions are valuable and that different people have different strengths. These profiles may be created and updated periodically using the confidential survey technique described in Section 13.7.

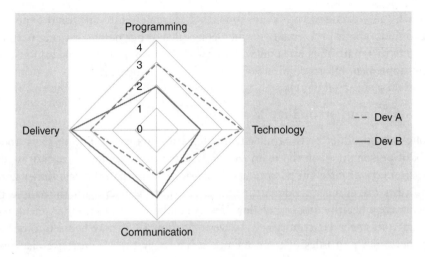

Figure 10-2 *Developer skill profile*

Skill profiles can also lead to better recruitment. In interviews, we tend to approve of people who have the same strengths as we do. Skill profiles help us become aware of this tendency. A manager looking to add some delivery-focused people to a team would do well to ask similarly abled team members to interview candidates.

10.3.4 Avoid Part-time Assignments

Given the talent crunch (Section 10.1), it is tempting to assign scarce specialists part-time to multiple teams. This is tolerable if the teams are in close physical proximity so the shared person is always at hand. Otherwise, the limited availability reduces responsiveness, and the repeated context switching between teams reduces the shared person's ability to focus. It also weakens the shared person's accountability for team outcomes.

A quick way to get out of dependence on a shared specialist is to nominate a pairing partner from each of the teams. Any time the shared specialist works for team X, she pairs with the nominated person from team X. This may slow down the shared specialist and increase team cost in the short term, but in the medium term we end up developing a second line of capability for the scarce skill. Since the full-time pairing partner has better team context, this also helps the shared specialist contribute more effectively.

The pairing partner needs to have some basic skill in the specialist area—this can be obtained by self-study or taking a training course. Even with this groundwork, an impatient specialist may suffer greatly from the curse of knowledge[4]—a cognitive bias that makes it extremely difficult for the specialist to think about problems from the perspective of her newbie pairing partner. Despite this, pairing is a useful way of growing poly-skilled talent in-house. It can supplement efforts to hire T-shaped people (Section 5.4.4).

10.3.5 Team Personality Mix

Long-lived product or capability teams have the luxury of aiming for a good mix of personalities on the team. A good personality mix lets a team draw on the strengths of different personality dimensions. Although the best dimensions and tests are subject to debate, some assessment is useful on the whole to encourage a healthy mix of personalities. A combination of self-assessment and group assessment via confidential surveys (Section 13.7) may be used to derive the personality profiles of team members. The very exercise raises consciousness about the value of different dispositions. In the absence of such team consciousness, the dispositions of the most powerful and influential members come to be valued more than the others.

Though not directly related to personality mix, gender mix is also important. Almost anyone who has worked on an all-male team and a more balanced team will attest to the fact that the team is better off with a balance of genders.

10.4 Summary of Insights

- Often, IT has an inherent bias for the latest technology, and business has a bias for making scope as comprehensive as possible. Put the two together, and we get situations where the original need and corresponding staffing requirements are blown out of proportion.

- Capacity-based budgeting lets us move away from project teams to stable long-lived capability teams without an increase in cost. The resulting absence of regular ramp-ups and ramp-downs lets the staffing team pay some attention to team mix rather than just scrambling to meet demand. It also reduces the need for short-term temp hiring.

- Long-lived teams don't necessarily incur more cost than project teams.

- Specialization-oriented job titles are out of place with cross-functional teams of T-shaped people.

- Skill profiling helps achieve a good mix of skills in stable long-lived teams. Personality profiling and gender balancing also help in their own ways.

---

4. http://hbr.org/2006/12/the-curse-of-knowledge/ar/1

10.5 Summary of Actions

- Bridge the demand-supply gap for IT talent from both ends. Choose buy over build (make) except for systems of differentiation. This bridges it from the demand side. Training, pairing, and selective outsourcing bridges it from the supply side. Where the gap persists, business and IT need to pare scope and sophistication respectively.

- Cultivate T-shaped people by moving to skill- rather than role-based staffing. It also helps transition a cross-functional team of specialists to a team of cross-functional (poly-skilled) people.

- Reduce part-time assignment of scarce specialists by instituting pairing.

Chapter 11

Tooling

This chapter unmasks a frequently overlooked agent of IT dysfunction: tooling. It describes how the toolchain and access landscape can affect collaboration. Organizational agility thrives on unscripted collaboration (Section 3.4.5). Designing for unscripted collaboration is one of the key themes of this book. It needs unfettered access to tools and information. We'll uncover toolchain-induced silos and ways to mitigate them in general. We'll also counter the argument that silos are a people problem wherein tools play no part. Finally, we'll see how tool evaluations done right can help increase adoption and limit proliferation of different tools for the same job.

11.1 Access Control for Unscripted Collaboration

Most organizations share information with employees only on a *need-to-know* basis. However, for any given employee, very little information (relatively) falls in the need-to-know category. She is cut off from information that she might just be curious about. But wait, isn't this a good thing? Why distract employees with irrelevant information? Fair enough, let's not push unnecessary information to everyone. However, let's not restrict it behind access control either. Let people pull freely. Someone might just find a serendipitous use for the information. Protect just the information that absolutely needs protection and free up everything else. Rather than share on a need-to-know or need-to-use basis, *protect on a need-to-restrict basis*. Sometimes, industry regulations don't allow this inversion of access control, so we revert to the old scheme where unavoidable.

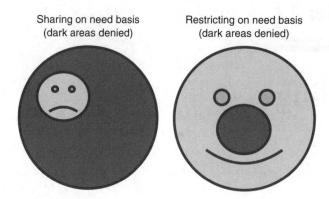

Sharing on need basis
(dark areas denied)

Restricting on need basis
(dark areas denied)

Figure 11-1 *Inversion of access control*

The outer circles in Figure 11-1 represent the entire tooling and information landscape of an organization. The dark shading represents the restricted information for a given employee, and the lighter shading is the permitted information. In a traditional setup, we look at what someone needs in order to do their daily work and just provide access to that part. In a collaboration-friendly setup, we look at what needs to be off limits and only restrict that much. When an organization shares freely with employees, employees in turn are also likely to share freely with each other. If the organization believes in sharing only on a strict need basis, then people in the organization can't be faulted for adopting the same policy with their colleagues.

Wikis are a great example of a technology that turns access control on its head. They are the technology behind Wikipedia whose rise has disrupted the business models of commercial encyclopedias. In a typical wiki, not only can everyone read everything by default, they can even edit anything. This feature used to invite ridicule in conservative circles. However, the adopters mostly thrived. Hell did not break loose. Wikis have a robust cure for mischief. All edits are traceable. Author traceability discourages frivolous edits. Besides, admins can revert a page to any earlier version. Since the very existence of these features discourages mischief, reverts are only occasionally put to use in practice. Authentication is essential. Authorization is less so.

There is also the issue of scale. Within an organization, a deny-by-default type of access control doesn't scale as well as allow-by-default. New team members commonly experience delays and denials in grant of access. Mechanisms that offer cheap cures in case of problems often scale better.

11.2 Subtle Effects of the Toolchain

A cross-functional IT-B team has people playing roles like analyst, developer, architect, sysadmin, database expert, UX person, etc. Silo-like conditions may develop if they choose to use different tools for similar activities. This also applies to specialty tools. If everyone has access only to their primary tools, it becomes difficult to gain adjacent skills and grow toward being the generalizing specialist described in Section 5.4.2.

11.2.1 Silos of Tool Access

So what's the problem with the team in Figure 11-2? We have a cross-functional and co-located team alright. But they are isolated from each other in terms of their tooling and access. Product analysts can't access the sales lead management tool to see ongoing communications with prospective customers. The marketing and sales teams can't access the product backlog management tool to see the most up-to-date set of feature priorities or a likely launch date. Developers can't access monitoring dashboards to see how the production servers are holding up—they have to ask their ops colleagues. This is far from advocating for login rights to production servers—it's just about having read access to monitoring systems.

It's okay if everyone doesn't have access to specialty *creational* tools like editors for graphics, video, mockups, code, or diagnostic tools like code profilers. All the earlier examples are of tools that have a reporting component—good candidates for information radiators (Section 2.4.4). Information radiators

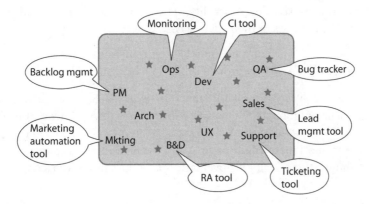

Figure 11-2 *A co-located team siloed in cyberspace*

need to be universally accessible. Otherwise, a team that is cross-functional and co-located in physical space may be disconnected in corporate cyberspace.

For example, if you only have enough Salesforce licenses for your sales team, it means people from product development cannot access Salesforce on demand to gather intelligence about features wanted by lost prospects. They'd have to ask busy salespeople. Now, salespeople are generally friendly and up for a chat, but they tend to dislike data-extraction jobs. Restricted access to tools thus reduces effectiveness.

To begin with, procurement mindset needs to come around to recognizing the need for near universal access. The days of providing access only on a need-to-use basis are over. However, it can be expensive to procure licenses for everyone. This is especially the case when the product vendor does not offer tiered licensing, that is, a cheaper license for read-only users and a regular license for read-write users. Although it is quite an important criterion, it is often absent from procurement checklists. Vendors will oblige when more customers ask for it.[1,2,3] Alternately, a company could negotiate with the vendor for a sharable read-only account that may be made available to everyone in the organization.

Segregated access isn't so bad if everyone is sitting in the same room. But that is often not the case. Not having access is limiting in many ways. It reduces our visibility of our colleagues' spheres of activity. It may lead to poorer decisions for want of autonomous access to information or for want of awareness of the existence of such information.

Some may say this is stretching things too far. Tools don't make or mar collaboration, people do. Unfortunately, tools aren't value neutral. While we may consciously want to be collaborative, our tooling landscape may subtly alter our habits and create challenges for collaboration. Before going further with this argument against value neutrality, let's see how tool usage and tool specialty contribute to silos in their own ways.

11.2.2 Silos of Tool Usage

When people use different tools for similar activities (e.g., version control, work tracking, documentation), they tend to form groups (camps) around tool usage boundaries. Thus, we have the Windows, Mac, and Linux camps and their subgroups, the vi and Emacs editor camps, and the myriad programming languages camps. Although their rivalry is mostly friendly, it does turn serious on occasion.[4]

1. http://service-it-remedy.web.cern.ch/service-it-remedy/clients/aruser/login5.html
2. https://success.salesforce.com/ideaView?id=08730000000BrT7
3. https://answers.atlassian.com/questions/171528/read-only-jira-user-without-license
4. http://discuss.fogcreek.com/joelonsoftware/default.asp?cmd=show&ixPost=13940

> A sage has respect for tools but does not confuse
> personal identity with the identity of the tools.
> —Tweet by Kevin Behr, coauthor of the Phoenix Project

The more we are invested in certain tools, the greater the likelihood of deriving a part of our identity from the tool and its ecosystem. Given that our self-esteem feeds on contrasting our identity favorably with other identities, a situation of rival tool-influenced identities in a team has potential for developing into silos. This has parallels in the world of ethnicities, languages, ideologies, and even currencies. We have enough challenges as it is, to be aiming for pluralism and multiculturalism with respect to tools used within a single team. On the other hand, when different types of specialists use common tools, techniques, and practices for similar activities, it creates a fertile common ground for cross-functional collaboration.

Sometimes, we see different teams using different tools for similar problems. This is a tolerable exercise of team autonomy as long as it does not lead to huge problems in reporting, consolidation, or coordination between teams. At other times, we may find the same tool being used extensively by one team and sparingly by another even though their requirements are similar. In one case, I learned that this behavior was because the second team did not have a say in tool evaluation. Section 11.4 addresses evaluations.

11.2.3 Silos of Tool Specialty

Too much tool specialization within a team leads to silos. Examples:

- Although digital marketing is just one aspect of digital transformation (Section 1.4), it brings with it a dizzying array of specialist tools for e-mail marketing, mobile marketing, social media marketing, search and social ads, events and webinars, communities and reviews, loyalty and gamification, and so on. Going by the principle of organizing by outcome rather than activity (Section 4.1), it is more effective to have a couple of marketing generalists per outcome leveraging all these tools. It works better than creating a shared marketing service having one specialist per tool.

- It is a bad idea to use one tool for continuous integration for use by developers and a completely different one for deployment for use by release engineers. Doing so may lead to silos as developers will rarely look at what's going on in the deployment tool and vice versa.

From the point of view of greater cross-functional collaboration, tools that *blur boundaries* between specialists are better than those that reinforce them.

11.3 Technology Isn't Value Neutral

Some say tools and org charts don't cause silos, people do. They point to individual examples of people collaborating despite a challenging environment. Usually, these heroes are a small minority in the organization and they run out of steam after a year or two (and a different minority of heroes may take their place). However, in the aggregate, the presence of silo-inducing design elements will lead to silos. Therefore, we shouldn't dismiss the problem of silos as merely a people problem. Yes, it is a people problem, but organization structure, culture, and policies (including policies regarding tooling) have the potential to amplify or attenuate the problem.

It is generally thought that we are the absolute masters of technology—we invent and control technology and exercise conscious choice over its use; technology doesn't control or influence us. While this may be true for some alert individuals, it isn't so for society or organizations as a whole. The media theorist Marshall McLuhan was one of the most influential voices behind the argument that technology isn't value neutral. He famously said:

> We shape our tools, *and thereafter our tools shape us.* . . . Our conventional response to all media, namely that it is how they are used that counts, is the numb stance of the technological idiot.[5]
>
> —M. McLuhan

For example, research shows that spoken language influences the way we think.[6] And what is language really? It is one of the earliest invented technologies of communication. Thus, a communications technology has been shown to influence the way we think! Could this be true of other communications technologies as well? McLuhan answered an emphatic yes for technologies of mass communication when he said, *"The medium is the message."*[7]

Later, the technology historian Melvin Kranzberg coined his six laws of technology,[8] the first of which asserts:

Technology is neither good nor bad; nor is it neutral.

---

5. (McLuhan 1994)
6. http://edge.org/conversation/how-does-our-language-shape-the-way-we-think
7. http://en.wikipedia.org/wiki/The_medium_is_the_message
8. Kranzberg, M. 1986. Technology and history: Kranzberg's laws. *Technology and Culture* 27:545-60.

He explained this is so because the introduction of a technology frequently has unintended human and social consequences. Its impact radius goes well beyond the intended radius of the immediate problem space. Besides, the impact is context sensitive—similar interventions have dissimilar effects in different contexts.

Language influences thought, tools influence action. Therefore, it matters a lot how we choose our tools. We shape our tooling and access landscape, and thereafter they shape the contours of our collaboration. When we choose a lot of different specialty tools, they in turn nudge us into different specialty groups. New techniques may be better in some respects and worse in other. For example, the practice of writing automated unit tests and doing test-driven development has increased the use of the debugger and reduced the value of logging during development. As a result, developers tend to omit logging[9] until a tech lead or someone from IT operations educates them of the importance of logs in a production environment.

The non-value-neutrality argument can be extended beyond technology to processes and structures. Our environment affects our attitudes and beliefs. Tribes and villages encourage community; nuclear families and cities encourage individualism. As an example of team structure influencing the shape of software, Conway's law[10] suggests that the interface structure of a software system will reflect the social structure of the team(s) that produced it. In the aggregate, interaction is always mutual—we shape our environment and we are shaped by it. E-mail is a case in point.

11.3.1 How E-mail Shapes Us

In the days prior to the advent of e-mail, the inbox was physically separate from the file cabinet (Figure 11-3). Read-and-done items were carefully filed away or trashed. The inbox was only meant for fresh arrivals. We didn't attend to the inbox constantly. Just once a day, maybe twice. People didn't expect a two-hour turnaround for written correspondence; they just used the telephone for urgent matters. Corporate announcements, bulletins, and circulars were often stuck on notice boards (bulletin boards). A copy of the notice wasn't thrust in the face of every employee in the middle of the working day. Communication, although a part of work, was still considered distinct from actual work.

---

9. http://programmers.stackexchange.com/questions/230131/do-we-need-logging-when-doing-tdd
10. http://www.thoughtworks.com/insights/blog/demystifying-conways-law

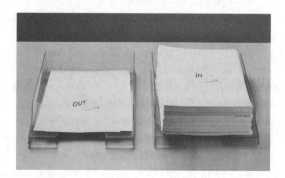

Figure 11-3 *The file cabinet used to be separate from the inbox.*
(Left) Source: jojje11/Fotolia. (Right) Source: pogonici/Fotolia.

E-mail has altered the balance of communication and actual work. McLuhan observed that technology shapes us even as we shape it. How has e-mail shaped us?

- **The inbox is also the file cabinet:** Say we decide to wrest control from the ever-brimming inbox. Check e-mail only twice a day at fixed times, keep it closed otherwise, let's say. But no, closing our e-mail clients (whether on the laptop, tablet, or mobile) also means locking our file cabinet. Thanks to multi-gigabyte inboxes and terrific search algorithms, our e-mail clients are also our file cabinets to which we often need access during the course of actual work. There we go, looking at our inboxes again. Filters, rules, labels, or folders may help us avoid looking at what's new, but now we begin cutting against the grain of the technology.

- **By the truckload, by the minute:** Because it is so cheap, we send and receive loads of it. Never mind spam, why have corporate notice boards disappeared? All sorts of corporate announcements flood our inboxes through the working day. At the very least, corporates should make it a rule to send announcements near the close of business. But then, there is no suitable time for a global corporation. IT matrixes compound the problem. Half a dozen function leads and their lieutenants are cc'ed on every e-mail.

- **A new addiction:** Of course, social media is the new addiction. Inside a corporation, though, e-mail offers a formidable alternative, more so where corporate firewalls block social media. Many IT people spend a big part of their days reading and writing e-mail. E-mail notifications provide endless distraction for those to choose to be interrupted. New e-mail provides a psychological kick. Some get bored and go for a break when there is no new e-mail for half an hour. E-mail addiction results in less actual work, more communication, most of it not addressed directly to the reader.

- **Frivolous documentation:** E-mail has bred a culture of excessive documentation. The ability to get things on record easily has increased the tendency to do so. This is another reason why people don't use the telephone for not-so-important but urgent matters. They write an e-mail to put it on record and wait for a quick reply, even if the recipient is only meters away. This needs to be discouraged.

11.4 Tool Evaluation

In enterprise IT, the activity of tool evaluation has the potential to make or break tool adoption. Uneven adoption could lead to silos of tool usage described earlier. Few places have documented guidelines for tool evaluation. Having one is invaluable because evaluations can be tricky—especially when migrating from an existing tool. The shortcomings of the tool in use are well known but not those of the ones under evaluation. We can check that the new tools don't have the old shortcomings, but we may not have evaluation scenarios to uncover new shortcomings.

A good evaluation is never merely technical. For instance, it has to consider whether the new tool will find adoption and whether training is needed. Evaluators need to appreciate that *best fit* is more important than *best tool* and come up with criteria accordingly. Different features are important to different constituencies and so it helps to have a representative evaluation team with one leader authorized to make tradeoffs. It is an anti-pattern to exclude end users from the evaluation team or to evaluate based on a procurement checklist with little regard for end-user input.

In case of tools that help manage business processes, there might be suggestions to buy and customize in order to fit the tool to the existing process. But what if the existing process could do with some improvement? This is a good opportunity to revisit the process and simplify it before codifying it into a new tool. Besides, the customizations may get expensive to maintain as newer releases of the tool become available. Unless the customizations provide competitive advantage, it might be better to take a one-time hit and tweak the process to align with the tool.

Extraneous considerations may implicitly influence tool evaluation—for example, what tool best enhances my résumé? These factors cannot be eliminated, but they can be contained by having one person (the lead evaluator) ultimately accountable (outcome owner) not only for the resulting tool recommendation but also for its successful adoption. A transparent decision record (Section 6.7.1) will help ensure that inputs from others aren't ignored. It is nearly impossible to measure actual ROI for money spent on tools. Tool adoption and extent of use is the second best indicator.

In the spirit of team autonomy, tool standardization is nice to have but not mandatory if users manage the tool themselves. For tools managed by IT-I, some standardization is essential.

11.5 Summary of Insights

- We shape our organizational tooling and access landscape, and thereafter it shapes the contours of organizational collaboration.

- Organizations that are straitlaced about providing employees with unrestricted access to information cannot expect them to have a different attitude toward sharing information with their colleagues.

- When specialists use common tools, techniques, and practices for similar activities, it creates a fertile ground for cross-functional collaboration.

- In tool evaluations, best fit is more important than best tool.

11.6 Summary of Actions

- Deny access on a need-to-restrict basis rather than allow access on a need-to-use basis. This better facilitates unscripted collaboration.

- Choose tools that blur rather than reinforce boundaries between specialists.

- Choose tools for which you can afford to have at least read-and-query licenses for almost everyone on the team.

- Develop guidelines for tool evaluations and rollouts. Assign outcome owners and maintain decision records to drive accountability for tooling decisions and tool adoption.

Chapter 12

Metrics

Scaling supervision using metrics is one thing; scaling results is quite another. The former doesn't automatically ensure the latter. This chapter examines how an organization's attitude to metrics influences agility. It first looks at some general shortcomings of metrics, dashboards, targets, and incentives. It cautions against overreliance on metrics and goes on to suggest ways to reform the metrics regime to bring it more in tune with the key themes laid out in Chapter 3.

12.1 Metrics Don't Tell the Whole Story

Software development is a *social activity*. As such, it does not lend itself very well to measurements. Sure, we can measure a whole lot of things about software development, but we can never contend that a given set of metrics is exhaustive—that it reliably paints the full picture. We could try expanding the set of metrics in an attempt to make it exhaustive, but it is costly to regularly measure and track a slew of metrics. Therefore, as illustrated in Figure 12-1, we restrict ourselves to a subset of what is feasible to measure. This subset may include metrics that, even though feasible to measure (measureable), aren't so useful (e.g., number of bugs found per tester per week). On the other hand, although ROI is a useful metric, it is often not feasible to measure and track it for a piece of software. Thus, in practice, we settle for things that *only paint part of the picture*. It is important to acknowledge this. Often, enterprise IT loses sight of this truth. It deludes itself that the reported metrics constitute the full picture. The roots of this way of thinking may be traced to the school of "If you can't measure it, it doesn't exist," or "If you can't measure it, you can't

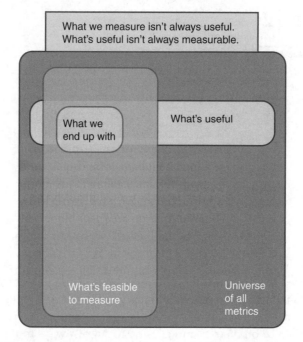

Figure 12-1 *What we measure*

manage it and so it doesn't matter that it exists." As we will see in this chapter, this is unwholesome doctrine.

12.1.1 Can Measure, Can't Forecast

Even where it is possible to measure things, it is hard to make future projections based on these measurements. Despite all the measurement, organizations routinely struggle to accurately answer questions like:

- When will we be done with the planned scope of work?
- By how much will a new feature improve a product's sale or an internal application's adoption? By how much will trimming scope on a planned feature affect adoption?
- How will the addition or removal of people from a team affect velocity?
- What is the chance of technical debt turning into an issue in the next 3, 6, 12, or 24 months? How big of an issue?

This is because all of software development is a design activity (Section 3.1). It doesn't lend itself to exhaustive, objective, quantitative measurement and even less to projections. Velocity is a case in point.

12.1.2 Velocity

Velocity is a measure of functionality delivered by a team in a given sprint or iteration. It is commonly used to track progress of software delivery. For example, if 72 points worth of functionality are to be delivered in 4 sprints (or iterations), the average velocity required is 72/4 = 18 points per sprint. 72 is the distance to be covered in 4 iterations. The velocity achieved during any given sprint is also the distance covered in that sprint (in this sense, *velocity* is not the best name for this metric). A graph called a *burnup chart* is commonly used to track the cumulative distance covered to date against the destination.

However, organizations routinely fail to use velocity correctly. A poor definition of *done* is the most common cause. Ideally, velocity only accrues when a story is done in all respects—developed and tested for functionality, regression, end-to-end integration, cross-platform/browser/device readiness, performance, operational readiness, and security. It is impractical to go through all of this for each story unless it is all automated and orchestrated via a continuous delivery pipeline. Very few teams are at this level of automation.

Therefore, we compromise on the definition of done and say that it counts as done as long as it tested for functionality, regression, and integration and it is signed off by tester and product owner. To account for the other tests, we set aside some time and budget later in the development cycle. This is okay as long as the new meaning of velocity is acknowledged throughout the reporting chain.

Any further compromise on the definition of done undermines the utility of the metric. For example, end-to-end integration tests are left out because it is the responsibility of a different team in another part of the organization. This is poor team design. Some teams simply define dev-complete as done and report an essentially worthless velocity. Occasionally, I come across egregious cases where user stories are split into tasks, tasks are estimated in points, and velocity is then earned by completing tasks. Stories are meant to be independent and valuable. Tasks aren't. By earning velocity at the level of tasks, it is possible to be 70% dev-complete for a release without a single story being dev-complete.

Thus, measurement doesn't tell the whole story.

12.1.3 Dealing with Unknown Unknowns

Why do we put so much effort into measuring and tracking software development? Because we wish to predict the process. However, as explained in Section 3.1, predictability continues to elude because a design process has unknown unknowns. It is not possible to measure what we don't know about. In these situations, adaptability is more important than predictability. Therefore, metrics that track speed of feedback (e.g., build time,[1] cycle time) are at least as important as those that help with prediction.

12.2 Dashboards Promote Ignorance

Balanced scorecards[2] came about in an attempt to provide some balance to management reports laden with financial metrics. A balanced scorecard balances financial perspective with customer perspective, and internal business perspective (what must we excel at) with innovation and learning perspective. By incorporating nonfinancial metrics, a balanced scorecard attempts to offer a well-rounded view of an organization's state of affairs.

Dashboards are similar to scorecards. IT-B dashboards tend to be delivery oriented and could do with some balance as well. A long-lived cross-functional team could use a dashboard that includes a customer (outcome) perspective, a quality perspective (health of code, architecture, and documentation), a performance perspective (availability, response time, etc.), and a team perspective. However, even balanced dashboards have their problematic aspects.

A dashboard is like the executive summary of a report. We read executive summaries and skip the body of the report if the summary is more or less in line with our expectations. Trouble is, measurement is never exhaustive. It is only when we dive in that we realize what areas may have been missed. For example, it is possible to collect a wide range of metrics on an IT development effort (e.g., codebase metrics, test metrics, build metrics, delivery progress). It is also possible to define red, amber, and green thresholds for each metric. Teams are then asked to assess themselves on various metrics, and the results are fed to a dashboard that uses a weighted formula to roll up all of these metrics into a single red, amber, or green project status indicator. Some large organizations have developed maturity scales consisting of a number of progressive levels and have defined level-specific thresholds for each metric (e.g., level 4 requires minimum test coverage of 70%).

However, an overall green status indicator doesn't mean anything most of the time. All it says is that the things under measurement seem okay. But there always will be many more things not under measurement (Section 12.1). To celebrate green indicators is to ignore the unknowns. One may argue that it is only a matter of measuring even more so that the overall green becomes truly indicative of overall project health. This is somewhat unrealistic in a fast-paced knowledge work environment. Tools and technologies keep changing. Measurement tools don't keep pace. It takes significant effort to maintain the measurement

---

1. http://blog.sriramnarayan.com/2011/03/build-time-impacts-team-performance.html
2. Kaplan, R. S., and D. P. Norton. 2005. The balanced scorecard: Measure that drive performance. *Harvard Business Review.* 83:172–80.

infrastructure on a project. The tendency to roll up metrics into dashboards promotes ignorance of the real situation on the ground. We forget that we only see what is under measurement. We only act when something is not green.

Rolling up fine-grained metrics to create high-level dashboards puts pressure on teams to keep the fine-grained metrics green even when it might not be the best use of their time. This happens when middle managers don't relish the prospect of explaining ambers and reds to project sponsors at status update meetings. However, fine-grained metrics such as test coverage are not so useful when green as they are when red. They exhibit unidirectional utility. Is 100% test coverage a cause for celebration? What if most tests don't have any assertions? On the other hand, coverage of 50% at least tells us unambiguously that half the code is not covered (or there is an error in measurement).

One may argue that a dashboard is only a tool and it is up to the user to use it well. This argument is called the *value neutrality argument* and has been used for everything from television to nuclear fission. We have addressed it in Section 11.3. There may be a few alert users, but in the aggregate, dashboards have a dumbing-down effect, and we begin to believe they tell the whole story.

12.3 The Problem with Targets and Incentives

> "Do this and you'll get that" makes people focus on the "that," not the "this." Do rewards motivate people? Absolutely. They motivate people to get rewards.[3]
> —Alfie Kohn

Measurement is different from targets or incentives. It is possible to use metrics for measurement only. Measurements don't necessarily have to imply targets or incentives. They can be useful simply as an indicator of where things are (e.g., we look at the speedometer on our cars just to know how fast we are going, not necessarily because we have a target speed in mind).

The conventional approach to managing the performance of a team or unit goes something like this:

1. Put in place mechanisms to measure performance along various dimensions.

2. Establish a baseline for current levels of performance along these dimensions.

3. Set targets for improved levels of performance over the next several reporting periods.

---

3. (Kohn 1999) and http://www.alfiekohn.org/managing/fbrftb.htm

4. Optionally introduce explicit incentives for meeting or exceeding targets.

5. Monitor closely.

This is a common approach at different levels of the organization. Targets cascade—org-level targets drive unit-level targets, which in turn drive team-level targets, and in some cases it goes all the way down to individual targets. It may seem like a methodical approach and it often delivers the goods along some dimensions. It helps individuals and teams focus their efforts. It allows managers to exert control by prioritizing one dimension over another or by increasing the frequency of reporting or monitoring. So what's the problem?

The problem is that systems and people interact and influence each other (Section 11.3). We shape our metrics regime and, in turn, it influences our behavior. The introduction of targets or incentives turns informational measurements into motivational measurements.

Austin[4] defines motivational measurements as those explicitly intended to affect the people who are being measured, to provoke greater expenditure of effort in pursuit of organizational goals. By contrast, informational measurements are valued primarily for the logistical, status, and research information they convey, which provides insights and allows better short-term management and long-term improvement of organizational processes. Note that while incentives are explicitly motivational, targets are also motivational, albeit implicitly (Section 12.3.7). Motivational measurements are problematic for several reasons detailed below.

12.3.1 Targets Tempt Local Optima

When a team is held to targets, it begins to look out for itself. It prioritizes the achievement of its own targets over that of its neighboring teams or parent organizational unit. We know from systems theory that local optima do not necessarily lead to global optimum. On the contrary, a global optimum may call for all subsystems to be at local suboptima.

Scenario 12-1 Testing Shenanigans

On one assignment, I found that an outsourced development team had no knowledge of the test scenarios that the end-to-end testing team was using to test their builds. Every run of end-to-end tests resulted in several defects being logged. I asked the development team manager if they could

---

4. (Austin 1996)

ask for the scenarios beforehand. The manager said no, the end-to-end tests were outsourced to a different vendor and they would not share the scenarios. It was as if the test scenarios were some sort of exam question paper that could not be leaked before the exam. Later, it turned out that there was one more factor influencing this behavior: The utility of the end-to-end testing team was being gauged by the number of defects they reported. Doing anything that would reduce number of defects reported would also reduce the perceived utility of the team!

The same reason surfaced inside a development team on another occasion. This team had developers and testers sitting side by side. Yet, the testers never directly reported potential bugs to the developers by simply calling one of them over and showing them the scenario. Instead, they would always first log a bug in the bug-tracking system, complete with screenshots and steps to recreate. They'd do this even if they knew that a developer was working in the same area of code and it would be simpler just to get it fixed immediately. They offered several reasons when quizzed:

1. A logged bug provided traceability for the corresponding code fix check-in.

2. Not logging it would skew defect metrics such as defect rate and defect density.

3. It would disturb the developers and interrupt their flow.

4. They might miss that scenario during regression tests if it wasn't logged.

5. It would reduce the perceived utility of the testers.

#1 and #4 could be addressed by the practice of writing an automated test that recreated the bug and then fixing the code. #3 wasn't a given—they'd know from the card wall and standup meetings if the developers had moved on to other areas. Besides, they could approach the developers by default and back off on the odd occasion when they didn't want to be interrupted. Doing so would save developers the effort of dealing with bugs that are invalid because the tester looked at the wrong version of the story or because some part of the story was out of date (i.e., it did not reflect changes from a recent conversation between analyst and developer).

After all, this is the reason for having co-located cross-functional teams—to encourage direct communication and resolution where possible. In a culture that values working software over comprehensive documentation, fixing bugs is valued over documenting them. That leaves with #2 and #5, a metrics issue. Going back to the arguments on revisiting software development (Section 3.1), defect rate and density are more appropriate as production process metrics than design process metrics. #5 shows how collaboration suffers when the worth of a team is judged by metrics.

The above scenario is an example of what may be called a *local optimization in space*—one team achieving its targets at the possible expense of another team. We have a *local optimization in time* when we optimize for the immediate term at the expense of the medium term.

Scenario 12-2 Targets Over Profits

It's the last week of yet another sales quarter at a privately owned ISV. Although there are quarterly sales targets, there is no fear of disappointing analysts or the market with less than expected earnings. As things stand, they are short of the target for the region by about $350K. Sanchez, a sales manager, has been trying to close a million-dollar renewal and expansion deal with an old client. The deal itself is a sure thing, but the client's procurement team is taking its time and Sanchez isn't too optimistic about the purchase order coming through this week. He hopes some other win will take care of the $350K shortfall for the quarter. Time passes, but it doesn't happen.

It's now the last day of the quarter and the gap is still looming large. In a desperate bid, Sanchez calls the million-dollar client and asks point blank, "How can I help to have the purchase order today?" The procurement team senses his desperation and audaciously asks for a 50% discount. Sanchez balks and tries to offer more free seats (user subscriptions) at the original price. Procurement isn't interested—they say they'll need more time to figure out whether it makes sense to stock up extra seats. Sanchez doesn't want to offer a huge discount on a sure deal, but even more than that, he doesn't want to miss his target for the quarter. He gives in and ends the quarter with a $500K purchase order. The target is exceeded by $150K but at a loss of $500K in annual revenue as a side effect of target chasing!

12.3.2 Targets Are a Control Mechanism

In order to control where a team devotes its energies, all you need to do is to impose a bunch of targets and track progress at regular intervals. For greater control, increase the range of targets and track more frequently. This is called *micromanagement* and is universally detested by teams. Doing so increases reporting overhead but rarely improves team performance. For example, it isn't useful to insist on breaking stories into tasks and estimating tasks in order to track progress at a task level. It is even more absurd to track that a task is 70% complete. If the story is small, independent, and valuable to begin with, it is likely that its tasks aren't independent or valuable. Time spent in the busywork of fine-grained tracking may be better used in alleviating bottlenecks or even by helping out with the work at hand.

12.3.3 Targets and Incentives Erode Intrinsic Motivators

> **Scenario 12-3 A Sell-out**
>
> An ISV has a portfolio of three products—Kappa, Omega, and Zeta. Over the last few years, Kappa has been faring much better in the market than Omega or Zeta. However, the company leadership believes in the potential of Omega and Zeta and is committed to help them grow. They want the sales team to share this commitment. Everyone agrees publicly that Omega and Zeta are exciting, innovative products in a space that does not have a well-established market. They are fun to sell.
>
> But the sales team privately realizes that it can earn greater commission by focusing on Kappa since it has much better lead-conversion ratios than Omega and Zeta. Naturally, this lack of attention further diminishes prospects for Omega and Zeta. One may argue that the problem here is not the incentive but rather the lack of dedicated product-specific sales teams. However, the decision to go with a common sales team was taken in order to encourage cross-selling between the three.

Targets and incentives tend to erode intrinsic motivators. This is arguably the biggest issue with having them. Intrinsic motivation for the job at hand is replaced by the motivation to meet or exceed targets and earn incentives. Recall that we said in Chapter 3 that autonomy, mastery, and purpose are the ingredients for intrinsic motivation. Targets erode the autonomy of intrinsically motivated people and distort their sense of purpose. Meeting targets and earning incentives becomes the new purpose. Mastery also suffers in the face of targets because it encourages us to do just enough to meet targets and not care so much about aspects that don't have targets around them.

A software team can get severely constrained when a velocity target is imposed on it. Velocity works well as a measurement, not as a target. Targets limit choice of actions. A team may find itself unable to address technical debt if it is constrained by velocity targets. At a certain threshold of constraints, team members lose the sense of empowerment (autonomy).

Public healthcare and education often exhibit similar characteristics. It is not just bureaucracy. In an effort to scale and centrally control efficient delivery of services, a raft of metrics and targets are imposed on service providers. Performance of schools/hospitals is then tracked accordingly. Teachers and doctors get frustrated, lose initiative, and just play by the book. Goal displacement[5] occurs—targets displace the original goals of social good.

The urge to scale without devolution of control is a root cause of this phenomenon. A report by an NGO called Locality and Professor John Seddon of Vanguard Consulting challenges the assumption that economies of scale should be sought in the running of public services in the United Kingdom.[6] It finds large-scale subversion of a system based on intrinsic motivators to one based on extrinsic motivators. As the report notes, it is not about public versus private but rather about the unsuitability of a conventional scaling mindset for service delivery.

Teams motivated by targets tend not to take ownership of problems. They attend only to those aspects that affect targets and leave the rest to be picked up by someone else. To some extent, the problem isn't the target itself but rather the incentive behind the target. However, all targets in an organization come with implicit or explicit incentives. KPI targets carry the implicit incentive of a good score in performance reviews. Sales commissions and variable pay are examples of explicit incentives. In recognition of these factors, some companies have abolished sales commissions[7]—a topic we'll soon return to.

Self-organizing teams need autonomy. They need a more meaningful purpose than just targets. A meaningful purpose is intrinsically motivating and provides opportunities for exercising individual discretion. These opportunities go to waste when there isn't enough autonomy to exercise discretion. The greater the range of targets to be met by a team, the smaller the scope for the team to exercise its discretion. Autonomy allows us to act on the opportunity that purpose provides. Mastery then lets us service the opportunity with a degree of excellence. Targets distort purpose, limit autonomy, and disregard mastery.

12.3.4 Targets Lead to Gaming

Targets inevitably lead people to game the system. Gaming may be innocent or deliberate as the scenarios below illustrate. It may be reduced by devising

---

5. (Merton 1968)

6. http://locality.org.uk/wp-content/uploads/Locality-Report-Diseconomies-web-version.pdf

7. http://www.nytimes.com/2013/11/21/business/smallbusiness/for-some-paying-sales-commissions-no-longer-makes-sense.html

smarter criteria for targets, but that is beside the point. Intrinsic motivation flies out the window when there is a constant cat-and-mouse game between those who design incentives and those who have to work under those incentives.

Scenario 12-4 A Recruitment Game

A recruitment team is given a target of hiring five developers in the next month. They soon find all candidates being rejected sooner or later in the recruitment process. It could be that the candidates are genuinely not good enough, or it could be that the interviewers are being too picky. The interviewers obviously think it is the former. The recruiters, after talking to the interviewers, think it is the latter. However, it is recruiters who are responsible for the target, not the interviewers. They have limited options:

- Try sourcing better candidates.
- Try escalating concerns about the pickiness of interviewers.
- Somehow make it the interviewers' problem.

The first option involves working with agencies and has large turn-around times. The second option may have no effect given interdivision relationships and politics.

With the target hanging over their heads, the recruiters flood the system with lots of candidates. The interviewers are unable to service this volume, but under pressure from recruiters, they agree to let their junior colleagues conduct the interviews. The juniors find the candidates okay and the hiring goes through. Recruitment target achieved! Did we get the right people in? Only time will tell.

Scenario 12-5 Green Dashboards and Red-faced Users

UpAndDown Inc. had a problem with the uptime of a critical internal application. Their CIO decided to make uptime a KPI for the IT operations team. Accordingly, variable pay was tied to 99% uptime. However, the real problem was in the way code was being written. Some operations engineers had tried to explain that the developers needed to be trained to write better code, but the suggestion was viewed as being outside the jurisdiction of the operations manager. The operations team couldn't do much except monitor the app and restart it when it crashed. Prior to the KPI, this process was manual. They'd only know that the app was down when they did a manual check or when a user reported the problem.

After the introduction of the KPI, they automated the task of monitoring and restarting the app if it was down. This solution satisfied the availability-monitoring app, which began reporting good availability numbers. KPI satisfied! However, the solution did not satisfy the users of the app because the automated restarts simply ignored in-flight user journeys. Users found that they often had to start all over again in the middle of their work. It was a hard problem to surface and bring to the attention of the IT manager in charge of the app. Whenever an infrequent user tried logging in, it would work. Only when one tried to complete several user journeys over a couple of hours would they find that many of them failed midway and had to be redone.

12.3.5 Goodhart's Law

The preceding sections illustrate how a measure begins to lose its value when a target is set on it. This effect is not limited to IT. Way back in 1975, Charles Goodhart, an advisor to the Bank of England, made a similar observation about economic policy targets. This is now known as Goodhart's law[8] and, per Wikipedia,[9] its most popular formulation is "When a measure becomes a target, it ceases to be a good measure." Designers of organization-wide metrics would do well to take note of this effect. Ignorance of this effect leads to management taking decisions on the back of metrics that have lost their significance. In Section 12.5, we discuss ways to mitigate this effect.

12.3.6 Implicit Targets

The very act of measurement may lead to unintended or even unconscious changes in behavior. Here is an example from day trading. What is more important—making more winning trades than losing trades, or making money? Obviously, it is the latter. However, the moment we start tracking win-loss ratio, it may become an implicit target. Emotional conditioning also comes into play, and we try to have fewer losing trades. In other words, we have a tendency to become self-conscious and alter our behavior when a new metric is brought into our field of attention. This alteration in behavior may not be in favor of the larger goal.

This isn't a reason to refrain from measurement but rather to be watchful about how it influences behavior. This effect may be put to good use by simply publishing key metrics (e.g., sales for the quarter, velocity, outstanding bug

---

8. http://lesswrong.com/lw/1ws/the_importance_of_goodharts_law
9. http://en.wikipedia.org/wiki/Goodhart%27s_law

count, net promoter score) in a public space via information radiators (Section 2.4.4). Note that it is just measurement without the pressure of targets. Stop measurements that lead to counterproductive behavior, and stop at measurements (i.e., don't continue to targets) that lead to desired behavior. More isn't better when it comes to metrics.

12.3.7 Targets Imply Incentives

Some people argue that while incentives may be problematic, targets are okay and even necessary. However, targets invariably imply incentives. Even when incentives aren't explicit in the form of commissions, bonuses, or variable pay, targets usually come with implicit incentives. For example, consistently beating targets might lead to a raise or a promotion. Therefore, all the dangers of incentives described in the preceding sections apply to targets that are only partially aligned with outcomes. Can targets ever be fully aligned with outcomes? As noted in Section 12.1, exhaustive measurement is usually not possible, and therefore targets based on non-exhaustive measurement will not address all aspects of the outcome. See Austin[10] for a comprehensive treatment of this topic.

12.4 Reforming the Metrics Regime

As discussed so far, it can be counterproductive to automatically impose targets on everything we measure. When measurements indicate something is wrong, it calls for a *conversation in context*, not for a rating downgrade. Conversations in context may reveal that things are still okay in the larger scheme of things; the measurements only point to local suboptima. We need a *data-informed* approach as opposed to a *data-driven* approach that relies exclusively on metrics.

It Works!

An article in *The Atlantic*[11] describes Finland's unique education system. The PISA survey,[12] conducted every three years by the Organisation for Economic Co-operation and Development (OECD), compares 15-year-olds in different countries in reading, math, and science. Despite having a relatively easy-going education system, Finland has ranked at or near the

---

10. (Austin 1996)
11. http://www.theatlantic.com/national/archive/2011/12/what-americans-keep-ignoring-about-finlands-school-success/250564/
12. http://www.oecd.org/pisa/keyfindings/PISA-2012-results-snapshot-Volume-I-ENG.pdf

top in all three competencies on every survey since 2000. Finland's system is nowhere as grueling for students as those of super achievers such as South Korea and Singapore.

Why is this relevant to a chapter on metrics? Finland has no standardized tests (i.e., no standardized measurement). The only exception is what's called the National Matriculation Exam, which everyone takes at the end of a voluntary upper-secondary school, roughly the equivalent of American high school. Instead, the public school system's teachers are trained to *assess* children in classrooms using independent tests they create themselves.

To reform the metrics regime, we need to address all three aspects of it: metrics, targets, and incentives.

12.4.1 Get Rid of Incentives

Incentives are the most corrosive aspect of a metrics regime. They are generally easier to dismantle than targets.

It Works!

A 2013 article in *The New York Times*[13] reports how some companies, IT and non-IT, have made a radical departure from the time-honored practice of paying sales commissions. Describing the situation at ThoughtWorks (an IT consultancy and the author's employer at the time of this writing) before 2012, the article reports that some people in sales appeared to be operating at cross purposes. So the leadership decided to move away from individual incentives while still retaining sales targets. Based on their total earnings under the prevailing arrangement, salespeople were offered an adjusted, new, straight-salary structure. Even though a few people quit, the company did well in terms of revenue growth.

As of 2014, Keith Dodds, Director of Sales at ThoughtWorks said:

> "Internally, it meant much less competition between salespeople over scarce resources. In the old days, if you didn't get your project staffed, it directly limited your income. In the new world, salespeople weren't incentivized to argue for their prospect or client's needs over another's just to maximize

---

13. http://www.nytimes.com/2013/11/21/business/smallbusiness/for-some-paying-sales-commissions-no-longer-makes-sense.html

their income. It enabled a much more healthy discussion about priorities when resources were tight."

The referenced article names a number of other companies who successfully abolished sales commissions including a car dealer and manufacturer. However, it also mentions another software company that started off without commissions but introduced them later. What do we make of this? With reference to Schneider's culture model (Section 2.3), it appears that sales commissions are best fit for competence and control cultures. Abolishing sales commissions has a better chance of working out in Agile cultures (collaboration and cultivation).

12.4.2 Ease Targets Progressively

The *imposition* of targets hurts autonomy and erodes intrinsic motivation as much as the targets themselves. Here is one way of gradually moving from imposition toward greater autonomy for the team:

1. Usual prevailing situation: Targets are imposed on the team and tracked frequently.

2. Decide targets with the team and track frequently.

3. Decide targets with the team and track infrequently. Balance greater latitude with greater accountability.

4. Decide measures (not targets) with the team and check infrequently.

12.4.3 Allow Assessments

Conventional management wisdom says:

> If you can't measure it, you can't manage it.

A more useful credo for IT-B management is:

> If you can't *assess* it, whether objectively or subjectively, quantitatively or qualitatively, then you can't manage it.

Of course, measurement does not preclude assessment, but there is a tendency to aim for self-explanatory metrics (i.e., to eliminate the human element from assessment). Apparently, this helps management at scale. Clearly this is flawed, for if it were true, we could automate management. Humans are needed to make an assessment because it is essential to have a mental model and some hypotheses first and then validate or invalidate them against the measurements and other inputs. Otherwise, it's just a lot of data without any means to obtain insights. Assessment is like picking stocks using fundamental analysis—we don't just go by the numbers in the books, we also do a qualitative assessment of the industry sector and the company leadership.

Besides, when we have many things to measure, we have to automate measurement. Thus, we rely on reports from marketing analytics tools, sales management systems, CRM and customer support systems, project management, and engineering tools. It takes time and effort to develop and maintain custom reports. It also requires good data-entry discipline on the part of the users of these system—the reports are only as good as the underlying data. The users, on the other hand, don't like being nagged about data entry—they'd rather focus on doing the job at hand: running marketing campaigns, converting leads, providing support, or building the product. They might even have slightly different conventions about data entry, for example, different salespeople have differing ideas of what "60% sold" means. In sum, automated measurements (reports) are not self-explanatory, more so when the process under measurement is a design process rather than a production process (Section 3.1).

Human assessment, on the other hand, is tolerant of measurement deficiencies. It can be achieved with subjective and qualitative reports that supplement not-so-reliable, quantitative, objective measurements. The result is a *data-informed* approach rather than a *data-driven* approach. It is inconsistent to maintain on the one hand that individuals and interactions are valued more than processes and tools while on the other hand ban individuals and interactions from metrics/data and their interpretation. Here are a couple of examples of allowing for human assessment:

> **Alignment maps for metrics:** Creating metrics maps on the lines of alignment maps described in Section 7.2.3 can help with assessments. The map would indicate what outcome (or suboutcome) is served by each metric. It would help guard against metrics that aren't aligned to outcomes. It would also serve as a good information radiator about the purpose of each metric.

> **RAG reports:** In the spirit of assessment over measurement, it is often more useful to report a metric as red, amber, or green (RAG) rather than as a raw number. This also does away with the false accuracy of a raw number—most IT-B measurements can be off by a few percentage points due to data entry or measurement errors.

When a metric oscillates around single-point thresholds (edge), the RAG indicators change back and forth. This is illustrated in the top bar of Figure 12-2. The

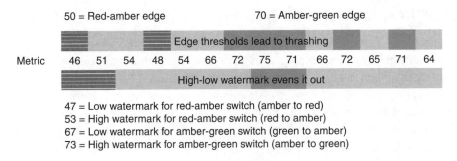

Figure 12-2 *An example of high-low watermark thresholds for RAG metrics. In greyscale image, note that "red" refers to areas with a striped pattern, "amber" refers to light-grey areas, and "green" refers to dark-grey areas.*

metric thrashes between red and amber even for small changes around 50 and between amber and green for small changes around 70. These switches can be problematic to explain while reporting to higher-ups.

The high-low watermark approach shown in the lower bar does away with single-point thresholds and evens out RAG indicator switches. The thresholds now depend on the direction of transition—this helps even out oscillations. When the metric turns amber, it stays amber under the metric falls below 47— the low watermark for red-amber. Similarly, it stays amber until the metric rises above 73—the high watermark for amber-green.

Note that this discussion on RAG metrics is not a vote in favor of dashboards. It is meant to be an aid to the assessment process and an approximate one at that. It avoids the false picture of accuracy painted by raw measurement numbers.

Once we embrace assessments, we find that the RAG status need not always be derived from an objective measurement. It can just as well be the subjective assessment of someone who is accountable.

12.5 Designing Better Metrics

Even without targets, metrics can benefit from better design. In this section, we'll see how to design better metrics along different axes. Note that well-designed metrics aren't a panacea—the very fact that we have to design them carefully is symptomatic of the prevalence of teams with little intrinsic motivation, power, or understanding to do the right thing. Besides, a well-designed metric is a longish learning journey, not something we can come up with on day one. Finally, reporting frequency matters. Even well-designed metrics may exhibit irregular variations inside short windows of time—it doesn't help to ask explanations for hourly, daily, or even weekly variations.

12.5.1 Outcome-oriented Metrics over Activity-oriented Metrics

In Section 4.1, we saw the difference between activities and outcomes. The distinction can be applied to metrics as well. Velocity is an outcome-oriented metric when it has a good definition of *done* (Section 12.1.2). It becomes an activity-oriented metric when the definition of done is dev-complete. Although they are often easier to measure, activity-oriented metrics are less valuable than outcome-oriented metrics. Since activity-oriented metrics relate only to a part of the value stream, acting on their basis runs the risk of local optimization (Section 2.4.3). As they are not actionable, they are closer to what Eric Ries—author of *The Lean Startup*—calls as *vanity metrics*.[14] Besides, as activities tend to be more numerous than outcomes, moving to outcome-oriented metrics will also help reduce the number of metrics under observation.

12.5.2 Aggregate Metrics over Specific, Fine-grained Metrics

Grouping a bunch of related fine-grained metrics into an aggregate metric works better than handling them individually. This is commonly achieved by defining an aggregate metric as a weighted sum of contributory metrics. It is the sort of technique used in credit scoring, insurance risk scoring, or the points system for immigration. Thresholds are then set on the aggregate score to define different categories of eligibility.

Value velocity[15] is a good example of an outcome-oriented, aggregate metric. Regular velocity sums up effort estimates in points. What if each user-story also had an estimated value assigned by the product owner? Value velocity aggregates the value added by a team in a sprint or iteration. Code toxicity[16] is another example. It aggregates different aspects of static code quality into a single number. Aggregate metrics are also well suited for reporting to higher-ups because they cut down detail without loss of signal.

12.5.3 Adaptability Metrics over Predictability Metrics

It is common practice to track the execution of a release plan using metrics like velocity and artifacts like burnup charts. It is also common knowledge that actual scope and effort greatly differ from what was planned. After all, a release plan is an elaborate prediction. However, as argued in Section 3.1, these predictions seldom materialize because software development is not a production process. If we can't get predictability, let's settle for reliability. How do we reliably

14. https://hbr.org/2010/02/entrepreneurs-beware-of-vanity-metrics
15. http://www.jamesshore.com/Blog/Value-Velocity-A-Better-Productivity-Metric.html
16. http://erik.doernenburg.com/2008/11/how-toxic-is-your-code/

deliver useful results in the face of changing business and technology? It calls for a well-oiled adaptive process (responding to change over following a plan). How do we track the level of adaptability of a process? We measure the length of the feedback loops. On the engineering side, this can be done with metrics like build time. On the process side, what matters is end-to-end story cycle time (Section 2.4.3).

12.5.4 Get Comfortable with Lagging Indicators

Let's take a couple of software examples to understand leading and lagging indicators. Velocity is a lagging indicator because it a measurement of past activity. By contrast, the trend line on a burnup chart is a leading indicator because it uses past performance data to forecast when the team will be done. Plans and business cases are also mistaken for leading indicators when they are treated as promises rather than projections. Even though leading indicators are often unreliable, we obsess over them when we chase predictability. This is counterproductive to predictability eluding design processes like software development.

What's more, leading indicators are simply unavailable for important attributes like scope and value. On the other hand, lagging indicators are readily available. Short feedback loops help ensure that the information provided by lagging indicators is timely and not too late to be acted upon. Velocity and backlog size are lagging indicators of finished and unfinished scope. Usage analytics from production and sales data are lagging indicators of value. It is important to get comfortable with using the feedback provided by lagging indicators to steer the work with the aim of improving outcomes.

12.5.5 Compensating Metrics

Since metrics can never be exhaustive, performance under one metric may be achieved at the expense of something that is not tracked as a metric. If this can be anticipated or detected, a compensating metric can be tracked to restore balance. Note that the compensation is rarely foolproof, but the intent is not to make it so. That path leads to an unhealthy game of cat and mouse. The intent of the compensating metric is to serve as a first-level check and a reminder against unintentional suboptimization. Here are some examples of this.

- Customer satisfaction at a call center may correlate with average call duration. Tracking only customer satisfaction may lead to longer call durations, and this might undermine the viability of the call center. To compensate, wait times and unanswered calls are tracked. Satisfaction points are reduced when wait times increase beyond acceptable thresholds.

Agents are trained to deliver higher customer satisfaction without a corresponding increase in average call duration.

- In Scenario 12–3, awarding commission based on overall sales resulted in less attention for low-performing products Omega and Zeta. To compensate, we could cap commission from Kappa based on sales of Omega and Zeta. So, even if someone qualifies for $10,000 commission on account of sales of Kappa, it would be capped to, say, ten times the commission earned from Omega and Zeta. So, if commission from sales of Omega and Zeta only adds up to $800, the commission from Kappa would be capped to $8,000.

- Calculating toxicity per thousand lines of code helps normalize the aggregate metric. It is used to compare toxicity across codebases or to understand the growth in toxicity of a codebase over time relative to its size. The result can be skewed by the presence of duplicated code. If the duplicated code is of low toxicity, it provides a false improvement to the result. To compensate, duplication per thousand lines may be tracked alongside toxicity per thousand lines.

- Test coverage can be skewed by tests that exercise lots of code but actually test very little or even nothing. This can usually be detected by looking at the test-to-code ratio—a ratio of the number of lines of test code to the number of lines of production code. High coverage should correlate with high test-to-code ratios.

12.6 Objections to Metrics Reform

If you have read this chapter closely, you will agree that it isn't against metrics per se. It is against overreliance on metrics and the tendency to scale management by instituting a raft of targets and incentives against all manner of measurement. However, we tend to harbor reservations against arguments that seem contrary to long-held convictions. The following objections are common.

12.6.1 Conversations in Context Don't Scale

It is true that in theory, conversations in context don't scale as well as quantitative reports and dashboards promise to. However, in practice, the latter don't work either because they fail to present the true picture. The industry track record for large IT programs stands as testimony to the fact that scaling management (supervision) does not automatically scale results.

For software lifecycle management, the true picture cannot do without some subjective and qualitative interpretation. Besides, the scaling challenge can also be addressed by reducing the number of reporting touch points (e.g., by having cross-functional teams with greater autonomy for achieving a business outcome). Greater autonomy for decisions coupled with adequate mechanisms for alignment (Chapter 7) and accountability (Chapter 6) reduces the need for constant oversight.

12.6.2 My Team Only Responds to Carrots and Sticks

It might appear as if extrinsic rewards and punishments are the only way to encourage desired behavior. After all, it is what we have been exposed to right from school. However, a carrot-and-stick workforce will keep on needing ever-juicier carrots and ever-stouter sticks to move forward. They will constantly figure out ways to achieve targets by not caring for things outside the measurement radar. By contrast, intrinsic motivation stems from universal needs and is latent in everyone, waiting to sprout under the right conditions. Read Dan Pink's book called *Drive*[17] to convince yourself of this.

12.6.3 Nice Try (at Cost Savings)

A hard-boiled cynic may view all this talk of intrinsic motivation as an attempt to cut cost by avoiding incentive payments. However, organizations can move from *if-then* incentives to *now-that* incentives,[17] (i.e., post facto payments without prior agreement). Also, moving away from a regime of incentives does not have to mean a net reduction in income for its beneficiaries. For example, if you abolish sales commissions, you could compensate your sales team with a one-off pay revision.

12.7 Migration

How can a traditional metrics-oriented organization migrate to being assessment oriented? First, decide on a subunit to run a one-year pilot. Educate all the managers and other senior people in that unit about what is being attempted and why. Start by reducing the footprint of metrics by moving from activity-oriented metrics to outcome-oriented ones and from highly specific metrics to

---

17. (Pink 2009)

aggregate metrics. Reorganizing the subunit so that its teams are organized along outcomes will help the introduction of outcome-oriented metrics. Next, abolish incentives and replace if-then rewards with now-that rewards. Next, attempt a progressive easing of targets as described in Section 12.4.2. Any potential loss of focus can be addressed by clarifying lines of accountability as described in Section 6.3.2. Next, create metrics maps with RAG indicators derived from measurements or from the judgment of accountable people. Use these maps for periodic assessments that include a conversation about the indicators rather than automatic acceptance/rejection based on color.

Targets and incentives form the apparatus for extrinsic motivation. When we take them down, we need to set up another apparatus for intrinsic motivation. Suggestions on how to do this are found in almost every chapter of this book because the topic of fostering conditions for intrinsic motivation is a big underlying theme here.

12.8 Summary of Insights

- Scaling management by numbers is easy. However, it mostly ends up scaling supervision without scaling results.

- Metrics never convey the whole picture. Management by metrics and dashboards needs to be supplemented with management by context and conversations.

- It is inconsistent on one hand to maintain that individuals and interactions are valued more than processes and tools while on the other hand to ban individuals and interactions from metrics and their interpretation.

- The introduction of targets or incentives turns potentially useful, informational measurements into potentially counterproductive, motivational measurements.

- Measurements can be valuable without targets. Targets can have harmful side effects such as erosion of intrinsic motivation, local optimization, and gaming. Incentives are even worse than targets in that they tend to amplify side effects.

- Autonomy allows us to act on the opportunity that purpose provides. Mastery then lets us service the opportunity with a degree of excellence. Targets distort purpose, limit autonomy, and disregard mastery.

- The urge to scale without devolution of control is a root cause of attempting to manage by targets and incentives. On the other hand, we scale by devolving control when we grant autonomy along with clear accountability.

- When we govern for value over predictability, tracking numbers that predict a completion date are less important than tracking numbers that indicate the degree of adaptability of the process.

12.9 Summary of Actions

- Avoid overreliance on metrics. Avoid targets or use them sparingly. Try progressively easing the imposition of targets.
- Don't turn KPIs into targets. A measure turned into a target ceases to be a good measure.
- Get rid of incentives. Instead, create structural alignment with outcomes, give people autonomy, and then hold them accountable for outcomes.
- Stop measurements that lead to counterproductive behavior and stop at measurements (i.e., don't continue to targets) that lead to desired behavior.
- Prefer outcome-oriented metrics to activity-oriented ones. Prefer aggregate metrics to fine-grained ones.
- Get comfortable with lagging (or trailing) indicators. When fast feedback is available, lagging indicators are a reliable alternative to speculative leading indicators.
- Use compensating metrics as a check against *unintentional* suboptimization.
- Use metric maps as information radiators to indicate what outcome (or suboutcome) is served by each metric.
- Scale non-quantitative management by reducing the number of reporting touch points and by giving teams greater autonomy (with commensurate accountability) to realize outcomes.

Chapter 13

Norms

This chapter and the next are the only two that address deliberate interventions to influence organizational culture. Other than that, culture change is mostly a by-product of changes in leadership behavior, org structure, policies, and operational practices. This chapter argues for the recognition and reinforcement of a few organizational norms that help with day-to-day decision making. It also describes a set of potentially applicable norms for organizational agility. In terms of the key themes outlined in Chapter 3, the discussion here is about designing for intrinsic motivation (autonomy, mastery, and purpose) and unscripted collaboration.

13.1 What Are Norms?

The work ethic of an organization is partly shaped by unwritten rules and codes of behavior.

"That's how things work here," said the tenured employee to the new hire.

Scenario 13-1 Fear of Freedom

On the first day of work at her new job with Edgy Inc., Mariam was shocked to find that she had been given full administrative access to her company laptop. She could install whatever software she wanted—the company trusted her to be responsible about it.

This was in stark contrast to her previous job. Her laptop there was so badly locked down she couldn't browse the Internet freely on it even from home. She had to use a personal laptop for using tools not whitelisted by the company IT-I team. She could not transfer the resulting work to her office laptop with USB stick or cloud storage. She had to e-mail them as attachments from her personal e-mail account to her official account. The company even enforced an attachment size restriction on e-mails from free web-based e-mail providers. They had provided rationalizations for all the restrictions, and that was that.

Mariam was unnerved by her newfound freedom. She went to the IT helpdesk at Edgy Inc. and inquired. How could they be unworried about so many unlocked laptops? They told her that they do have cases of occasional abuse. Depending on the infraction, people are either warned or grounded (i.e., their laptops are locked down for three months). In one serious case, an employee was fired. "But you can't pre-emptively put everyone in jail just because one or two might break the law," they said matter-of-factly. Besides, they had much tighter controls on access to sensitive information, production systems, and customer data.

Thus, organizational norms are an informal, collective understanding of what's normal for a place. In some ways, they reflect the values and culture of the organization. Every social system—and an organization is one—has its norms. They may be acknowledged implicitly, explicitly, or not at all. While they don't need to be turned into formal policy documents, it is useful to select valuable norms and propagate them through the organization. They can serve as a useful guide to conflict resolution and decision making.

13.2 Reinforcing Norms

In the absence of regular reinforcement of norms from the leadership, culture evolves on its own depending on whoever is influential in the local units. This is why many organizations have strong subcultures at the level of local units. However, a diversity of core values and work culture does not help the cause of the business. On the contrary, it works against efforts to decentralize. Reiterating organizational norms is a way of centrally establishing and sustaining the principles that form the basis of daily decision making so that the decisions themselves may be decentralized. A well-thought-out set of norms provides a healthy framework for greater autonomy.

When propagated well, norms can influence daily behavior. Storytelling is a promising way of propagating these norms. This is nothing new. Organizations routinely broadcast stories of successful deals and projects internally. By doing so, they propagate the values that directly influence business results, for example, execution excellence, putting customers/clients/stakeholders first, getting things done, winning against odds, or innovating under constraints. Why not do the same to disseminate cultural cues that help shape the character of the organization?

13.2.1 Mechanics of Reinforcement

How do we go about reinforcement? Here is one way to do it for some organizational norms: Create an internal blog for each norm. Explain the value of the norm in an introductory post from leadership. Use subsequent posts to narrate supporting stories. Employees subscribe to the blog, vote up or like stories, and comment on posts.

Crowdsource stories from the entire organization. As for publishing them, allow self-service publishing or get the submissions curated by internal comms. In the most open scenario, everyone is allowed to post new stories. The good ones are picked up by the leadership for e-mail broadcasts. If that sounds too scary, publish an inbox to which employees can send new stories. Someone from internal comms then curates and publishes selected stories on the blog.

How do we keep this from degenerating into a lame "leader's speak" section full of vague homilies that is the butt of private ridicule? As a first rule, leaders comment more than post. Except for an introductory post explaining the value of a norm, leaders mainly post only to narrate or highlight the story of regular employees. Second, exercise restraint regarding the use of incentives for posting stories (e.g., story of the month). Finally, not everyone is keen to post their stories; so, whenever leaders hear of a promising story, they should assign someone from internal comms to tease it out.

This type of reinforcement is required because it is common for those mired in the daily details of running the business to lose sight of the big picture. Top management knows and understands the big picture, but they need to realize that those on the ground need regular doses of guiding narratives to be able to see daily work through the frame of organizational norms.

Without calling it out as a norm, we discussed "best fit over best tool" in Section 11.4 on tool evaluation. A number of other potentially applicable norms are described in the rest of this chapter.

13.3 Cooperation over Competition

At every quarterly examination a gold medal was given to the best writer, and a silver one to the best cypherer.

... When the first medal was offered, it produced rather a general contention than an emulation; and diffused a spirit of envy, jealousy, and discord through the whole school; boys who were bosom friends before became fierce contentious rivals, and when the prize was adjudged, became implacable enemies. Those who were advanced decried the weaker performances; each wished his opponents abilities less than his own, and they used all their little arts to misrepresent and abuse each other's performances.

—Robert Coram. (1791). *Political Inquiries,* pp. 102–103.

When it comes to winning in the external market, there is perhaps no alternative to competition. However, it doesn't have to be so inside an organization. Internal competition is often corrosive. It isn't a natural fit for an Agile culture (Section 2.3).

There is no such thing as "healthy" competition within a knowledge organization; all internal competition is destructive.

—Tom DeMarco in *Slack,*[1] p. 175

Efforts to create a climate of *healthy* competition inside an organization mostly backfire in other ways. Common reasons are as follows:

- A culture of internal competition leads to rivalry among contributors to a common outcome, thus compromising the outcome.

- Competing for a reward (e.g., most innovative solution, employee of the month) shifts the focus from the business outcome to the reward. The reward acts as a target and, as we saw in Section 12.3, it leads to local optimization.

The following are examples of cases in which it is better to foster cooperation than competition:

- Measuring individual productivity in a team and tying productivity to compensation: Not only is the whole idea dubious[2] for a design process such as software development (Section 3.1), a focus on individual productivity will discourage individuals from taking the time to help each other.

---

1. (DeMarco 2002)
2. http://martinfowler.com/bliki/CannotMeasureProductivity.html

- Openly comparing performance of two different product teams: This is like parents comparing the academic, sporting, or extracurricular performance of one child against another. It only builds up resentment.

- Gamification: Regular activities at work may be *gamified* by keeping score and turning it into a competition for the highest individual score. Again, this can lead to undesirable behaviors. For example, a certain team held a monthly competition called the *bug bash*. Testers would head into a room and perform manual exploratory testing for a couple of hours. The person who found the most bugs during this session was the winner. One day, a developer found a small bug during the course of her work and reported it to a tester. The tester informed her that she already knew about the bug. The developer asked her if she had recorded it in the bug database. The tester replied in the negative stating discreetly that she was saving it for the bug bash!

Migrating from a competition culture to a cooperation culture might need intermediate steps. The first step is to move away from what author Alfie Kohn calls *mutually exclusive goal attainment* programs.[3] This is any program or contest that has a single first rank. Since there is only one top prize, there is never a win-win situation between the contestants. It is better to have a rank-less contest. Pick the winners from a group of contestants, but don't rank-order them. Also, don't try to make it too exclusive by having only one or two winners. Artificial scarcity may help create the illusion of value, but it also breeds non-cooperation among those in the race. For example, *employees*-of-the-month works better than employee-of-the-month does. An award for innovative solutions works better than one for the most innovative solution.

13.4 Living Policies

Organizations are bound by policies and processes. Some policies are high-level principles (e.g., equal opportunity employer, corporate social responsibility). HR policies tend to be much more concrete (e.g., business travel and expense, benefits and entitlements, non-harassment). HR processes include performance appraisal, on-boarding and exit processes, etc. IT policies and processes include things like laptop policy, bring-your-own-device (BYOD), software purchase, product development process, incident management process, and change request process.

---

3. http://www.alfiekohn.org/article/competition-ever-appropriate-cooperative-classroom/

Policies may be at the organization level or unit level. The unit may be a functional, regional, or business unit. Traditionally, policies are engraved in wood, if not cast in stone. They are slow and hard to change. However, many organizations have begun to update their policies regularly in tune with changing business realities. These updates are influenced by a circle of input providers. The radius of this circle is an indicator of the extent of openness.

One very open approach is to maintain all policies as living documents in the organization's content platform accessible to all employees. Everyone can read and comment; only the policy owner and other authorized people can edit. Queries raised via comments are expected to be answered within a reasonable period. The policy is revised periodically taking the comments, among other inputs, into consideration.

How do we migrate from the existing setup to a living policies model? We could start by identifying owners for each policy and having them post the current version on the content platform. Better yet, it might be useful to conduct a rules audit[4] to rationalize policies prior to starting life as living policies. In short, a rules audit reviews existing rules (written or unwritten) for present-day relevance, ownership, effectiveness, and unintended consequences. They are then kept intact, marked as inadequate, or discarded. Once owners are identified for the rules that are retained, they can go about fixing inadequacies.

The next section describes how these policies need to be administered not just by the letter and not always by the letter. This is aided by stating the purpose and intent of the policy at the beginning of the policy document. It is also useful to document provisions that were considered but not included in the policy along with the reasons for doing so. This will reduce the need for saying, "We already considered that but…" when someone offers the same suggestion via comments.

All of this documentation might feel heavyweight, but in practice, it turns out to be less than the cost of administering a poorly documented policy. The act of documentation also forces policy makers to think clearly about the issue and address any shortcomings that become evident. At any rate, a shift to living policies should not result in the formation of a new policy-making team. Line and staff managers responsible for policy administration should own the policy and periodically seek approval for revisions from senior management.

Once living policies become a norm, teams naturally adopt the idea to document and evolve team-level standards, conventions, and rules.

---

4. (Rieger 2011)

13.5 Consistency over Uniformity

Business organizations are not democracies. Equality before law is very important in a democracy. In a business, though, policies and processes are secondary to business goals. Deviation is allowable as long as it remains ethical, safe, and legal. Although fairness is important when it comes to HR policies, there is a risk of achieving fairness by being equally unfair to everyone.

Scenario 13-2 Keep the Baby, Never Mind the Bathwater

Indicode Ltd. had a policy of providing interest-free loans to employees to cater to one-time needs such as house rental deposit, wedding expense, etc. The loan would be recovered from the employee's future salary in ten installments. There were guidelines around the size of the loan, minimum employee tenure, etc. Loan requests were to be approved by HR and finance. Requests could be partially approved or even rejected if the business was in a tight cash flow situation.

Although the policy proved to be quite helpful to employees, some of those whose requests weren't granted began to view the process as inconsistent and unfair. The HR head was frustrated by the allegations. It was not possible to make the process transparent to all. She could eliminate all complaints by discontinuing the policy, that is, achieve total fairness by being equally unfair to everyone.

However, it had proved to be useful to many employees at little cost to the company. She finally decided to keep the policy, added some explanatory notes to the policy document to explain the ostensible inconsistencies, and pretty much ignored any further controversy.

In the above scenario, the disgruntled employees were demanding uniformity, not consistency. Irrespective of the situation, they wanted all loan requests that were superficially identical to be treated the same. But unlike uniformity, consistency is a dynamic attribute. The HR head realized that the policy administration was consistent with the aims of the policy although the results appeared inconsistent to an external observer.

Outside HR, we often play the consistency card in the support of an argument:

"I want this UI (form) to be laid out this way for the sake of consistency."

Or

"Let's be consistent and use the corporate presentation template."

Used as above, the word *consistency* is an inappropriate substitute for *uniformity*. To check, ask, "Consistency with what?"
Example #1:

"Let's be consistent and use the corporate presentation template."

"Consistent with what?"

"With each other and with corporate guidelines, of course."

"Guidelines don't demand uniformity. *We could use our own templates as long as they are* consistent *with the image we want to portray as a company."*

Example #2:

"I want this UI (form) to be laid out this way for the sake of consistency."

"Consistency with what?"

"With the rest of the UI."

"You mean uniformity *with the rest of the UI?"*

"Isn't it the same thing?"

"Well, laying it out this other way is consistent *with the aim of keeping the user from making an incorrect assumption about the feature."*

Consistency is a higher-order goal than mere uniformity. Figure 13–1 illustrates the push-pull door example made famous by design guru Donald Norman.[5] It is misleading to have a uniform interface on a door that only opens one way (push-pull). The non-uniform interface on the right is consistent with the door's

---

5. Design guru Donald Norman is the author a popular book called *The Design of Everyday Things.* 2002. New York: Basic Books.

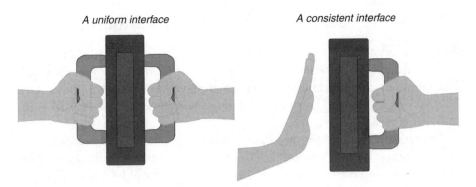

A uniform interface   A consistent interface

Figure 13-1 *Consistency is more than uniformity.*

behavior. It is intuitive to use. The uniform interface on the left annoys users by leading them to believe it is pull-pull. Yet, we commonly encounter a pull-pull design on push-pull doors, perhaps because their designers valued visual symmetry afforded by mindless uniformity over enhanced user experience afforded by a consistent but asymmetric (non-uniform) interface.

It requires some deliberation to decide whether a certain course of action is consistent with broader objectives. On the other hand, uniformity is easily achieved by mechanical application of a rule book. This is what call center agents are trained to do (much against their wishes, usually). We know what the resulting customer experience feels like. On the other hand, Wikipedia's editing guidelines[6] are a great example of aiming for consistency without a strict, detailed ruleset.

Why, then, do organizations regress to uniformity in the name of consistency? Often, it is just laziness to listen and think. Sometimes (as in the case of call centers), it is a side effect of organization design. Decision makers and policy makers sit on top of corporate hierarchies. They attempt to scale execution without devolving discretionary powers to subordinates. The subordinates learn to function uniformly, without regard to context. Organizational newspeak[7] soon substitutes "consistency" for "uniformity".

The other reason is what Rieger[8] calls *parochialism*. Owners of policies and standards begin to act as overzealous guardians. They need to be reminded from time to time that the policies are meant to serve a larger purpose. This can be achieved by recognizing *consistency over uniformity* as an organizational norm and using techniques like those described in Section 13.2 to reinforce it in people's minds.

---

6. http://en.wikipedia.org/wiki/Wikipedia:Editing_guidelines
7. http://en.wikipedia.org/wiki/Newspeak
8. (Rieger 2011)

13.6 Ask for Forgiveness, Not for Permission

This is a catchy way of saying, "Don't wait around for approval. Get the job done. If it displeases someone, we can always ask for forgiveness after the fact." In an organization that embraces this norm, forgiveness is usually granted. This is a tricky norm as it can be abused. But at the same time, it is essential in order to let people take initiative.

To prevent abuse, emphasize that the norm is primarily meant for cases of business gain (e.g., delivering the goods on a sale based on e-mail confirmation instead of waiting for purchase order) rather than personal gain (e.g., proceeding on leave without approval). Also, emphasize the need to stay ethical, legal, and safe at all times.

Be cautious while publicizing stories of this sort. Take care to acknowledge the magnanimity of the approver to forgive the infraction in the interest of business expediency. Otherwise, the bypassed approver comes across as a stodgy bureaucrat.

Waiting for permission can lead to inaction in two ways. The first is when people are reluctant to suggest to their bosses a different way of doing things. They fear rejection and disapproval or they are not confident of the proposal. The second is when superiors are reluctant to recommend to their subordinates a different way of doing things. They'd rather have voluntary adoption.

Asking for permission spreads accountability for the action between the requester and the approver. If something goes wrong, the requester can get away by saying she asked for permission. Thus, a permission culture is a risk-averse culture.

On the other hand, a system can only harbor a small number of insubordinate idealists—else there is a risk of anarchy. A healthy organization needs a large proportion of conforming behavior and a small proportion of nonconforming behavior. Therefore, even if we are uncomfortable advertising this norm, it has to be an underlying motif in how infractions are dealt with. In this aspect, an organization can afford to be slightly more discerning than democratic society in that some law-breaking acts may be condoned if they are judged to be for the greater good (e.g., a skunkworks[9] effort that violates IT procurement policies).

Won't this norm encourage a cavalier attitude toward information security? Yes, this is a genuine risk, but good information security is better achieved by moderate policies supported by good stories that explain the risks rather than by periodic e-learning tests and strict policies that frustrate people into subversion.

---

9. http://en.wikipedia.org/wiki/Skunkworks_project

13.7 Confidential Surveys

Uncommonly high levels of personal maturity and integrity are required to handle 100% transparency in an open culture. For example, it is very common that, in peer reviews, X's evaluation of Y is influenced by Y's evaluation of X, thus compromising the integrity of the review. Yet, peer reviews and 360-degree reviews are essential to reduce bias in assessments. We could make reviews anonymous to encourage honest feedback in order to limit behaviors like scratching each other's back or pulling each other down. However, anonymity may give rise to extreme assessments. We need an approach that strikes a balance between complete anonymity and complete transparency. This is where confidential surveys enter the picture.

Unlike an anonymous survey, in a confidential survey, input is collected *nonymously* (identity is captured) but presented anonymously as an aggregate. Several people may fill out a survey about X, but X will only see aggregated results. Survey admins can still access individual input. This helps avoid the issue of extreme ratings. A confidential survey can be achieved with software or face to face in a room. In case of the latter, a trusted survey facilitator uses sticky notes to collect input from a bunch of people in a room. Respondents sign each note so that the inputs are transparent to the facilitator. The facilitator can then filter outlier inputs if required and aggregate the information for presentation to the recipient.

Confidential surveys are not a norm per se, but nevertheless it is useful to institutionalize the practice of conducting surveys in this manner. In avoiding the disadvantages of complete anonymity and transparency, confidential surveys provide a reliable way of obtaining good-quality first-hand input on subjective matters. One-on-one hearings (meetings) are a poor but common alternative. They are subject to biases and problems of translation, and they lead to a culture of hearsay.

13.8 Balance Theory and Practice

He who loves practice without theory is like the sailor who boards ship without a rudder and compass and never knows where he may cast.
—Leonardo Da Vinci

Business, in general, rightly prefers practice to theory—for example, implementations over plans, prototypes and proofs-of-concept over proposals, experience reports over bookish wisdom. Being result oriented, it favors what works over what could work or ought to work. This bias for action serves business well where the modes of action are established or prescribed. However, in the rapidly changing landscape of IT, established and prescribed modes of action (e.g., ITIL,[10] COBIT,[11] CMMI,[12] PMP,[13] PRINCE2,[14] TOGAF,[15] Zachman[16]) are under strain from demands of higher responsiveness. We need a little theory in order to tweak existing modes or choose new modes of action. Even a trial-and-error method of choosing right action converges faster when aided by a little theory.

Since Agile isn't prescriptive, it was omitted from the list of examples above even though it is somewhat established under different methods like Scrum and XP. Since it is nonprescriptive, we hear of the difference between doing Agile and being Agile. We can't *be* Agile just by doing what someone says. We need to understand the theory—the underlying principles, the whys, the different schools and the current trends, not just the hows. This helps us make better decisions in new situations where there are no ready answers. I'm not advocating a transfer of power to theory spewing Agile coaches, only that theory also be given a seat at the table.

The legitimacy of theory may be obvious to you, but there are many organizations or teams where theory is implicitly illegitimate. They say they are too busy doing stuff in the real world to bother about books, blogs, or conferences. To be sure, there is a fair bit of self-promotion masquerading as knowledge sharing in these media, but to ignore them completely on this account is to throw out the baby with the bathwater. A bias for action is great except when it turns into a disdain for theory and thoughtfulness.

In his book *Drive*, author Dan Pink[17] repeatedly points out the gap between what science knows (about motivation) and what business does (persists with targets and incentives). This gap can be bridged by cultivating an organization-wide habit (norm) of reading and discussing books and tweaking the work where it makes sense. It is part of continuous improvement.

An organizational norm that says, "We value practice over theory but we value theory-informed practice over ad-hoc practice" helps to restore some respect for theory. We then reinforce this norm by encouraging specialist communities of practice (Section 5.7) to include books and theory in their activities. Internal knowledge-sharing sessions, brown bag lunches, and conferences should be encouraged to discuss practice in the context of theory. In the absence

---

10. https://www.axelos.com/itil
11. http://www.isaca.org/cobit
12. http://www.sei.cmu.edu/cmmi/
13. http://www.pmi.org/Certification/Project-Management-Professional-PMP.aspx
14. https://www.axelos.com/prince2
15. http://www.opengroup.org/subjectareas/enterprise/togaf
16. http://www.zachman.com/
17. (Pink 2009)

of organizational backing, legitimacy of theory becomes dependent on the disposition of the leaders of local units or communities of practice.

13.9 Summary of Insights

- Culture change is mostly a by-product of changes in leadership, behavior, org structure, policies, and operational practices. Propagating select norms is an attempt at direct intervention.

- A well-thought-out set of norms provides a healthy framework for greater autonomy.

- Reinforcing organizational norms helps to centrally establish and sustain the principles that form the basis of daily decision making so that the decisions themselves may be decentralized.

- Storytelling is a promising way of propagating norms.

13.10 Summary of Actions

Shortlist an initial set of norms worth reinforcing. Operationalize the practice using internal blogs, crowdsourcing of stories, and curation as needed by the internal comms team. Here is a summary of potentially applicable norms in designing an organization for agility:

- Discourage internal competition and mutually exclusive goal-attainment contests. They do more harm than good.

- Adopt living policies. They are more in tune with an Agile organization. Along with the recognition that consistency is a higher-order goal than uniformity, they provide an institutional safeguard against slow-moving bureaucracy.

- Recognize that a permission culture is a risk-averse culture. Embrace (perhaps tacitly) the norm of asking for forgiveness rather than permission. It encourages people to take initiative without being too fearful of breaking rules.

- Use confidential surveys to collect all manner of sensitive feedback without fear or favor.

- In a rapidly changing environment that calls for experimentation and learning, it pays to know a little theory. This mindset can be cultivated with an organizational norm that values theory-informed practice over ad hoc practice.

Chapter 14

Communications

The communication culture of an organization may be viewed as a dynamic aspect of organization design. For instance, is it considered okay to talk to your boss's boss without informing the boss first? Is it okay to question company policies on public internal forums? Are all-hands and unit-level meetings a forum for active dialogue, or just one-way broadcasts from the leadership to the teams? Is everything meant to be driven by e-mail or forms and backed by an audit trail, or does work routinely get accomplished on the back of unrecorded verbal communications? Granted, the last item may not be advisable in all situations and may even be constrained by industry regulations, but in general, a culture of open, purposeful, hierarchy-effacing communication energizes everyone toward greater organizational agility.

14.1 Intrinsic Motivation

Effective collaboration between business and IT needs good levels of motivation because of the pressures and constraints commonly involved. If organization design is to play its part toward fostering the intrinsic motivators of autonomy, mastery, and purpose then it needs to address the communication culture as well. In a healthy culture, communication is purposeful and, hence, intrinsically motivating.

It pays to deliberately influence the communication culture rather than let it take shape based on the habits and styles of unit-level leaders. This includes addressing aspects such as:

- General style of interpersonal communications
- Broadcast communications
- Communications that lead to important decisions
- Appropriate media of communications (e.g., speech, written text, visual aids)
- Presentations, reports, and templates

14.2 Interpersonal Communications: Problems

The wheels of routine, business-as-usual activities are greased by interpersonal communications. This includes formal and informal exchanges at one's desk, cubicle, or office; at meetings; and during encounters in the corridors, at the cafeteria, or in the parking lot. The protocol followed in these exchanges reveals the culture of the organization. Hierarchical cultures tend to have rank-sensitive protocols whereas open cultures tend to have easy-going protocols.

14.2.1 Pulling Rank

Anything more than just enough hierarchy is detrimental to an Agile work culture. Many organizations recognize this and have minimal hierarchies. However, this doesn't go far enough. It is also essential that senior peers/leaders/managers *exercise authority sparingly*. By contrast, an authoritarian organization like the army emphasizes rank all the time. Salute the senior. Seniors address juniors by their rank. Juniors address their seniors as Sir/Madam. These organizations are all about giving and taking orders. They may perfunctorily ask, "Any questions?" at the end of each briefing, but that's about it. Many business organizations still function this way or close to it. Even inside the technology and knowledge industry, there are unit leads that function this way—their units gradually turn into feudal subcultures.

On the other hand, at a workplace more in tune with the times, we address each other by first name. Whoever gets to the door first holds it open to let their colleagues, irrespective of relative rank, pass. The boss routinely walks over to the subordinate to discuss something rather than always summoning the subordinate to her office. In meetings, people find it safe to voice an opinion opposite to what a senior might have already voiced.

Protocols of initiating and terminating communications affect people as much as the actual content of the communication. The number of levels of hierarchy does not matter as much as the exercise of hierarchy. Hierarchy manifests itself via protocols of communication—the hierarchy-in-effect may be more or less than the hierarchy on paper. Egalitarian protocols can make a law firm feel like a tech startup. Authority or turf protection-oriented protocols can make an ad agency feel like Victorian England.

14.2.2 Microaggression: Nonverbal

Few remain unaffected by negative vibes in routine interpersonal communications. Rare is the person who does not give it a second thought if her unit head does not respond to her smile when they pass each other in the corridor. An organization cannot assume that the vast majority of its employees are psychologically secure. The opposite is generally true regardless of a person's rank.

The seniors in a team want to be acknowledged and respected for their seniority, their hard-earned titles, and the competence that they imply. In the absence of sufficient signs of deference from the team in the content of communications, they begin to assert their seniority in the protocols of communication. They resort to microaggression in management.

The juniors, on the other hand, want to be in the good books of seniors without having to turn into yes men (or women) in order to get there. They want to have their say in the content of communications. They resent it when disagreements in the content of communications translate into hardening of the protocols. Here are some examples of hardened-protocol behavior by Tom, a fictional manager, in his interactions with Peter, who reports to him. Some of it is culture specific, but this is the general drift.

- Tom almost never answers the phone when Peter calls. He chooses to call back at his convenience. However, he does not allow Peter the same privilege. Peter is expected to take all of Tom's calls.

- Tom may ignore or answer Peter's e-mails after considerable delay but expects prompt replies from Peter.

- Peter is expected to show up for meetings called by Tom even if Tom's invitation conflicts with his prior appointments. But Peter is expected to book time on Tom's calendar with due care if he expects Tom to show up. Even then, Tom won't respond to Peter's invitations with an Accept or a Decline. He'll keep Peter guessing and expect him to take it in stride if he doesn't show up.

- Tom may show up late to a one-on-one meeting but Peter had better not.

- Tom may choose to take calls or check e-mail on his smartphone in the middle of a one-on-one with Peter, but Peter is expected to behave more professionally.

- In an open office layout, Tom may sometimes call out to Peter expecting him to get up and walk over to him, but Peter may not.

- Tom would barely turn around to face Peter when he walks over and approaches Tom at his desk with a question/issue, but Peter had better stand up if Tom approached his desk.

- When Tom sends Peter links to various articles on the Internet, it is considered education. But when Peter sends links to Tom, it is evidence of aimless Internet surfing and not focusing on work.

- Even though a team lunch is scheduled for 12:30, Tom may show up 15 minutes late and expect the team to wait and understand that he was busy. However, no team member may behave so and have Tom wait.

All of this is unnecessary power symbolism and display of authority. It's the opposite of exercising authority sparingly. It is difficult to go about one's job with a sense of purpose in the face of such daily acts of microaggression. Purpose suffers death by a thousand slights. If left unchecked, this leads to good people leaving the organization. It is wrong to condone this behavior as that of a high-flying alpha male (or female). It may be okay in a control culture, but is out of place for an Agile culture (Section 2.3). Companies that boast of a no-jerks policy ought to discourage this behavior.

14.2.3 Microaggression: Verbal

Microaggressive behavior also turns verbal. Let's continue the example above:

- If Tom disagrees with Peter's ideas, he decides what level of detail he will provide by way of explanation. If Peter probes further, Tom gets to label him as a poor listener, sulker, or just plain slow. On the other hand, if Peter disagrees with Tom's ideas, he'd better have an explanatory slide deck ready before he even states his disagreement. If after hearing Tom's counterarguments, Peter persists in his disagreement and politely points out flaws in the counterarguments, he is obviously dissenting, showing insubordination, misaligned, or antiestablishment.

- Tom may probe Peter for information without explaining why or giving any context, but Peter may not do so.

- Tom may poke fun of Peter in a group and expect him to take it well, but Peter dare not attempt the same.

- Tom may speak to Peter in any tone, but if Peter's tone is anything but cordial, his speech may be dismissed using the tone argument.[1]

Another kind of verbal microaggression results from poor listening skills or from a this-is-not-worth-listening-to attitude. Especially with junior colleagues, we tend to sum up a situation without granting them a full hearing. A symptom of this is the use of stock phrases to sum up a situation, for example, "It's not rocket science," "Let's not over-engineer it," "I know the situation is less than ideal but…," "Let's take baby steps," etc. These phrases may annoy the receiver; she may take them as an insult to her intelligence.

Note that the same phrases sound obviously inappropriate when delivered by a junior to a senior in the middle of a conversation. It is an act of microaggression to be on the stronger side of a power relationship and pass judgment in an off-hand manner. It implies one or more of the following:

- The senior has given the junior a polite hearing more out of courtesy rather than a genuine desire to understand the other perspective.

- The junior is being unreasonable if he still doesn't get it.

- The senior wants the junior to get on with it without making an effort to convince her.

This behavior could also occur without a formal hierarchical relationship. It could be an old-timer talking down to a newcomer at the same level. Verbal acts of microaggression create lasting negative impression in the minds of those at the receiving end. They may conclude that the only way to be heard is to grow in authority—intrinsic motivation goes out of the window.

14.2.4 War Metaphor

Our everyday business language is peppered with metaphors of violence and war: shoot an e-mail, fire a print, kill a project, etc. Could violent language contribute to violent, competitive, or non-cooperative thoughts? Research indicates that language influences how we think[2,3] (although there are refutations[4] as well). This is no surprise if we consider that language is just a communication technology invented by early humans and, as pointed out in Section 11.3, technology influences user behavior.

---

1. http://rationalwiki.org/wiki/Tone_argument
2. http://edge.org/conversation/how-does-our-language-shape-the-way-we-think
3. (Lakoff 2003)
4. McWhorter, J. H. 2014. *The Language Hoax.* Oxford, UK: Oxford University Press.

Table 14-1 *Alternatives to War Metaphor*

War/Violence Metaphor	Milder Alternative
After many years in the trenches	After many years in the thick of things
Armed with information/data	Prepared with information/data
Attack an argument	Refute/challenge an argument
Beat the competition	Overcome the competition
Blast someone	Admonish/castigate/reprimand someone
Bullet points, bullets	Points
Don't shoot the messenger	Don't blame/scold the messenger
Double-edged sword	Double-edged knife
Fire a print	Take a print
Fire up the BitLocker wizard (from a disk encryption manual)	Bring up the BitLocker wizard
Kill a process	Terminate a process
Kill a product	Discontinue a product
Kill two birds with one stone	Fix two problems with one solution
No silver bullet	No magic solution
Please cascade to your troops	Please cascade to your team
Shoot an e-mail	Write/send/drop an e-mail
Spearhead the effort	Lead the effort
Take a stab at it	Try, make an attempt, guess
Pick your battles	Pick your struggles

As part of propagating norms of healthy communication, it might be useful to consider alternatives to war metaphors. This is illustrated with some examples in Table 14-1. It turns out to be much harder to replace established idioms such as kill two birds with one stone. Even if it doesn't make a real difference, the value of this exercise lies in raising awareness to the fact that we use these phrases in everyday language without being conscious of how violent the words actually are.

On the other hand, it is possible that the urge to turn every argument into a competition will be tempered by the conscious choice of less competitive language. As called for in the section on avoiding internal competition (Section 13.3), it is a possibility worth working toward even if it comes at the cost of some loss of color from everyday language. Note that many other common business metaphors aren't warlike (e.g., door that swings both ways, trying to boil the ocean, rain on someone's parade, steal someone's thunder).

Avoiding war metaphor is relevant to marketing efforts as well. A lot of digital marketing is social—a space where we want to tone down our competitive streak. In an article in the *Harvard Business Review*, Phil Granof, winner of a 2014 CMO leadership award, admits that although the war metaphor may have served traditional marketing well, digital marketing is more about co-creation than war. He makes the case[5] that digital marketers need to be *more dancer than soldier*.

14.3 Interpersonal Communications: Mitigation

It is quite difficult to institutionalize the detection and correction of microaggressive behaviors. Sometimes, the aggressors are genuinely unaware of their behavior or of how it is perceived. Feedback or coaching may be enough in this case. At other times, microaggression is a deliberate technique of exerting control. This requires more work on the part of the organization to contain and correct. Here are two ways by which an organization can signal that it is serious about addressing microaggression.

14.3.1 New-Hire Orientation

New-hire orientation is a good place to impart awareness of rights and responsibilities in this area. Many organizations already have a non-harassment module as part of orientation. Microaggression could be added to this module to sensitize new hires to what microaggression is and how it affects the organization. Ed Schein's book *Humble Inquiry*[6] could be made required reading as part of the orientation. Before adding this module to new-hire orientation, it is important to get existing employees on the same page via office-wide sessions.

14.3.2 Pulse Charts

A pulse chart is an information radiator (Section 2.4.4) that provides a glimpse of the emotional pulse of a team. Simple flip charts like Figure 14-1 may help keep microaggression in check. HR explains what qualifies as microaggression and puts out guidelines for legitimate uses of this chart. Any team member can add a bar to the chart at any time. They can also scratch out a bar they added if they feel that the situation has been addressed. The whole team discusses the

---

5. https://hbr.org/2012/05/marketing-needs-a-new-metaphor/
6. (Schein 2013)

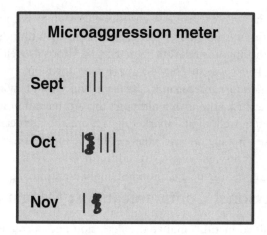

Figure 14-1 *Team pulse chart*

pulse during retrospectives. People who are comfortable talking about instances without naming names do so. Others can have a one-on-one with the team manager. Mostly, the existence of a public and transparent device like this is enough to deter bad behavior. If the bars continue to persist on the chart, someone from HR is expected to reach out to the team and understand the concerns. They may choose to run a confidential survey (Section 13.7) to get to the bottom of the matter.

14.4 Scaling Employee Engagement through Internal Communications

> If you want people to feel ownership, having 1% of 1% of 1% of the shares is way less important than having a voice in decisions that matter.
> —Gary Hamel[7]

Autonomy, mastery, and purpose can work wonders for employee engagement inside the domain of their jobs. Cross-functional teams confer a measure of autonomy upon team members and outcome owners. When aligned around business outcomes, they serve to instill a sense of purpose in the team. However, it is very difficult to devolve autonomy to the level of individual contributors in a team. How do we ensure their engagement? There is also the issue of

---

7. http://blog.loomio.org/2014/06/17/management-hacker-gary-hamel-interviews-loomio/

organizational involvement—being engaged in company-wide events, development programs, and discussions. For example, a product manager may engage well with her team and immediate product organization but may not choose to participate in office-wide activities.

Engagement comes from participation. Participative forums drive engagement whereas nonparticipative ones turn people into mute spectators. Post facto participation (i.e., having team members/employees *respond* to decisions) is lame. It doesn't drive engagement. Participation here implies being fully heard and considered; it does not mean having a vote. Decision makers are free to make decisions that run contrary to input as long as they stay accountable for it.

However, designing for participation *does* rule out one-way communications. An e-mail announcement of a corporate-level decision from the internal comms department is an example of one-way communication even if it ends by saying, "Feel free to reach out to your local manager or people representative for further clarity," because employees only get to respond to the messengers, not to the decision makers.

The challenge, then, is to come up with a means of two-way communication that is truly participative and scales beyond one-on-one meetings. Let's examine common approaches to scale two-way communications.

14.4.1 Group Meetings

Group meetings are all right for a group of up to eight or ten people. Participation breaks down beyond that. All-hands meetings are two-way in name only. Less than a quarter of the total time is usually allotted for Q&A. Each person gets to ask *one* question so that maximum number of people can "participate." Besides, the questioner doesn't get to probe the response further. Knowing this, the responder may skirt the question. That's more of a press conference than a meeting. Group meetings have to be time-boxed to an hour for fear of wasting everyone's time. Group discussions over important issues often need much more than an hour. Meetings in which people join in via teleconferencing or videoconferencing fare worse. By demanding that all attendees be available at the same time, meetings lose out as effective means of two-way communications for big groups.

Sometimes, organizations attempt to "share" an important update via several meetings of smaller groups instead of one big meeting. While it improves participation, this divide-and-conquer approach has two problems. First, it demands a lot more time on the part of the conveners of the meeting—this has the side effect of leaders nominating proxies to conduct the meeting with the result that employees don't get to talk to the real decision makers. Second, all employees don't get to hear all the discussions—only those in their meeting. This type of throttled two-way communications is a good approach to divide-and-conquer dissent but not a good one to drive engagement.

14.4.2 Blogs and Videos

In some places, important updates are conveyed via internal blogs or videos. Note that these are primarily a form of one-way communication. They can serve as weak two-way channels when employees can respond via comments and can expect at least a consolidated reply from the decision makers. Some people prefer to watch video while others prefer to scan through text at their own pace rather than having to watch a 7-minute video. Video updates would therefore do well to include a text summary.

14.4.3 Surveys

Sometimes, surveys are used to solicit input before a decision is made. Since this isn't an interactive mode of communication, it is actually two separate channels of one-way communication rather than two-way communications. Besides, employees don't get to see others' responses to the survey. Therefore, in general, surveys don't drive engagement.

14.4.4 Online Forums

Scenario 14-1 WFH (Work From Home)

Woohoo Inc. was going through a rough patch. Among other actions to turn things around, the leadership team discussed suspension of the work-from-home policy (unless approved by exception). Work-from-home was very popular in the company, and not everyone in the leadership team thought it was such a good idea to suspend it. After some debate, the decision was put on hold. Instead, it was decided to announce it in a company discussion forum as something the leadership was considering. The topic would stay open for comments in the forum for ten days. After that, the leadership team would reconvene over the topic and take a final decision. A representative was chosen to respond to employee comments on the forum on behalf of the leadership team. This was done to avoid differences of opinion inside the leadership team from spilling out.

The announcement triggered a flood of responses—some in favor of the proposal and many against. Most of the arguments against the proposal were things that had already figured in the leadership debate. The representative responded with the leadership group's position on those arguments. A couple of arguments were new and noteworthy. To these, the representative acknowledged that they hadn't considered these points but that her gut feeling was they weren't strong enough to sway the proposal. This triggered a fresh flurry of posts in support of the new arguments. After ten days, the leadership team reconvened, discussed the new arguments as summarized by the representative, and still decided to go ahead with the suspension. The representative announced the final decision along with a summary of the deliberations over the new points.

Although there were strong murmurs of discontent to the final decision, it is likely that the reaction would have been worse had the decision simply been announced without prior discussion. People would have felt that they were at the mercy of the leadership with no say in policies that affected them. The honest acknowledgement and subsequent consideration of new and noteworthy arguments also helped. The leadership was genuine about reconsidering the proposal after the public discussion. The decision was by no means a foregone conclusion. The public discussion was never thought of as just a device to soften the inevitable blow. On another day or topic, the leadership would have deferred to the employees if it found greater merit in their arguments.

In a later meeting, the leadership team wondered what they'd have done had the very first leadership discussion been unanimous. Would they have simply gone ahead and announced the decision? In retrospect, it was felt that the prior consultation was a good practice for important decisions that touched the lives of employees. There were concerns that it would slow down decision making, but then it wasn't going to be an indefinite delay. The model had three clear stages. Leadership takes a position first, then it is put forth for company-wide discussion for a fixed period, and finally leadership takes a final call. It wasn't meant to democratize decision making, either. It merely served to *engage* all stakeholders in the decision-making process.

Online forums hold the greatest promise of scaling engagement via two-way communications. Being asynchronous and always available, they let people participate in their own time and from their own location. There is no notion of local and remote participants. By requiring participants to state their views in writing, they foster a certain due diligence—a point the next section expands on. Finally, discussions in forums can be accessed later to understand the context of past decisions.

Any of the following styles of forums may be effective depending on context:

- A simple mailing list that is archived and searchable
- Web-based discussion forums
- Stack Exchange[8]-style web-based Q&A forum
- Structured discussion formats that allow for collaborative decision making (e.g., Loomio; described in Section 6.7.2)
- Google Moderator[9]-style forum that collects input (questions, suggestions, ideas) from the community and ranks them based on community votes
- IdeaBoardz[10]-style app that helps with distributed retrospectives

Some people feel intimidated or are otherwise uncomfortable to participate in online forums. They are unlikely to air their views in a big meeting as well. Requiring a friendly posture in forums (by publishing a code of conduct, for example) can alleviate some discomfort. Additionally, they could be encouraged to have private conversations with local managers. The other common objection is that people don't like to write. They'd rather speak than write. Unfortunately, speakers require real-time listeners, and this requirement doesn't scale. We all have learned to read and write, so it isn't unfair to include it in the definition of basic communication skills—a hiring requirement.

14.5 Deliberating in Writing

> When you have to write out your ideas in complete sentences,
> complete paragraphs, it forces a deeper clarity.
> —Amazon.com CEO Jeff Bezos

It's not just about scaling engagement; we arrive at better-informed decisions by a process of written deliberations. Whether it is a leadership team, task force,

---

8. http://stackexchange.com/tour
9. https://sites.google.com/site/moderatorhelpcenter/getting-started/guide
10. http://www.ideaboardz.com/page/faq

SWAT team,[11] tiger team,[12] or any other team, they all have to take decisions collectively in the face of imperfect information. However, the discussions leading to these decisions are often flawed when conducted verbally. This is due to various factors:

- Glib tongues talking others down.

- Relative seniors intimidating others by tone, impatience, patronizing comments, and nonverbal cues.

- The inability of non-native speakers of English to match the articulation of native speakers. They may lack fluency, vocabulary, or panache in English. Fumbling or pausing mid-sentence for a word or a phrase makes for a weak impression.

- Lack of time to reflect and counter an argument that sounds good superficially but feels flawed intuitively.

- Lack of time to collect one's thoughts and answer a question effectively. Extempore podcast interviews feel a lot more like mere commentary than an article or book.

- Spur-of-the-moment emotional reactions to perceived slights.

- Westerners have a habit of maintaining and expecting eye contact with the person whom they are addressing. Absence of eye contact is treated with suspicion sometimes. Asians, who don't have this habit or expectation, find themselves at a double disadvantage (the first being a lack of English fluency).

After all, do we really want important business decisions to be settled by whoever wins the day in a verbal battle of wits? Real-time, spoken arguments frequently fail the test of a *minimum viable argument* and are therefore a waste of everyone's time. A minimum viable argument is one that:

- Has understood the purpose of the conversation

- Has taken the conversation so far into account

- Is reasonably free of biases and errors of reasoning

---

11. http://softwaredevelopmenttoday.com/2011/01/swat-team-a-pattern-for-overloaded-multi-project-organizations/
12. http://washingtontechnology.com/articles/2009/08/10/upfront-tiger-teams.aspx

By contrast, conducting these deliberations over written media like e-mail-friendly, self-archiving discussion forums has many advantages:

- It levels the playing field for non-native English speakers. This bodes well for a multicultural workforce. Embracing diversity does not stop at hiring. The environment has to be adjusted to suit the needs of a diverse workforce.

- It promotes accountability for decisions and discourages HiPPO decisions as described in Section 6.7.

- It discounts the smart turn of phrase or the cavalier argument and allows time to expose errors of fact and logic.

- By allowing all concerned to weigh in at their own time (within limits), it avoids hurried decisions taken in a 30-minute window when everyone (or almost everyone) has to be available.

- By allowing for a greater interval between stimulus and response, it helps reduce emotional reactions.

To be fair, there is the risk that written trolls and flame baits will replace verbal duels, but we will be free to ignore them rather than stand by and wait for verbal duels to finish. Perhaps the advantage will swing toward those with a flair for writing rather than speaking, but the written record will guard against mischief. Written communications may also be misconstrued more than face-to-face communication because of the lack of nonverbal cues. Therefore, interpersonal communication is best conducted face to face. In decision-making situations, other considerations weigh heavier. Besides, pre-existing relationships help to reduce misunderstandings in written communications.

Won't written deliberations slow down decision making? Well, meeting-based decisions rarely come to a resolution in a single sitting. Frequently, the primary outcome of a meeting to decide on something is the realization that further discussion is required. Besides, a decision taken after a day or week (elapsed time) of offline written deliberations is likely to be much better informed than one taken after a half-hour showdown.

Except for emergencies, the extra effort of writing is a small price to pay for decisions that result in significant deployment of business resources. Strangely enough, written records are the norm for operational business-as-usual work at many places (refer to frivolous documentation discussed in Section 11.3.1). By contrast, decision records (Section 6.7.1), are much more important for infrequent but high-stakes decisions.

If you are still unconvinced, think of it this way: Spoken arguments require us to get it right the first time in real time. It's like directly deploying software to production with minimal testing. It may be heroic, and those who pull it off regularly may be really sharp, but it doesn't make business sense as a practice. On the other hand, written arguments by their very nature force a modicum of scrutiny and reflection (i.e., testing), even when they say "Sent from my smartphone" at the end.

14.6 The Use and Misuse of Visual Aids

Visual aids are a medium of communication. Poor use of visual aids diminishes the quality of communications and can lead to misunderstanding. Although this is true for any medium, I see enough misuse of visual aids inside organizations to warrant this section.

A picture (visual) is worth a thousand words when it is a photograph of the real world. Even in this case, an accompanying narrative can provide valuable context, for we may be led astray in our attempt to make sense of a visual without its context. Propagandistic television news and advertising understand and exploit this well.

When the visual in question is a mere illustration or graphic, the accompanying narrative becomes even more important. Yet, there is a disturbing trend of trying to make sense of the visual without providing, asking for, or reading the narrative. For example:

- Graphing metrics without a narrative to provide context for the measurements.

- Archiving presentation slide decks without speaker notes in document repositories.

- Demanding or preparing reports in the form of presentations rather than the more traditional form of a document. Tradition makes sense sometimes.

Presenting visuals without a narrative is risky in multiple ways.

14.6.1 Visuals May Mislead Inadvertently

The so-called *cone of uncertainty* (Figure 14-2) is a good example of the perils of visuals without narratives. The cone, first proposed in 1981 by Boehm,

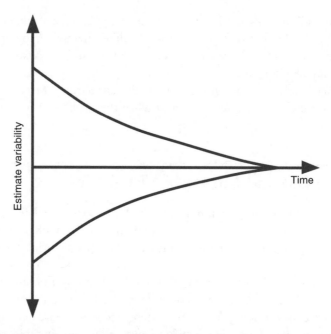

Figure 14-2 *The misleading cone of uncertainty (Boehm, Barry W., Software Engineering Economics, 1st Ed., ©1982, p. 310. Adapted and electronically reproduced by permission of Pearson Education, Inc.)*

visually suggests that variability in estimates of project scope decreases exponentially with time. Since then, a number of publications referenced the cone and it acquired the status of a basic truth. Bossavit[13] points out several problems with the cone:

- In reality, variability is not symmetric with respect to overestimates and underestimates.

- There is no data to suggest the decrease is exponential rather than linear or quadratic.

- Common experience suggests that the variability doesn't decrease monotonically; it may stay constant or even go up for a while.

Bossavit uncovers that the cone is not based on any data at all. It was a subjective observation by Boehm simply to illustrate that estimates get better as work unfolds! To be fair, Boehm said as much in a footnote in his book, but the

---

13. Bossavit, L. 2015. *The leprechauns of software engineering.* Leanpub.

author of another book that popularized the cone omitted or neglected to include this narrative along with the visual. Thus, the visual took on an unintended meaning without the narrative.

14.6.2 The Primacy of Words

Text is in danger of going out of fashion. People say *tl;dr* (too long; didn't read) to anything longer than a tweet. Until recently, book lovers could spend hours absorbed in a book without any illustrations. Now there is greater emphasis on having text punctuated by illustrations. Sometimes, a perfectly fine page of text is pejoratively referred to as a *wall of text*. It is one thing to have some illustrations interspersed in pages of text and quite another to have a few words interspersed in pages of illustrations. Yet, that is what a slide deck is when it isn't accompanied by a narrative.

The world of ideas and arguments needs the language of words. The mounting disapproval of text does not augur well for business communications. Pictures and illustrations can be useful adjuncts, but words and numbers are of greater importance in business communications. The claim that 93% of information is transmitted by nonverbal cues is a myth.[14] Nonverbal cues have their place in contexts that are naturally face to face (e.g., deal making, negotiating, selling, and hiring). Even here, they supplement the discussion carried out in words. Nonverbal cues appeal to emotion, and that's why they form a big part of advertising, selling, and entertainment. Internal business discussions need to be rational, and they would do well to refrain from appeals to emotion.

14.6.3 Meaning Trumps Aesthetics

Unlike the case of art, where form is all important, the maxim of design is *form follows function*. We might counter that in case of consumer devices like smartphones, form (desirability) precedes buyer evaluation of function. However, the purpose of internal business communications (as opposed to advertising or selling) is to inform, to convey the meaning intended by the originator. This is hard to achieve if text is granted a lower status than a visual.

One kind of visual targets the recipient's analytical faculty. Another kind targets her aesthetic faculty. Aesthetics are in vogue among consumer devices like tablets, smartphones, and smartwatches. This has spilt over to the kind of visuals favored by us. Thus, we encounter graphs where a table would be more

---

14. See https://en.wikipedia.org/wiki/Albert_Mehrabian#Misinterpretation and http://publicwords
    .com/debunking-the-debunkers-the-mehrabian-myth-explained-correctly/

informative, a 3-D visual where 2-D would do, and only a visual where a paragraph is also needed. In internal business communications, the visual is best used as a means to tap into the pattern recognizing, parallel-processing prowess of the brain rather than as a means to catch the eye.

14.6.4 Slide Decks

Slide decks are a type of visual aid since good decks are meant to be more visual than textual. However, slide decks without narratives are useless after the presentation. This statement flies in the face of the popularity of web sites such as SlideShare, which have tons of slide decks without any narrative. Perhaps they get used more to harvest slides for internal use than for any real exchange of meaning (unless the slides have speaker notes or sufficient explanatory text).

It Works!

The Amazon Exemplar

Did you know that slide decks are discouraged at Amazon? Instead of a presentation, all meetings are structured around a six-page memo prepared by the presenter. The meeting begins by everyone reading the memo in silence. At an interview by Charlie Rose[15] in 2012, Amazon CEO Jeff Bezos said, "When you have to write your ideas out in complete sentences, complete paragraphs it forces a deeper clarity."

We still behave as if a projector can only handle slide decks. We have come a long way from the days of the analogue projector that could only project transparencies. Modern projectors can project whatever is on our laptop screen, not just slide decks. This is obvious. But then, shouldn't we be more comfortable projecting a report in the form of a document or a live dashboard rather than a slide deck?

Slide decks used to be an adjunct to presenting a report or a proposal in a meeting; they have now taken the place of the actual report or proposal. Almost all reports and proposals are now submitted as slide decks with very limited narrative text. They are only understandable when the author is present. They have little value when stored in a document or knowledge repository. It is not necessary to ban slide decks as long as we ensure that they accompany the real thing,

---

15. http://www.charlierose.com/watch/60148245

i.e., a long form report, proposal, or a video of the presentation. If nothing else, at least include detailed speaker notes along with an archived slide deck.

14.6.5 Ditch the Pitch

Section 11.3 introduced McLuhan's adage: the medium is the message. When the medium is a slide deck, what is the message? In my experience with slide decks, the emphasis shifts from a deep and nuanced exchange of information and meaning to making an impression with a slick presentation. It might be the right approach for making a pitch, but isn't that supposed to be only a fraction of all business meetings? Unfortunately, a pitch culture is on the rise.

Decision makers seem to be taking a stance of, "Impress me with your pitch and then I may allocate time and resources for your idea." On the face of it, there is nothing wrong with this stance. However, it absolves the decision maker of the responsibility to listen deeply. If the decision maker is distracted, it is up to the pitch maker to grab her attention. It is okay for prospective investors and customers to act this way; they are not paid to listen to pitch makers. However, inside an organization, making an effort to listen to people's ideas is implicitly part of the job description of every leader. It should not *require* a slick presentation. On the contrary, many a project has failed to deliver partly because it was approved based on little more than a slick presentation. The Adobe Kickbox[16] program, for example, is an attempt to bypass the severe judgement of impress-me-first decision makers by saying it's okay to try out different ideas without a successful initial pitch.

Some decision makers say they have too much on their plate. Therefore, they can only attend to the most arresting pitch (hence the *elevator pitch*). This is disingenuous. The psychological aspects are never acknowledged. It feels good to be wooed by pitch makers. The feeling soon turns into one of entitlement. It is a false entitlement. Decision makers aren't paid to confer their largesse on those who woo them best. A pitch culture is a lobbying culture. Corporate lobbying wrecks democracies by putting corporate interest ahead of public interest. Within an organization, a pitch culture wrecks the business by putting pitch makers' interests (funding for pet projects, empire building, visibility, and career growth) ahead of business interests. Just as lawmakers have a responsibility to be wary of lobbyist spiel, corporate decision makers have a responsibility to not just listen to pitch makers and their pitches.

---

16. https://hbr.org/2015/02/inside-adobes-innovation-kit

Of course, merely discouraging slide decks is not going to address the pitch culture. Confidential surveys (Section 13.7) may help. Ask everyone to evaluate those who hold the purse strings to see whether they make an effort to understand their ideas and suggestions.

14.7 Documents, Reports, and Templates

Organizations transitioning from CMMish processes to Agile are often surprised to learn that it is not mandatory to have documents called a project plan, test strategy, communication plan, configuration management plan, etc. Even for the documents that we choose to maintain, there is no need to define templates. Fearing anarchy and chaos, they go ahead and define their own templates and mandatory documentation requirements. Yet, many other places that follow Agile principles without the baggage of legacy processes function just fine without template-based mandatory documentation.

Minimally prescriptive templates are sometimes useful. For example, it is common for the marketing or internal communications department in a company to issue corporate presentation templates). Even here, the thinking has evolved to provide just a set of recommended fonts, a color palette, and a set of logos. Not insisting on the use of a template is respectful of the presenter's autonomy.

Besides, what is the difference between a detailed template and a form? Application and registration forms work out well because they are used to collect information in repetitive and well-defined scenarios. But issuing a detailed template for a project status report is problematic for several reasons:

- It is an attempt to scale project oversight with standardized reports. Without a template, a project manager might have begun with what she considered most pertinent. With templates, all reports look the same.

- By attempting to cover all possibilities, templates end up with a lot of boilerplate. Documents based on a template tend to have many redundant, non-applicable sections. This reduces readability.

- With increased software automation, a lot of the information needed can be generated out of project management tools, issue-tracking tools, continuous integration tools, etc. A project manager could simply pull up these reports during a review meeting rather than waste time translating the information into a template.

- The time spent in preparing a template-based report and going through it in a review meeting may be better utilized in a quality conversation about the project situation.

Ultimately, a regime of templates and mandatory documentation is another example of enforcing uniformity in the name of consistency (Section 13.5). Consistency without uniformity can be achieved by providing guidelines and optional checklists instead of templates. For example, guidelines for a project status report would indicate what questions are to be answered and would leave the *how* to the individual.

14.8 Summary of Insights

- It pays to deliberately influence the communication culture rather than let it take shape based on the habits and styles of unit-level leaders.

- Unnecessary exercise of authority and acts of microaggression in interpersonal communications vitiate the climate, erode the sense of purpose, and reduce motivation levels.

- Online forums are the most viable channel to scale two-way engagement between knowledge workers and management.

- Real-time, spoken arguments frequently fail the test of a minimum viable argument. Yet, decision-making meetings are full of them. Important decisions are better made by deliberating in writing outside of meetings.

- A regime of templates and mandatory documentation is an example of enforcing uniformity in the name of consistency and is not a good fit for an Agile work culture.

14.9 Summary of Actions

- Contain microaggression by appropriate new hire orientation and the use of pulse charts.

- Encourage written deliberations for important decisions.

- Reinforce that meaning trumps aesthetics when it comes to the use of visuals in internal business communications.

- Discourage slide decks without written narratives.

- Use confidential surveys to keep the pitch culture in check.

- Provide document guidelines and optional checklists instead of templates.

Chapter 15

The Office

The physical layout of the office may be off topic for organization design, but it has a bearing on organizational agility. It serves to reinforce ideas of autonomy, non-hierarchy, open communications, and purpose. Recall that we stated the need for unscripted collaboration as a key theme in Chapter 3. However, offices are commonly laid out without a thought for ease of collaboration. In this chapter, we take a brief look at optimizing layout for encouraging collaboration and for alignment with an open culture while not losing sight of the need for privacy, quiet, and comfort.

15.1 Open-plan Layouts

From the point of view of greater face-to-face collaboration, open-plan layouts are preferable to cubicle farms or individual offices. As illustrated in Figure 15-1, the organizing unit of an open-plan layout is a big table (much like a conference room table). Members of a team sit around one or more such tables, usually without any notion of preassigned seats. Sitting around a table is an invitation to interact as everyone sits facing each other. Being within earshot of conversations around the table facilitates serendipitous communication.[1] However, there are several aspects to getting open layouts right; it does not mean simply strewing several big tables across an open floor.

---

1. http://c2.com/cgi/wiki?SerendipitousCommunication

Figure 15-1 *Open-plan seating*

15.1.1 How Open?

Open layout does not mean having absolutely no partitions other than the walls along the periphery of the floor. A good layout aims to encourage interaction while at the same time limiting distraction. Aligning the seating plan with business outcomes helps this cause. Teams bounded by the same business outcome sit together. Cross-functional teams occupy one or more tables without dividing along functional lines. Installing big movable partitions between unrelated teams reduces distraction and provides much-needed wall space.

An open layout generally means no personal offices for anyone, at least in the IT organization. It is an unnecessary display of hierarchy to have personal offices for senior folks and an open layout for everyone else. Sometimes, people in functions like admin, facilities, HR, and finance find it difficult to manage their desks with an open layout. They do a lot of paperwork and prefer to have a private desk where the papers are undisturbed. They could have cubicles if they so choose.

15.1.2 Wall Space

Paper-based information radiators like flip charts, physical card walls, and posters require lots of wall space. Wide-open layouts without any partitions limit wall space to just the periphery of the floor. This is one more reason to

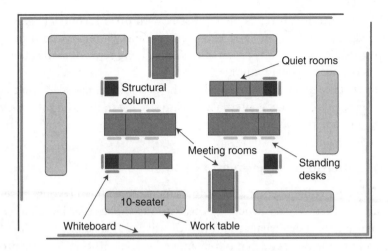

Figure 15-2 *Balanced open-plan layout*

have some partitions in a big floor. One way to introduce partitions naturally is to locate all meeting rooms in the middle of the floor away from the edges as shown in Figure 15-2. The sides of the rooms serve as whiteboards or walls for sticking things up. Speaking of whiteboards, it is a good idea to affix big glass panels along all walls of the floor. Glass panels can serve as whiteboards (assuming the wall behind is white) or walls, depending on the needs of a team at different points in time. They are easier to maintain than regular whiteboards that often get soiled and hard to use after lots of writing and erasing.

15.1.3 Solitude and Privacy

Sometimes, we just need some peace and quiet at work. We might want to:

- Write an important memo or article without interruption.
- Untangle a section of code.
- Work through some ideas in isolation.
- Have a call in private.

A free pool of private individual rooms is necessary to cater to these needs. These rooms can only be booked for private use and not for meetings. An open layout thus needs more rooms than a cubicle farm to cater to individual private use. This may not be the most space-efficient way of seating, but it is a worthy tradeoff for greater interaction. The need for quiet can also be met by designating some floors or sections as silent zones with a free pool of seats that people can walk into and occupy for a few hours.

Computer screen privacy is also an issue with open layouts. This is rarely acknowledged, but it is common to see the people who arrive in office early take up seats along the walls or partitions. Supplying screen guards along with laptops is one way to deal with this.

When we take away cubicles, we lose the private storage space that comes with it. Some places provide alternate private storage in the form of a locker in a common locker room/rack.

15.1.4 Criticism of Open-plan Layouts

Claims of better collaboration and performance in open-plan layouts have been questioned. A *New Yorker* article[2] quotes various studies that indicate reduced performance due to disturbance and loss of privacy. Those from the Joel Spolsky school of thought argue that old-fashioned private offices are more productive as they respect the individual's rhythm of work.[3] Some even allege that open-plan layouts are a conspiracy to cram more workers into less space.

> The amount of space per employee shrank from 500 square feet in the 1970s to 200 square feet in 2010.
> —A statistic quoted by Susan Cain in her book *Quiet*[4]

On the other hand, supporters of open-plan layouts counter that distraction doesn't go away in private offices. Social media, Internet, instant messaging, and e-mail notifications offer plenty of opportunity to those susceptible to distractions. Besides, if the work requires collaboration, we'll have to interact electronically if not face to face. Aren't they equally distracting? No, says Susan Cain in her book *Quiet*. She argues that unlike face-to-face collaboration, online collaboration is a form of solitude all by itself. It is what helps creators of open-source software to concentrate, yet collaborate. I think there is merit to this argument to the extent that electronic collaboration is asynchronous.

15.2 Ergonomics[5]

Laptops are problematic for ergonomics. Good adjustable-height swivel chairs with lumbar support are necessary but not sufficient. Good posture demands that:

---

2. http://www.newyorker.com/business/currency/the-open-office-trap
3. http://blog.stackoverflow.com/2015/01/why-we-still-believe-in-private-offices
4. (Cain 2012)
5. This section does not provide medical or health advice. It is for information only.

- The monitor is at eye level with the head held erect.

- The forearm is at right angles or slightly obtuse to the arm.

- Forearms don't rest on the table. This may lift the shoulder causing strain.

This is impossible to achieve with a laptop—we have either to tilt our heads down toward the screen or lift our shoulders to use the keyboard. For good posture, we can use either the laptop's keyboard or monitor, not both. A common solution is to use an external keyboard and/or monitor. However, external keyboards placed on the table may still require us to lift our shoulders to use them. One of the following is needed:

- Tables attached with pull-out drawers for external keyboards. This is common in cubicle furniture.

- Increased chair height to eliminate shoulder lift while using the laptop keyboard along with an adjustable-height external monitor to avoid looking down at the laptop screen. However, this might require raised footrests.

External monitors with a glassy surface cause glare that in turn drives people to draw window blinds and shut out natural light. Choose non-reflective monitors. Having too many large monitors on a table tends to block people out from seeing each other, thus undermining the purpose of sitting around a table. This is generally the case with a table full of developers, so it is another reason not to sit by functional division.

Standing desks[6] are an excellent addition to the office floor. They allow people to stand and work for a while as a break from sitting in the same posture for long hours. It gets the blood circulation going. When built around the sides of meeting rooms, they also allow people to work while waiting for the people from an earlier meeting to finish up and move out.

Other than this:

- Carpeted floors absorb sound and serve to reduce the level of noise.

- Keeping meeting rooms away from the edges of the floor maximizes natural lighting in the work area (assuming window blinds aren't drawn). Meeting rooms can do without natural light as they are meant for temporary use compared with the regular work area.

- Screen guards for laptops reduce eyestrain.

---

6. http://lifehacker.com/5735528/why-and-how-i-switched-to-a-standing-desk

15.3 Remote Working

Proponents of remote working (from home) argue[7, 8] that:

- An interruption-free remote location improves productivity.
- It helps being able to mind home-related affairs from time to time.
- It forces a shift toward managing by output rather than input (hours on the seat).
- It helps recruitment of top talent from other locations (since they don't have to relocate).
- It eliminates time wasted in commuting to an office.
- It encourages a shift from synchronous to asynchronous collaboration. This is easier on everyone's calendars.
- It reduces office space requirements.
- Thanks to technology, effective remote collaboration is more feasible than ever.

On the other hand, opponents argue the following: IT-B work is not well suited for working from home, especially when requirements are in flux. Software development is a social activity in which we learn iteratively. It helps to be co-located and face to face. Even with all the technology, it is difficult to recreate the experience of a bunch of people discussing around a whiteboard. Some teams are good at working remotely, but it requires a lot of discipline and breaks down if people don't have very good written communication skills and good prior relationships with each other. Granted, we all like the flexibility to work from home occasionally to take care of personal matters. Allowing people to work from home one day a week may be a happy compromise. Longer stretches may be approved by exception. It may also be useful to make sure that the whole team works from office at least two days a week.

I used to be opposed to the idea of remote working, but I increasingly see the merit in it. Face-to-face interactions are useful to establish professional relationships, but once these are established, remote interaction can be just as effective in most situations. Here are some things that help remote working:

- Team chatroom and a discipline to avoid one-on-one chats so that all exchanges are visible to the whole team. @user notifications allow people

---

7. (Fried and Hansson 2013)
8. http://blog.stackoverflow.com/2013/02/why-we-still-believe-in-working-remotely

to work undisturbed until called out. During logical breaks, they can scan the transcript to update themselves of team conversations.

- Ability to use VOIP and screen casting without bandwidth limitation.
- Ability to access all company infrastructure (e.g., through VPN).
- Use of tools for remote pair programming.[9]
- All information radiators need to be available remotely (over the wire). Unfortunately, this usually means no physical information radiators in the office because someone would have to keep them in sync.

However, professional services firms (IT consultancies) will have a tough time convincing their clients to let their consultants work remotely. After all, they charge for input (billable hours), and their clients are understandably keen to have them within line of sight. Besides, the consultants need to be co-located with their clients in order to establish relationships and understand client context. Note that offshore work isn't remote work in this sense because offshore workers are expected to report to a local office and work together in a team with a manager.

15.4 Summary of Insights

- Open-plan layouts encourage collaboration and deemphasize hierarchy.
- There is more to an open layout than just strewing big tables across a room. It should be planned from the point of view of effective collaboration rather than maximizing space efficiency.
- Open layouts need to cater to our needs for quiet and privacy.
- Remote work can be very productive. It also helps recruit people who don't wish to relocate.

15.5 Summary of Actions

- Plan co-located seating for teams bounded by the same business outcome (as far as possible).
- Discourage intrateam division of seating along functional lines.

---

9. http://en.wikipedia.org/wiki/Pair_programming#Remote_pair_programming

- Provide for lots of wall space by using movable partitions between unrelated teams. It also helps teams focus.

- Locate meeting rooms in the middle of the floorplan so that the work tables receive natural light. This arrangement also lets us use the walls of the rooms or whiteboards for card walls and other information radiators.

- Design open layouts with more cabins or silent zones in addition to the regular meeting rooms.

- Include standing desks in addition to regular work tables.

- Consider remote working options seriously in view of the benefits they promise.

Chapter 16

Wrap-up

We started this book with the aim of achieving organizational agility through organization design. We set out to explore how to design an IT organization that optimizes for value over predictability, for responsiveness over cost-efficiency, and for intrinsic over extrinsic motivation. We examined several contributory aspects—structural, cultural, operational, political, and physical. Admittedly, this is beyond the conventional scope of organization design, but we deliberately took an expansive view of the term in order to address all the important ingredients for organizational agility. In this last chapter, we wrap up the discussion with a few summaries and take a quick look at how the contents of this book may apply to IT services companies and Global In-House Centers (GICs).

16.1 Summary of Effects

Table 16-1 summarizes org agility problems and solutions described in preceding chapters in terms of the three themes set out in Chapter 3. Some line items are relevant for more than one reason and are repeated under different heads.

Table 16-1 *Problems of Org Agility and Their Solutions*

Theme: *Govern for value over predictability.*		
What Hurts Pursuit of Value	**What to Do Instead**	**Reference Section**
Plan-driven projects, release plans.	Capability teams and value-driven projects.	3.1, 8.1, 8.2
Project-based budgeting (funds are sanctioned against plans).	Team capacity-based budgeting (funds are sanctioned against outcomes for which outcome owners are accountable).	8.2, 9.5, 9.6
Over-reliance on business cases.	Rely on actual benefits validation.	8.4
Early determination of full solution.	Shape as you go.	8.5
Letting accounting considerations influence team design.	Use alternate mechanisms to track CapEx and OpEx.	9.4
Predictability metrics.	Adaptability metrics.	12.5.3
Focus on individual/team productivity.	Focus on outcome realization.	12.5.1

(continues)

Table 16-1 *Continued*

Theme: *Organize for responsiveness over cost-efficiency.*		
What Hurts Responsiveness	**What to Do Instead**	**Reference Section**
High-cost handoffs (that result when a critical value stream is serviced by multiple teams).	Reduce cost of handoffs by servicing critical value streams with a single cross-functional team.	5.2
Obsessing over utilization of specialists.	Trade it off for greater responsiveness.	5.4
Ineffective decision making due to unclear accountability.	Clarify decision rights with accountability maps. Regularize the notion of a decision owner. Maintain a decision record to keep decision owners accountable.	6.5, 6.7
Agile IT, indifferent business.	Get business people to align with IT's execution model.	7.4
Permission culture.	Permissive culture.	13.6
Approval-based access to tools and information.	Allow access by default, restrict by exception.	11.1
Assigning enhancements and bug fixes to a separate maintenance team.	Merge maintenance and development teams.	5.7

(continues)

Table 16-1 *Continued*

Theme: *Design for intrinsic motivation and unscripted collaboration.*		
What Hurts Autonomy	What to Do Instead	Reference Section
Activity-oriented teams can't be given autonomy as activity silos are useless and a big drag.	Outcome-oriented teams can be given autonomy to fulfill outcomes. Outcome silos are still useful when they deliver primary outcomes.	4.1.1, 4.3.3, 8.7
Centralized configurations stifle autonomy.	Decentralize around product or region but not function.	4.2
Shared authority and accountability between outcome leads and function leads has the potential to lead to power struggles and compromise outcomes.	Use accountability maps to clarify accountability. Avoid sharing of authority between outcome leads and function leads. Set up things so that function leads can lead by influence rather than authority.	6.3, 6.4
Targets limit autonomy.	Shared understanding of outcome reduces the need for targets. Mere measurement can be effective without targets. Where necessary, decide targets with team; don't impose.	12.3, 12.4
True delegation is impeded by the absence of clearly defined and shared operating norms.	A well-thought-out set of operating norms provides a healthy framework for greater autonomy.	13.1, 13.2
Information and tooling access regime based on a need-to-use basis.	Invert the regime. Restrict access on a need-to-restrict basis.	11.1
Too much tool standardization.	Let teams choose their tools in cases where they are also responsible for managing them.	11.4

(continues)

Table 16-1 *Continued*

What Hurts Purpose	What to Do Instead	Reference Section
Shared service teams find it difficult to identify with a purpose beyond service-level targets.	Avoid shared service teams for important value streams. Embed the competency into outcome-oriented teams.	5.2.4
Absence of a business outcome to work toward (activity-oriented teams).	As far as possible, create teams such that they can directly contribute to business outcomes.	4.1
An inability to relate daily work to larger business objectives.	Use a combination of techniques to achieve and articulate alignment of IT with business.	7.2
Targets and incentives distort purpose.	Shared understanding of outcome reduces the need for targets.	12.3, 12.4
Fixed policies encourage bureaucracy and come in the way of purposeful execution.	Implement living policies.	13.4
Needless exercise of hierarchy and microaggression in interpersonal communications erodes the sense of purpose.	Discourage this via new hire-orientation and pulse charts.	14.3
Nonengaging style of organizational communications diminishes purpose.	Drive engagement by using online forums to scale two-way communications.	14.4

(continues)

Table 16-1 *Continued*

What Hurts Mastery	What to Do Instead	Reference Section
Absence of a functional organization has the potential to compromise a competency and hurt mastery.	Since functional organization has other big drawbacks, we can't have them. Instead, we rely on communities of practice to nurture competencies.	5.7
Separation of planning and execution roles affects planners' mastery of situations.	Overlap planning and execution.	6.8
Transient project teams don't allow mastery to take hold.	Move to long-lived, stable capability teams.	10.2
Prescribing the use of templates for documents, reports, and presentations risks leading to an unintelligent, ritualistic documentation culture.	Be less prescriptive. Provide guidelines and non-mandatory checklists instead.	14.6.4
Visual aids without accompanying narratives are useless without the presenter. It limits readers' ability to master their meaning.	Make sure that narratives accompany visual aids. Don't overemphasize the need for visual aids.	14.6
Role-based staffing.	Skill-based staffing.	10.3.1
Part-time assignments.	Pair part-time specialists with full-time team members.	10.3.4
Targets limit mastery to what is required to fulfill the target.	Shared understanding of the outcome reduces the need for targets. Mere measurement can be effective without targets.	12.4.1
Open-plan layouts without enough interruption-free spaces.	Plan for a combination of open and silent zones.	15.1.3
Decisions based on verbal arguments in meetings.	Decisions that are discussed in writing.	14.5

16.2 Order of Adoption

It is impractical to try to change many organizational aspects at once. Migration advice provided in some chapters might help with a gradual rollout. In addition, Table 16-2 is a quick, general guide to the difficulty versus benefit of various transformational actions. Your mileage may vary.

Table 16-2 *Order of Adoption*

Action	Benefit	Dependencies, If Any
Easy		
1. Publish business strategy and models of IT alignment.	Rich	
2. Clarify accountability and decision rights with an outcome map.	Rich	
3. Reduce dependence of important value streams on shared services.	Significant	
4. Roll out initial set of norms and a regime of reinforcement.	Rich	
5. Move away from templates.	Some	
6. Take steps to curb microaggression.	Significant	
7. Discourage the use of slide decks and visual aids without narratives.	Significant	
8. Establish communities of practice.	Significant	
9. Introduce pairing to help move away from part-time assignment of specialists.	Significant	
Less easy		
10. Move to skill-based staffing.	Some	16
11. Adopt team capacity-based budgeting.	Significant	16
12. Move to stable teams.	Rich	16
13. Move to an information- and tooling-access regime based on need-to-restrict basis.	Significant	
14. Move to a model of better engagement via two-way communications.	Significant	
15. Move to an egalitarian office layout.	Some	

(continues)

Table 16-2 *Continued*

Least easy			
16. Move to outcome-oriented, cross-functional teams.	Rich		
17. Recast function leads.	Significant		
18. Move to a regime of assessment over measurement.	Rich		

16.3 Information Radiators

Section 2.4.4 introduced information radiators. Subsequently, we made the case for quite a few new information radiators that go beyond highlighting activity at the level of individual teams or systems. Table 16-3 is a summary.

Table 16-3 *Information Radiators*

Name	Purpose	Described in Section
Accountability map	Clarifies who is accountable for what outcomes	6.3.2
Architecture-business alignment map	Shows how planned/ongoing architecture work relates to business objectives	7.2.3
Feature-business alignment map	Shows how planned/ongoing work on business features relates to business objectives	7.2.3
Portfolio wall (or Kanban board)	Provides an overview of planned, in-flight, and complete projects/features	8.8.2
All queryable information systems	Helps avoid tooling induced silos	11.2.1
Business metrics	To help everyone understand what matters	12.3.6
Metrics-business alignment map	Helps us choose outcome-oriented metrics instead of activity-oriented ones; helps guard against vanity metrics	12.4.3
Pulse charts	Helps contain microaggression by providing a quick insight into the pulse of a team	14.3

16.4 Sample Exercise

Finally, here's a sample exercise to see whether we can apply our learning to a situation that is more complicated than the topic-specific scenarios we encountered so far. Based on the arguments in this book, what is your analysis of the situation? What corrective measures would you suggest? My analysis is provided on the next page.

Scenario 16-1 Breakdown at ArmsLength

Farah used to be CTO at ArmsLength Inc. She headed a 500-member, mostly inexperienced IT organization. One day, a new CEO was appointed who came to disagree with her way of working. He decided that he didn't want Farah reporting to him and temporarily abolished the position of CTO. Farah became head of an enterprise architecture team and started reporting to the COO. Her small new team was to provide architecture guidance to the huge, inexperienced development organization headed by Yang—previously a subordinate of Farah, now her peer.

Farah's team drew up an enterprise architecture roadmap with lots of goals and acceptance criteria to test achievement of the goals. As part of every new business project (and sometimes as part of a dedicated architecture project), the development organization was expected to sign up for some self-determined contribution to these goals. Farah's team was wary of imposing themselves on the development organization, so they didn't prescribe how to go about achieving the goals, but they were ready to offer consultation if approached. Besides, they did not have any authority over Yang's organization.

Development teams began signing up for contributing to goals without a good understanding of what it would take. Yang did not encourage too much consultation with Farah's team and, at any rate, they were too small to handhold the huge development organization. As development progressed, project funding began running out without achievement of the promised contributions. In the face of competing business priorities, the funding team (separate from Farah's and Yang's organizations) began rejecting requests to extend funding.

The COO had asked Farah for a monthly report of progress toward goals signed up for by the development teams. This unwittingly set her group up as auditors to the development organization. Report after report would state that the promised contributions toward goals hadn't materialized. The reports demoralized developers, and business suffered from an architecturally weak technology platform and long development cycle times.

Analysis

We have two planning teams (Section 6.8)—funding and enterprise architecture—that are completely separated from execution (the development organization). Besides, all three are activity-oriented teams—they don't own business outcomes (Section 4.1). Authority and accountability are wrongly distributed. In the absence of authority over development, Farah understandably refuses full accountability for enterprise architecture. The new CEO may have distanced herself from Farah, but in doing so, she set it up as a power struggle between Yang and Farah.

It would have been much better to hire a new CTO and constitute Farah's architects as the office of the CTO acting as professorial function leads (Section 6.4.3) for development teams. They could now be held accountable for outcomes. Given the authority, the architects would no longer act from a distance in a consulting (planning) capacity. They would be able to be 20% hands-on with development teams.

Finally, the funding and project model are better transformed to a model of team capacity-based funding of stable, long-lived, outcome-oriented, cross-functional teams created around business capabilities (as described in Chapters 8, 9, and 10).

16.5 IT Services

Although this book is aimed at IT-B organizations that serve their own business, some observations on IT services firms (i.e., IT suppliers) are in order. IT services (ITS) tends to be a business of nurturing client relationships and growing accounts. ITS revenue is based on billable hours. Therefore, revenue is a function of utilization, billing rates, and headcount. Utilization and rates cannot be increased indefinitely, and so ITS firms tend to rely on headcount growth for revenue growth. The top ten ITS firms by headcount account for well over a million employees.

Running a business at this scale limits one's options of value disciplines (Section 7.1.1) to operational excellence. Processes and tools tend to matter over individuals and interactions. There is little choice but to manage by numbers, targets, and incentives. Any talk of intrinsic motivators appears like utopian idealism. An IT-B manager from an ITS firm might react to the contents of this book with incredulity.

However, the changes in the market are here to stay. It is no longer enough (or even desirable) to be able to produce a 100-member low-cost team at short notice. The availability of good SaaS solutions is making it increasingly attractive to buy rather than make. Custom builds will be reserved for systems of differentiation, and continuous delivery will matter in these cases. If the big ITS firms don't shape up because of their inherent constraints, their clients will simply reduce outsourcing or migrate to smaller, nimbler, and more clued-in alternatives.

Besides, headcount-driven revenue models create a situation in which margins depend on the spread between average billing rate and average employee wage. In a market where demand for IT labor outstrips supply, wages have to be competitive. Thus, the only way to sustain margins is to work on the average wage. Average wage on an engagement can be kept under control by staffing few high-wage employees and lots of lower-wage ones. This is called a leveraged team (or pyramid) and it has its pros and cons, as described in Section 10.1.

With the right mix and leadership, leveraged teams can work well. However, the people in charge of staffing often have little lead time or choice of available people or understanding of the situation to put together a good team. Staffing managers are only held accountable for utilization. Thus, clients have to be lucky to get a good team on their engagements. They are themselves partly to blame for this as they often refuse to pay for people (*resources*) before the start date of the project or in between projects. Any holding costs have to be borne by the supplier. Moving away from a projects mindset to a capability mindset, as described in Section 8.2, will help both parties. It helps client organizations build true capabilities even in the face of outsourcing, and it helps supplier organizations provide clients with a good, stable team.

Given the focus on utilization and operational excellence, IT-B managers in ITS firms invariably tend to organize for cost-efficiency rather than responsiveness—sometimes despite the willingness of clients to pay for responsiveness. The use of activity-oriented teams (Section 5.2) is a common example of this predilection. Since many ITS managers have little or no hands-on experience with software development, all they can do is track percentage complete and other metrics. When they see delivery slipping, they resort to even more measurement and tracking at finer levels in an attempt to control and direct the activity; for example, they start tracking percentage completion on tasks in addition to stories.

There are other hurdles on the road to organizational agility in situations of outsourcing.

16.5.1 Contracts

Formal, legal contracts go hand in hand with outsourcing. Parties to a contract try to ensure that the language of the contract protects their interests. In the process, considerations of designing a collaboration-friendly contract with the aim of project success take a back seat. Clauses that deal with upfront definition of deliverables, warranty, limitation of liability, etc. constrain negotiation *during* delivery. The situation represents another form of local optimization (Section 2.4.3) that minimizes the likelihood of litigation at the expense of the project outcome.[1]

16.5.2 Access to End Users

ITS firms face extra challenges in talking to end users. Even when the end users belong to the client's business organization, ITS firms find themselves having to negotiate access through client's IT organization—the people who brought them in. They usually want to mediate access to stay in the loop and to prevent the ITS firm from getting too close to the business. At other times, they simply deny access and claim to be the absolute representatives of end users. The situation worsens when the end users are customers of the client. Procurement decision makers in client organizations would do well to take note of this dynamic and structure the engagement model to allow for some access to end users. Otherwise, the application or product under development suffers from lack of first-hand feedback from end users.

16.5.3 Securing Client Involvement

As noted earlier, Agile software development is only successful when the people in charge of requirements are fully engaged. It doesn't help to throw requirements over a wall or be available for a couple of hours per week, more so when the wall is a contractual boundary between client and ITS firm. All client representatives (e.g., product owner, analyst, UX person, architect, IT operations people) and ITS people have to act together as a single team to realize valuable outcomes. We cannot have a supplier-client dynamic within a team where a client instructs and a supplier obeys. That makes for a crippled team. The supplier-client dynamic may be very real at the level of people who negotiate contracts and sign invoices and checks, but it should be prevented from leaking into the team. When this doesn't happen, ITS account managers are usually loath to be assertive about it. Instead of acting to secure greater client engagement, they put pressure on the development team to make do with existing

---

1. http://www.agilecontracts.com/agile_contracts_primer.pdf

levels of engagement. This is done in the name of relationship management. The result is a less-than-optimal delivery that meets contractual obligations but falls far short of what might have been achieved with adequate client engagement.

16.5.4 Intrinsic Motivation

How do ITS firms fare in terms of fostering autonomy, mastery, and purpose—the ingredients (Section 3.4) for intrinsic motivation? Autonomy for ITS teams depends on the client. A client that views the ITS firm as a trusted partner will grant more autonomy than one who looks at them merely as implementation capacity. Experts provided by the ITS firm may find their autonomy curtailed by having to convince their client counterparts before going ahead with significant decisions regarding the implementation.

When the outsourced piece of work is far removed from a client's business outcome, purpose suffers. Sometimes, the client outsources an outcome-oriented piece of work but the ITS firm divides it internally in an activity-oriented fashion (Section 5.9). Another issue is the frequent hopping of people between short-term projects. It doesn't foster purpose. Again, moving from a projects mindset to a capability mindset as described in Chapter 8 will help the cause of purpose.

Mastery suffers because an ITS firm is paid for its input (billable hours) rather than client business outcomes. Schedule and budget compliance acquire greater importance. Sometimes, when actual effort turns out to be much greater than estimated, ITS firms have a tendency to push their teams toward working longer hours without compensation. It is one thing to voluntarily work long hours under the influence of a state of flow afforded by mastery and quite another to have to do so because of a contract drawn up by someone who may not have their interests in mind. What's worse, sometimes these contracts are based on very ambitious promises made just to win the work in a competitive bidding situation.

ITS firms can do their bit to encourage mastery by recognizing professional excellence, for example, sponsoring and encouraging people to write books, speak at conferences, write for industry publications, or contribute to open-source projects. Unfortunately, these activities are often viewed as peripheral and not adding value to the business even though they can be a source of inbound leads. Instead, some ITS firms pursue a dubious strategy of building intellectual property via software patents (e.g., the patent filing on performance tests in a continuous deployment pipeline[2]).

---

2. http://patents.stackexchange.com/questions/12307/prior-art-request-for-wo2014027990-performance-tests-in-a-continuous-deployment

16.5.5 The Way Ahead

IT-B is being increasingly accepted as strategic by the traditionally big clients of ITS firms. As a result, they are in-sourcing new development efforts.[3] The make-versus-buy equation is changing from make *outsourced* versus buy to make *in-house* versus buy. If the trend catches on, the ITS industry will be disrupted. It will be relegated to maintaining legacy applications that don't have a future.

The other likely trend is a shift away from a project-centric IT-B execution model to a product- or capability-centric model with stable, long-lived teams. ITS firms will be increasingly asked to augment the staff of client capability teams rather than own the delivery of a project. Staff augmentation is traditionally not preferred by ITS firms because it is viewed as low value-add compared with owning a project. Nevertheless, the question is how to adapt in view of new circumstances in the market.

Staff augmentation can be high value-add if the staff in question is composed of influencers rather than just executors. Many ITS firms have not managed to be influential even while owning projects. Their corporate cultures have bred obedience rather than questioning or influencing. This has been a common theme of their clients' feedback. Besides, moving to high-value staff augmentation won't be easy for those who have a built a business on the back of highly leveraged staff mix.

16.6 GICs

Many companies have invested heavily in building offshore delivery centers (GICs—also known as captives) in lower-cost regions. They are often built out with first class infrastructure, roomy interiors (relatively speaking), and great campuses. It is common for a single campus or building to host thousands of employees.

A GIC reduces (or removes) dependence on third-party IT suppliers. It also reduces the need to share privileged information outside the company network. In theory, this model erects a lower barrier than outsourcing between business and IT. The reality is much more complicated. Several factors sustain the divide between business and GIC IT.

---

3. http://www.economist.com/news/special-report/21569576-developed-countries-are-beginning-take-back-service-industry-jobs-too-next-big

16.6.1 Business Attitude

Business often views GICs as dumb cost-centers. They don't realize the extent of collaboration that is required to create good software and continue to throw things over the wall (or ocean) for implementation. They also shoot themselves in the foot by holding IT-B teams to rigid upfront plans with fixed budget, schedule, and scope. Take, for example, the attitude of business consultants at a management consultancy toward their GIC-based IT-B colleagues. These business consultants routinely require their GICs to develop tools and models to be used or deployed on business consulting assignments. When IT-B developers ask them to devote more time to collaborating on requirements, they are known to snort, "I bill at $800 an hour, you are a $40 per hour cost. Don't expect me to be at your beck and call."

16.6.2 Cultural Differences

Cultural differences that show up as a big difference in the power distance index[4]—the extent to which the less powerful members of institutions and organizations within a culture expect and accept that power is distributed unequally. It results in an unquestioning obedience—even among managers—that is more suitable for plan-driven behavior than value-driven behavior.

Other cultural differences come in the way of relationship building even during business visits. For example, even by the age of 25, Americans and Europeans tend to have experienced more of the world in general than their counterparts in GICs, many of whom may have never lived in a big city outside of university education. There are big differences in leisure interests and in the ability to socialize and navigate relationships.

16.6.3 Old-style Managers

The IT managers in GICs are predominantly from other big ITS companies. Their attitude toward software development is the same as that described in the previous section. They view software as a production process, manage by numbers, and organize for cost-efficiency. They are comfortable being supervisors, assigning work down to the hour, and making sure the team is kept busy. In a different context, my colleague Nagarjun Kandukuru quipped, "Earlier we took orders sitting down; now that we are Agile, we 'stand up' and take orders." It sums up the situation at many GICs well.

---

4. (Hofstede, Hofstede, and Minkov 2010)

16.6.4 The Journey from CMM

GICs also suffer from the legacy of Capability Maturity Model (CMM).[5] Until some years back (circa 2005), ITS firms used to vie with each other to flaunt their CMM (or Capability Maturity Model Integration [CMMI]) level-5 status. This also meant having a process quality department—an activity-oriented team (Section 5.2)—that had nothing to do with testing software quality. This department generally had two groups. One group was called the *software engineering process group* (SEPG). It was in charge of defining processes, metrics, and documentation templates and defining acceptable thresholds for various metrics supposedly based on performance of projects across the organization. The other was a group of auditors called *software quality analysts* (SQA). They went around auditing projects for process compliance. In terms of net results, all the overhead around process compliance had a much smaller impact on actual software quality than code reviews and manual testing. However, the overhead was maintained in order to hold on to the certification label for marketing.

In due course, their clients saw that the heavyweight processes weren't working and demanded that they switch to lighter-weight Agile methods. The incumbent custodians of process quality would not concede that Agile didn't need them. They devised a heady cocktail of CMMI + Agile or some such combination and kept the process quality roles intact.

Unfortunately, as a side effect of recruiting from ITS firms, this legacy carried over into GIC IT even though GICs don't need a certification label for marketing. Not surprisingly, it did not help the cause of building good software. Under pressure from their parent organizations, GICs then embarked on wholesale Agile transformation initiatives. The same old process quality department hired dozens of Agile coaches and drew up new process templates (Section 14.7) and phased rollout plans.

Occasionally, an Agile coach would advise them to start small, go deep, and demonstrate success with one team instead of a big upfront plan for an organization-wide rollout. But apparently, the people responsible for the rollout were under tight deadlines from headquarters. Some of these efforts have unraveled while others are still on.

16.6.5 Prognosis

Realization has yet to dawn[6] that software is not a production process (Section 3.1) and cannot be managed as one, that chasing value is more important

---

5. http://en.wikipedia.org/wiki/Capability_Maturity_Model
6. http://www.business-standard.com/article/management/it-is-difficult-to-talk-of-value-when-you-cannot-measure-the-value-you-are-delivering-rohan-murty-114121400510_1.html

than chasing predictability, and that changes are required beyond delivery processes and engineering practices. But it is a paradigm shift to move from controlling a production process with the aim of meeting the plan, to participating and facilitating a design process with the aim of delivering value. Culture change is hard—a shift from a control culture to a collaboration culture is a shift (Section 2.3) from impersonal process to people-driven process; few are equipped for it. As Kuhn[7]—the originator of the term *paradigm shift*—argues in the case of scientific paradigm shifts, it may take the passage of generations, especially in the absence of strong clued-in leadership. In the meantime, frameworks like the Scaled Agile Framework may offer emergency relief[8] because they try to work with the existing control culture rather than oppose it. On the other hand, Steve Denning argues[9] that a paradigm shift toward greater people orientation is already underway.

16.7 Beyond IT

Some reviewers observed that the discussion in this book is applicable beyond IT. Although this is true, I retained IT in the title because most of the examples and narratives are from the world of software. Besides, I didn't want to diffuse the context of discussion by wandering outside of IT. However, the few non-IT examples that are included should provide an idea of how it is applicable beyond IT:

- Using cross-functional teams in a hospital emergency room (Section 5.5.1)
- Finland's education system that favors assessment over measurement (Section 12.4.1)
- The radical approach to budgeting adopted by the bank Svenska Handelsbanken (Section 8.2)
- Abolishing sales commissions (Section 12.3.3)
- Discouraging slide deck-driven meetings (Section 14.6.4)

The first three examples are completely outside the IT industry. The last two are from the industry but outside or not limited to the IT division.

There are other well-known examples of Agile organization design outside of IT. The celebrated story of Semco[10] has many a common thread with what

---

7. (Kuhn 1962)
8. http://xprogramming.com/articles/issues-with-safe/
9. http://www.forbes.com/sites/stevedenning/2012/10/31/dont-diss-the-paradigm-shift-in-management/
10. (Semler 1995)

has been described here. The book *Reinventing Organizations*[11] examines the design of a number of successful companies in sectors as varied as energy, healthcare, manufacturing, food processing, and apparel. Its observations regarding the need for autonomy (self-management) and intrinsic motivators aren't very different from the observations in this text.

The wider relevance of an Agile organization design is no surprise. The broad themes that underlie this book are by no means only applicable to IT. Not fixating on predictability and chasing value instead is a pragmatic course of action for any sector where the underlying dynamics make predictions risky. Trading cost-efficiency for greater responsiveness is a reasonable strategy for retaining customers who are increasingly spoiled for choice. And, once we realize that innovation and responsiveness thrive on the back of unscripted collaboration, we can begin bringing about the conditions for making it happen. For a discussion of similar ideas in a broader context, please refer to *The Upside of Turbulence* by Donald Sull and Steve Denning's book, *The Leader's Guide to Radical Management.*

Finally, I do not claim that Agile is the only way to build an effective organization. For example, many companies have benefitted from a culture of internal competition and extrinsic motivation. They are company-oriented cultures, whereas Agile is a people-oriented system (Section 2.3). The 20th century was dominated by company- (and institution)-oriented thinking, and now I see a groundswell toward humanizing the conduct of business. Happily enough, this shift also leads to better business outcomes.

---

11. http://www.reinventingorganizations.com/

Bibliography

Aaker, D. 2008. *Spanning Silos.* Cambridge: Harvard Business Review Press.

Ackoff, R. L. 1999. *Re-creating the corporation: A design of organizations for the 21st century.* New York: Oxford University Press.

Austin, R. D. 1996. *Measuring and managing performance in organizations.* New York: Dorset House.

Blackstaff, M. 2012. *Finance for IT decision makers: A practical handbook.* 3rd ed. Swindon, UK: BCS Learning and Development Ltd.

Cain, S. 2012. *Quiet: The power of introverts in a world that can't stop talking.* New York: Crown Business.

DeMarco, T. 2002. *Slack: Getting past burnout, busywork, and the myth of total efficiency.* New York: Broadway Books.

Fried, J., and D. H. Hansson. 2013. *Remote: Office not required.* New York: Crown Business.

Highsmith, J. 2014. *Adaptive leadership: Accelerating enterprise agility.* Boston: Addison-Wesley.

Hofstede, G., G. J. Hofstede, and M. Minkov. 2010. *Cultures and organizations: Software of the mind.* 3rd ed. New York: McGraw-Hill.

Hsieh, T. 2010. *Delivering happiness: A path to profits, passion, and purpose.* New York: Business Plus.

Humble, J., and D. Farley. 2010. *Continuous delivery: Reliable software releases through build, test, and deployment automation.* Boston: Addison-Wesley.

Kim, G., K. Behr, and G. Spafford. 2013. *The Phoenix Project: A novel about IT, DevOps, and helping your business win.* Portland, OR: IT Revolution Press.

Kohn, A. 1999. *Punished by rewards: The trouble with gold stars, incentive plans, A's, praise and other bribes.* Boston: Mariner Books.

Kotter, J. P. 2014. *Accelerate: Building strategic agility for a faster-moving world.* Cambridge: Harvard Business School Press.

Kuhn, T. S. 1962. *The structure of scientific revolutions.* Chicago: University of Chicago Press.

Lakoff, G. 2003. *Metaphors we live by.* Chicago: University of Chicago Press.

Lencioni, P. 2006. *Silos, politics and turf wars: A leadership fable about destroying the barriers that turn colleagues into competitors.* San Francisco: Jossey-Bass.

McLuhan, M. 1994. *Understanding media.* Cambridge: The MIT Press.

Merton, R. K. 1968. *Social theory and social structure.* New York: The Free Press.

Pink, D. H. 2009. *Drive: The surprising truth about what motivates us.* New York: Riverhead Books.

Reinertsen, D. G. 2009. *The principles of product development flow.* Redondo Beach, CA: Celeritas Publishing.

Rieger, T. 2011. *Breaking the fear barrier: How fear destroys companies from the inside out and what to do about it.* New York: Gallup Press.

Ries, E. 2011. *The lean startup: How today's entrepreneurs use continuous innovation to create radically successful businesses.* New York: Crown Business.

Ross, J. W., P. Weill, and D. C. Robertson. 2006. *Enterprise architecture as strategy.* Cambridge: Harvard Business School Press.

Schein, E. H. 2013. *Humble inquiry: The gentle art of asking instead of telling.* San Francisco: Berrett-Koehler Publishers.

Schneider, W. 1994. *The reengineering alternative.* New York: McGrawHill.

Semler, R. 1995. *Maverick: The success story behind the world's most unusual workplace.* New York: Grand Central Publishing.

Topinka, J. 2014. *IT business partnerships: A field guide.* Minneapolis, MN: CIO Mentor Press.

Treacy, M., and F. Wiersema. 1995. *The discipline of market leaders: Choose your customers, narrow your focus, dominate your market.* Cambridge: Perseus Books.

Index